GROUP DEVELOPMENT

Second Edition, Revised and Enlarged

Edited by

Leland P. Bradford,
Ph.D., L.H.D.

University Associates
8517 Production Avenue
P.O. Box 26240
San Diego, California 92126

Contents

Part 2. Research

1

Theory
&
Practice

Introduction

The introduction to the first edition of this book, written in 1961, made the following important points:

> The complexity—social and technological—of the world we live in makes cooperation among interdependent people mandatory. But the ability to cooperate is itself complex and difficult. Cooperation demands maturity in the individual, understanding of the problems of human interaction, and competence in resolving these problems. . . . Examples of the need for cooperation—and hence of the need for understanding group behavior—are found wherever individual goals must be merged with the goals of others.

Thus, it is crucial to understand the dynamics of group behavior and the complexity of group formation, and to realize that groups can consciously develop in smoothness of interrelationships, effectiveness of production, and the ability to confront intra- and inter-group problems openly and directly.

> In the area of international relations, the need to forge standards and set directions in a shrunken world has inspired the organization of many international agencies and prompted many international conferences. Though the implications are world-wide, the results are in large part measured by the ability of individuals to understand and work with forces of group behavior.
>
> In industry, research indicates that management decisions are increasingly team decisions. The ability of the company to keep abreast of changing competitive demands to a large degree reflects whether staff units have indeed learned to work as teams and, since management teams overlap, to work with other teams.
>
> In communities, the traditional American machinery for making decisions, solving problems, taking action, is the community organization and its committees and meetings. Sound community growth and individual satisfaction depend on how well this machinery works, that is, on how effectively people

are able to share their common concerns, to reach wise decisions, to plan together.

At every level of education, from elementary school to programs for adults, those teachers who know how to help groups form and mature can release powerful forces to support individual learning. And the school executive who knows how to mobilize the energies of groups—whether in staff conference, board meeting, or PTA committee—faces the critical problems of today's schools with strength.

The family itself is a group. Inability to bring about the kind of membership necessary to resist divisive forces lies at the heart of many of our social problems.

If these statements were important in 1961, they are infinitely more so now. International problems have increased in complexity. Population increases have brought resource, health, and educational problems to greater magnitude. Domestically, governmental misuse of authority has created the need for a more open relationship between citizens and government. Cities face difficulties that previously were unknown. Welfare, unemployment, and inflation add new crises. The focus of education faces review.

With all these problems, the use of groups has mushroomed. There are groups for obesity control, child abuse, and community improvement; there are groups for the socialization of the elderly and for the personal growth and learning of individuals and of couples. The list could go on and on and on. The need for increased understanding of group behavior continues to grow. The introduction to the 1961 edition of *Group Development* spoke of the importance of such understanding.

For all of us there are daily opportunities and daily necessities for establishing group membership and leadership. Our own satisfaction and the success of the enterprises we support demand that our membership be meaningful and effective. In a world where individuality is threatened by pressures toward conformity, the best guarantee for maintaining individuality is the ability to nurture groups which develop individual contributions. For a group will function adequately *as a group* only to the extent that the members carry out sensitively and appropriately the individual functions necessary to work on the group task and to maintain the group in good working order. . . .

Organizing for work, building a group goal from many individual perceptions of the task and from many individual purposes, developing work procedures, encouraging individual contributions, are complex dimensions of group membership. The facts of group life are still further complicated by the inevitable presence of interpersonal relationships, shifting emotional reactions, problems of status and individual ego needs, and complicated further still by the fact that none of us is a member of only one group. Standing behind us as "our invisible committees" are the silent but persistent spokesmen for the other groups to which we also owe loyalty.

Perhaps, then, the most important of all member skills is diagnostic sensitivity. Unless a member is aware of and sensitive to the fluctuating forces within the group, his actions will in all probability be inappropriate. . . .

. . . If the individual is to find greater and more responsible freedom in the group life which is a fact of our existence as social beings, he must learn to work creatively and productively in the presence of the emotional, social, and work aspects of groups. To do this demands *trained awareness.*

Articles selected for the first edition were perceived to be most applicable to the practitioner—the leader or member of a group. Some of these articles discussed potential dilemmas to be aware of, others were diagnostically oriented, and a few gave tips on what to do.

These articles, however, were based on important research, largely carried out during the nineteen forties and fifties, stimulated by the theories of Kurt Lewin and the establishment by him of the first Research Center for Group Dynamics at the Massachusetts Institute of Technology. The National Training Laboratory in Group Development, which began its pioneering efforts in 1947, was staffed with many of those doing research in group dynamics. Consequently, articles for practitioners, written by these researchers, quickly appeared. The gap between the knowledge gained through research and its use in practice was measurably narrowed.

This revised edition of *Group Development* endeavors to bring theoretical assumptions and research results more closely in touch with articles about application. Part 1 contains many of the articles written for practitioners that appeared in the original edition, as well as theoretical articles about group development. Part 2 samples some of the important research in the field.

It is hoped that this combination of "what to look for and what to do" articles with theoretical discussions and research reports will provide a more consistent presentation of the vitally important area of group behavior.

Group Formation and Development

by Leland P. Bradford

Group behavior is affected by the dynamic interaction of many factors, making possible varied approaches to understanding the behavior and the development of groups. One approach is described in this article. It assumes there are phases or major problem areas in the continuing life of a group, with each problem area, when adequately resolved, creating improvement in internal group functioning and consequent productivity. These phases are:

- Initial group formation and initial movement
- Confronting a difficult problem
- Overcoming the problem through cooperative problem solving
- Group reorganization of structure and function.

Groups seem to go through these phases over and over again; each time, hopefully, at a slightly deeper level. In a sense, a group reforms each time it meets. Intervening events for the individual members, new expectations, problems or pressures from outside sources, subgroup cliques, rumors and gossip—all conspire to create a new group at each meeting. Absent or new members produce a new set of interrelationships, and sociometric choices may change. Hence, observing a group's phases of behavior is a matter of examining a process of continuing dynamic change.

Much of this article draws on concepts included in a mimeographed paper prepared by the author and Thomas J. Mallinson for the staff of the 1950 Summer Session of the National Training Laboratory in Group Development held in Bethel, Maine.

THE PHASE OF GROUP FORMATION

A large number of factors enter into the formation of a group. Before making a commitment to be fully involved, each potential member usually assesses the personal importance of the group's purpose and what would be required. When persons first gather together, they have not yet become a group. Relationships with each other have not been formed and channels for communication have not been established. Their differing perceptions of the group's purposes and goals have not been clarified. An analysis of the task, preliminary to any movement toward solution has not been made.   A "psychological group" forms when:

- Patterns of interaction are proven effective;
- Differences in perceptions about task, communication, and procedures are clarified;
- Relationships to other persons and groups are delineated;
- Standards for participation are set;
- Methods of work that elicit rather than inhibit contributions are established;
- A respected "place" for each person is secured; and
- Trust is established among members.

   For such a "psychological group" to come into existence requires deliberate and conscious efforts by both leader and members to overcome as many barriers to good group formation as possible. Otherwise, the initial formation leaves unexamined and unsolved major problems that might plague and distort the work of the group in the future and make its continued growth unlikely.

   Most individuals enter a new group situation with some bewilderment, confusion, tension (frequently denied), and anxiety (often unrecognized). To dispel these feelings, sense must be made out of the situation, order brought out of apparent chaos, and meaning out of uncertainty. Most importantly, the individual needs assurance of acceptance and recognition. The members' concerns deal both with the task level and the level of social-emotional needs. For the individual to feel comfortable, trusting, and free to contribute without fear of rejection, these concerns must be met. The more satisfactorily they are resolved, the greater the individual's involvement in and liking for the group.

Task-Level Concerns of the Member

- How clear am I about the purposes of the group? Are all of them equally significant to me, or sufficient enough to make me wish to be involved? What pressures from certain members or outside sources worry me?

What are my concerns about possible solutions to the problems confronting the group? How clear do other members seem to be about purposes, problems, solutions, and consequences?

- How are we supposed to communicate in this group? Should we address questions or offer opinions only to the leader or feel free to communicate and respond to others? How will a common frame of reference be developed so that talk is not at cross-purposes? How are decisions going to be reached? By voting? By consensus? By the leader or some influential member or clique?

- What are the purposes and aims of the leader? Are they congruent with mine? Are the members supposed to rubber-stamp the leader's ideas? How will the leader treat contrary suggestions? By rejection? By ignoring? By argument? By a punishing response?

- Am I under much or little pressure from my other groups to take a particular stand? What "back-home" loyalties do I suspect that other members may hold? How should I respond to such pressures?

- What are the rules, procedures, and boundaries under which we will be expected to operate? Will I feel stiff, uncomfortable, and reluctant to disagree, or feel relaxed and involved? By disagreeing, what personal risk might I take with being accepted and with others' perception of me and my reputation? On the other hand, how will I feel if I "go along" against my beliefs?

- Will the group atmosphere encourage or discourage the free interchange of ideas? Will it permit the critical assessment of ideas or will such reactions be perceived as personal attacks?

- What will be the pattern of participation in meetings? Will a few persons monopolize the discussion—ignoring, interrupting, or blocking less assertive members? Will the leader or other members assume any maintenance roles, such as bridging between opposing ideas, seeking common grounds (rather than polarized positions), and encouraging others to participate?

Social-Emotional Concerns of the Member

- How will I be accepted in this group? Will other members really listen to me? Will my comments be interrupted or be considered and used? How much influence or power can I expect to secure?

- Will I be perceived as effective or ineffective, knowledgeable or unknowledgeable? Should I be highly participative in order to be recognized, or should I sit back and evaluate the situation before participating? Would the latter cause me to be stereotyped as weak, timid, and ineffectual?

- What are the expectations about member behavior? How are boundaries set and by whom? What are the penalties if one transgresses the boundaries?

- How do I perceive and react to others? Do those who are more talkative and aggressive evoke fear of conflict in me, causing me to draw within myself, or to compete with them? What persons do I feel most comfortable with in this group? Why?

- How can I gain a sense of security in this group? Who must I watch, if anyone, in terms of self-protection? What must occur before I can feel a sense of trust in the group?

- How do I react to the leader as a person? Does his or her leadership style and approach to people make me feel tense, fearful, and uncomfortable or relaxed, accepted, and warm? Does the leader take sides or push a purely personal point? Does he or she dominate the group or help members feel involved in what happens in the group?

- How warm do I feel toward the other members? How warm and friendly do I perceive their feelings toward me? Do I wish for warm feelings or do I perceive each group as a battleground in which I enjoy contending with others?

- How do I feel about attending group meetings? With anticipation or with reluctance and dread? Why?

Such concerns of members should be resolved satisfactorily during the early stages of group formation. If they are, members will feel relaxed, excited about being a part of the group, free to participate actively, released to disagree without anxiety about rejection, and responsible with others for the productivity and maintenance of the group. A group will have formed. Cohesiveness and pride in the group will be present, along with tolerance for conflicting ideas. Personal hidden agendas will be minimal and disagreement and conflict will tend to be used constructively. Leadership will have become shared in an atmosphere of trust and sensitivity. Group members will have their thoughts, insights, and abilities stretched.

If these concerns are ignored, less desirable results may occur and groups may continue at a low productivity level. There may be: meetings prolonged by argument over trivial points or irrelevant drifting; decisions postponed or hurriedly and ineptly reached and then not implemented; opinions offered as facts; covert struggles for power and place in a pecking order; interpersonal conflicts unresolved; participation skewed by interruptions and punishing responses; a limited range of ideas and information in the group; leaders forced to control disruptive members and the group's adherence to the task; and member uninvolvement in group maintenance.

The effective formation of a group, and its continued development, require time and patience. It requires active effort on the part of the leader to produce an atmosphere of trust and the involvement of group members in the functioning of the group—in short, to encourage shared leadership. By indicating through word and action the necessary group task and maintenance roles, a leader can encourage members to assume these roles whenever appropriate. The leader can suggest, or encourage members to recommend, different group methods to meet emerging problems, and can model methods of nonpunishing feedback as a way of improving member behavior. Through examples, the leader "teaches" members how to take responsibility for their own group. In this way, the leader demolishes the assumption that the leader possesses all group control and direction, reduces member dependency, and increases member responsibility.

THE PHASE OF CONFRONTING A DIFFICULT PROBLEM

The most destructive situation that can occur after a group has achieved trust among members and is functioning effectively is to reach such harmony that no difficult problem or disagreement confronts the group. If this happens, the mood and purpose of the group is to maintain peace and harmony at the cost of productivity and growth. Fortunately, this seldom occurs.

Most groups eventually encounter a barrier—a difficult problem requiring a major decision, a readjustment of structure, a different perception of the job at hand, or the repair of interrelationships. The barrier suddenly seems insurmountable to the group members. Their previous over-optimism is shattered and consternation occurs. Was all their progress and harmony a fantasy? Was their beloved group really not very competent? Had they ignored problems they should have handled earlier? Did the leader fail them? Did some member lead them down the wrong path?

This major barrier, this difficult problem, could result from a variety of causes. Perhaps the task the members were working on had been discarded or reversed by a higher authority and the group felt powerless. Perhaps new information appeared, creating a totally different perception of the task and the needed solution. Perhaps the consequence of a decision is now becoming apparent and has created anxieties among members. Perhaps a fundamental difference related to the task has become obvious and has divided the group into two irreconcilable camps. Perhaps an interpersonal conflict, erupting to the surface, has thrown the group into disarray. Perhaps group members do not believe they have the knowledge, skill, or authority to deal with the issue.

Whatever the cause, the group breakdown appears severe. The realization that the group faces a situation that seems unsoluable comes as a shock. The impasse is interpreted as a failure and failure produces guilt. Guilt can be reduced by finding a scapegoat. Who to blame? The leader may be blamed for allowing the situation to occur. Members who are in conflict may be painted as villains, while other members offer critical and punishing remarks. Other interpersonal differences that have lain latent may now surface, and what seemed to be a cohesive, caring group may now regress into a collection of warring individuals. Some members, fearful of conflict, may withdraw from participation.

Task Level

Regression occurs on the task level. Where common perceptions of the task existed, now disagreements as to what the task exactly encompasses begin to appear. Previous group decisions are now viewed differently by members. Methods by which those decisions were reached, previously considered acceptable to all, now are questioned. Comments imply that decisions were reached by manipulation.

There also is regression in the group's patterns of interaction and participation. Instead of each verbal contribution being related to the previous comment, an intervention now bears little relation to the previous contribution. Arguments develop over minor points. Subgrouping and clique formation begin to emerge and pressure is placed on uncertain members to "declare themselves." The noise level rises. Discussion avoids the major barrier and difficult problem and drifts into off-the-track talking about trivial points.

Social-Emotional Level

On the social-emotional level, the competition for power previously dampened, now reappears. Hidden agendas of a personal nature are voiced obliquely. Emotional commitment to the group is lessened and group morale is low. Differences develop in the group between those who question any decision and those who feel that some decision, any decision, that will move the group out of its present dilemma is imperative.

The major barrier has, for the moment, demoralized the group and seems to have destroyed the progress made in its formation and initial development.

THE PHASE OF OVERCOMING THE PROBLEM THROUGH COOPERATIVE PROBLEM-SOLVING

Frequently, because the problem arises so unexpectedly, the group reaction is unnecessarily intense. Cohesion and agreement, perhaps reached prematurely, have led group members to assume there are no great difficulties ahead. But the shock may well be salutary if the group can recover. However, the danger to a group at this point in its existence should not be minimized. If no effective efforts are made to raise group morale, involvement and productivity may sink to a low level. Future problems, ordinarily perceived as inconsequential now may appear insurmountable.

Task Level

For this phase to strengthen the group and its continued development, group members must see that their earlier formation plastered over a number of task and group problems. Individual concerns about the task, the quality and quantity of information collected, the real assessment of decisions, and the consequences of implementing the final solution were not voiced by members for fear of disturbing the atmosphere of agreement. Members should also see that an implicit norm of preventing conflict had pushed interpersonal conflict or task disagreements to the covert level, to remain unsolved. Earlier, the group may have rejected the use of brief, but open and legitimate, subgrouping for better data collection, fearing that subgrouping would shatter the cohesiveness of the group.

Social-Emotional Level

The letdown in the group requires efforts to disentangle emotional reactions, do something about the problems that have surfaced, and create a new group structure and appropriate procedures. If no member acts, the leader can begin the process of reviving the group by suggesting that the members look back at the history of the group. A review of past experiences may highlight the group's proven strengths and abilities, as well as pinpoint specific group problems that now can be resolved.

The leader, or any perceptive member, can respond to expressions of failure and doubt by suggesting that the group's sense of failure and futility has become overblown. An analysis comparing the severity of the damage to the group with the severity of the shock might bring greater realism to the group's discussion. The group members may then seek and find a better balance between effective productivity and harmony. The task role of *critical appraiser* can be related to the value of contributions, rather than to the rejection of individuals. Improved problem-solving procedures can be discussed and adopted. By reorganizing structure, methods, ground rules, and expectations, members collaboratively reform their group.

THE PHASE OF GROUP REORGANIZATION

Once the group has recovered its composure, reorganization can take place on both the task and social-emotional levels through the following actions:

Task Level

- Effectively clarifying the problem or point of discussion to prevent differing perceptions of what is being discussed;
- Securing relevant information before arriving at a decision;
- Assessing information in terms of the adequacy and practicality of a solution;
- Accepting individual contributions in order to encourage full participation among members;
- Developing the norm that contributed ideas do not have to be "right" and may stimulate further ideas;
- Replacing poorly considered, overly simplistic, and hurriedly reached decisions by thoughtful decisions that are based on maximum participation and related to the problems and the consequences of implementation.

Social-Emotional Level

- Reducing the stereotyping and judging of others, constraints inhibiting individuality and contributions, and anxieties about status and acceptance;
- Legitimatizing group resistance to emotional "bandwagon" pressures or efforts to force members to take sides on polarized issues;
- Seeking solutions rather than polarized conflicts;
- Increasing group ability to withstand shock and to reintegrate and reorganize without a drastic regressive period;
- Increasing tolerance toward group-oriented disagreements and greater appreciation of untapped resources within the group;
- Increasing the individual's sensitivity to the needs of the group and other members;

- Lessening volatile emotional reactions and achieving more individual self-discipline because of better problem solving;
- Increasing the members' individual learning, testing of previously unexplored ideas, and participatory ability, because of their greater security in contributing.

These four phases usually recur in different forms and under different conditions. Together, they form the cycle by which groups continue to improve and grow. When future problems on either the task or social-emotional level are left unexamined or unsolved, or when a group ceases to periodically examine and evaluate its process, this growth and development cycle is broken. Not only is growth slowed or stopped, but the breakdown causes a slow regression in group ability, a diminution of trust, and an increase in interpersonal conflict. On the other hand, the continued growth and development of a group increases the learning and ability of its members.

A Theory of Group Development

by Warren G. Bennis and Herbert A. Shepard

If attention is focused on the organic properties of groups, criteria can be established by which phenomena of development, learning, or movement toward maturity can be identified. From this point of view, maturity for the group means something analogous to maturity for the person: a mature group knows very well what it is doing. The group can resolve its internal conflicts, mobilize its resources, and take intelligent action only if it has means for consensually validating its experience. The person can resolve his internal conflicts, mobilize his resources, and take intelligent action only if anxiety does not interfere with his ability to profit from his experience, to analyse, discriminate, and foresee. Anxiety prevents the person's internal communication system from functioning appropriately, and improvements in his ability to profit from experience hinge upon overcoming anxiety as a source of distortion. Similarly, group development involves the overcoming of obstacles to valid communication among the members, or the development of methods for achieving and testing consensus. Extrapolating from Sullivan's definition of personal maturity we can say a group has reached a state of valid communication when its members are armed with

> . . . referential tools for analyzing interpersonal experience, so that its significant differences from, as well as its resemblances to, past experience, are discriminable, and the foresight of relatively near future events will be adequate and appropriate to maintaining one's security and securing one's satisfactions without useless or ultimately troublesome disturbance of self-esteem (19, p. 111).

From *HUMAN RELATIONS*, 1956, 9(4), 415-457. Reprinted by permission.

This theory is based for the most part on observations made over a 5-year period of teaching graduate students "group dynamics." The main function of the seminar as it was set forth by the instructors was to improve the internal communication system of the group, hence, a self-study group.

Relatively few investigations of the phenomena of group development have been undertaken. This paper outlines a theory of development in groups that have as their explicit goal improvement of their internal communication systems.

A group of strangers, meeting for the first time, has within it many obstacles to valid communication. The more heterogeneous the membership, the more accurately does the group become, for each member, a microcosm of the rest of his interpersonal experience. The problems of understanding, the relationships, that develop in any given group are from one aspect a unique product of the particular constellation of personalities assembled. But to construct a broadly useful theory of group development, it is necessary to identify major areas of internal uncertainty, or obstacles to valid communication, which are common to and important in all groups meeting under a given set of environmental conditions. These areas must be strategic in the sense that until the group has developed methods for reducing uncertainty in them, it cannot reduce uncertainty in other areas, and in its external relations.

THE TWO MAJOR AREAS OF INTERNAL UNCERTAINTY: DEPENDENCE (AUTHORITY RELATIONS) AND INTERDEPENDENCE (PERSONAL RELATIONS)

Two major areas of uncertainty can be identified by induction from common experience, at least within our own culture. The first of these is the area of group members' orientations toward authority, or more generally toward the handling and distribution of power in the group. The second is the area of members' orientations toward one another. These areas are not independent of each other: a particular set of inter-member orientations will be associated with a particular authority structure. But the two sets of orientations are as distinct from each other as are the concepts of power and love. A number of authorities have used them as a starting-point for the analysis of group behavior.

In his *Group Psychology and the Analysis of the Ego*, Freud noted that "each member is bound by libidinal ties on the one hand to the leader . . . and on the other hand to the other members of the group" (6, p. 45). Although he described both ties as libidinal, he was uncertain "how these two ties are related to each other, whether they are of the same kind and the same value, and how they are to be described psychologically." Without resolving this question, he noted that (for the Church and the Army) "one of these, the tie with the leader, seems . . . to be more of a ruling factor than the other, which holds between members of the group" (6, p. 52).

More recently, Schutz (17) has made these two dimensions central to his theory of group compatibility. For him, the strategic determinant of compatibility is the particular blend of orientations toward authority and orientations toward personal intimacy. Bion (p. 2) conceptualizes the major dimensions of the group somewhat differently. His "dependency" and "pairing" modalities correspond to our "dependence" and "interdependence" areas; to them he adds a "fight-flight" modality. For him these modalities are simply alternative modes of behavior; for us, the fight-flight categorization has been useful for characterizing the means used by the group for maintaining a stereotyped orientation during a given subphase.

The core of the theory of group development is that the principal obstacles to the development of valid communication are to be found in the orientations toward authority and intimacy that members bring to the group. Rebelliousness, submissiveness, or withdrawal as the characteristic response to authority figures; destructive competitiveness, emotional exploitiveness, or withdrawal as the characteristic response to peers prevent consensual validation of experience. The behaviors determined by these orientations are directed toward enslavement of the other in the service of the self, enslavement of the self in the service of the other, or disintegration of the situation. Hence, they prevent the setting, clarification of, and movement toward group-shared goals.

In accord with Freud's observation, the orientations toward authority are regarded as being prior to, or partially determining of, orientations toward other members. In its development, the group moves from preoccupation with authority relations to preoccupation with personal relations. This movement defines the two major phases of group development. Within each phase are three subphases, determined by the ambivalence of orientations in each area. That is, during the authority ("dependent") phase, the group moves from preoccupation with submission to preoccupation with rebellion, to resolution of the dependence problem. Within the personal (or "interdependence") phase the group moves from a preoccupation with intermember identification to a preoccupation with individual identity to a resolution of the interdependence problem.

THE RELEVANT ASPECTS OF PERSONALITY IN GROUP DEVELOPMENT

The aspects of member personality most heavily involved in group development are called, following Schutz, the dependence and personal aspects.

The dependence aspect is comprised by the member's characteristic patterns related to a leader or to a structure of rules. Members who find comfort in rules of procedure, an agenda, an expert, etc. are called "dependent." Members who are discomfited by authoritative structures are called "counterdependent."

The personal aspect is comprised by the member's characteristic patterns with respect to interpersonal intimacy. Members who cannot rest until they have stabilized a relatively high degree of intimacy with all the others are called "overpersonal." Members who tend to avoid intimacy with any of the others are called "counterpersonal."

Psychodynamically, members who evidence some compulsiveness in the adoption of highly dependent, highly counterdependent, highly personal, or highly counterpersonal roles are regarded as "conflicted." Thus, the person who persists in being dependent upon any and all authorities thereby provides himself with ample evidence that authorities should not be so trustingly relied upon; yet he cannot profit from this experience in governing his future action. Hence, a deep, but unrecognized, distrust is likely to accompany the manifestly submissive behavior, and the highly dependent or highly counterdependent person is thus a person in conflict. The existence of the conflict accounts for the sometimes dramatic movement from extreme dependence to extreme rebelliousness. In this way counterdependence and dependence, while logically the extremes of a scale, are psychologically very close together.

The "unconflicted" person or "independent," who is better able to profit from his experience and assess the present situation more adequately, may of course act at times in rebellious or submissive ways. Psychodynamically, the difference between him and the conflicted is easy to understand. In terms of observable behavior, he lacks the compulsiveness and, significantly, does not create the communicative confusion so characteristic of, say, the conflicted dependent, who manifests submission in that part of his communication of which he is aware, and distrust or rebellion in that part of his communication of which he is unaware.

Persons who are unconflicted with respect to the dependence or personal aspect are considered to be responsible for the major movements of the group toward valid communication. That is, the actions of members unconflicted with respect to the problems of a given phase of group development move the group to the next phase. Such actions are called barometric events, and the initiators are called catalysts. This part of the theory of group development is based on Redl's thesis concerning the "infectiousness of the unconflicted on the conflicted personality constellation." The catalysts (Redl calls them "central persons") are the persons capable of reducing the uncertainty characterizing a given phase. "Leadership" from the standpoint of group development can be defined in terms of catalysts responsible for group movement from one phase to the next. This consideration provides a basis for determining what membership roles are needed for group development. For example, it is expected that a group will have great difficulty in resolving problems of power and authority if it lacks members who are unconflicted with respect to dependence.

PHASE MOVEMENTS

The foregoing summary has introduced the major propositions in the theory of group development. While it is not possible to reproduce the concrete group experience from which the theory is drawn, we can take a step in this direction by discussing in more detail what seem to us to be the dominant features of each phase. The description given below is highly interpretive, and we emphasize what seem to us to be the major themes of each phase, even though many minor themes are present. In the process of abstracting, stereotyping, and interpreting, certain obvious facts about group process are lost. For example, each group meeting is to some extent a recapitulation of its past and a forecast of its future. This means that behavior that is "regressive" or "advanced" often appears.

Phase I: Dependence

Subphase 1: Dependence-flight. The first days of group life are filled with behavior whose remote, as well as immediate, aim is to ward off anxiety. Much of the discussion content consists of fruitless searching for a common goal. Some of the security-seeking behavior is group-shared—for example, members may reassure one another by providing interesting and harmless facts about themselves. Some is idiosyncratic—for example, doodling, yawning, intellectualizing.

The search for a common goal is aimed at reducing the cause of anxiety, thus going beyond the satisfaction of immediate security needs. But just as evidencing boredom in this situation is a method of warding off anxiety by denying its proximity, so group goal-seeking is not quite what it is claimed to be. It can best be understood as a dependence plea. The trainer, not the lack of a goal, is the cause of insecurity. This interpretation is likely to be vigorously contested by the group, but it is probably valid. The characteristic expectations of group members are that the trainer will establish rules of the game and distribute rewards. He is presumed to know what the goals are or ought to be. Hence his behavior is regarded as a "technique"; he is merely playing hard to get. The pretense of a fruitless search for goals is a plea for him to tell the group what to do, by simultaneously demonstrating its helplessness without him, and its willingness to work under his direction for his approval and protection.

We are here talking about the dominant theme in group life. Many minor themes are present, and even in connection with the major theme there are differences among members. For some, testing the power of the trainer to affect their futures is the major concern. In others, anxiety may be aroused through a sense of helplessness in a situation made threatening by the protector's desertion. These alternatives can be seen as the beginnings of the counterdependent and dependent adaptations. Those with a dependent orientation look vainly for cues from the trainer for procedure and direction, sometimes paradoxically they infer that the leader must want it that way. Those with a counterdependent orientation strive to detect in the trainer's action elements that would offer ground for rebellion, and may even paradoxically demand rules and leadership from him because he is failing to provide them.

The ambiguity of the situation at this stage quickly becomes intolerable for some, and a variety of ultimately unserviceable resolutions may be invented, many of them idiosyncratic. Alarm at the prospect of future meetings is likely to be group-shared, and at least a gesture may be made in the direction of formulating an agenda for subsequent meetings.

This phase is characterized by behavior that has gained approval from authorities in the past. Since the meetings are to be concerned with groups or with human relations, members offer information on these topics, to satisfy the presumed expectations of the trainer and to indicate expertise, interest, or achievement in these topics (ex-officers from the armed services, from fraternities, etc., have the floor). Topics such as business or political leadership, discrimination and desegregation, are likely to be discussed. During this phase the contributions made by members are designed to gain approval from the trainer, whose reaction to each comment is surreptitiously watched. If the trainer comments that this seems to be the case, or if he notes that the subject under discussion (say, discrimination) may be related to some concerns about membership in this group, he fails again to satisfy the needs of members. Not that the validity of this interpretation is held in much doubt. No one is misled by the "flight" behavior involved in discussing problems external to the group, least of all the group members. Discussion of these matters is filled with perilous uncertainties, however, and so the trainer's observation is politely ignored, as one would ignore a *faux-pas* at a tea-party. The attempts to gain approval based on implicit hypotheses about the potential power of the trainer for good and evil are continued until the active members have run through the repertoire of behaviors that have gained them favor in the past.

Subphase 2: Counterdependence-flight. As the trainer continues to fail miserably in satisfying the needs of the group, discussion takes on a different tone, and counterdependent expressions begin to replace overt dependency phase. In many ways this subphase is the most stressful and unpleasant in the life of the group. It is marked by a paradoxical development of the trainer's role into one of omnipotence and powerlessness, and by division of the group into two warring subgroups. In subphase 1, feelings of hostility were strongly defended; if a slip were made that suggested hostility, particularly toward the trainer, the group members were embarrassed. Now expressions of hostility are more frequent, and are more likely to be supported by other members, or to be met with equally hostile responses. Power is much more overtly the concern of group members in this subphase. A topic such as leadership may again be discussed, but the undertones of the discussion are no longer dependence pleas. Discussion of leadership in subphase 2 is in part a vehicle for making explicit the trainer's failure as a leader. In part it is perceived by other members as a bid for leadership on the part of any member who participates in it.

The major themes of this subphase are as follows:

1. Two opposed subgroups emerge, together incorporating most of the group members. Characteristically, the subgroups are in disagreement about the group's need for leadership or "structure." One subgroup attempts to elect a chairman, nominate working committees, establish agenda, or otherwise "structure" the meetings; the other subgroup opposes all such efforts. At first this appears to be merely an intellectual disagreement concerning the future organization of group activity. But soon it becomes the basis for destroying any semblance of group unity. Fragmentation is expressed and brought about in many ways: voting is a favorite way of dramatizing the schism; suggestions that the group is too large and should be divided into subgroups for the meetings are frequent; a chairman may be elected and then ignored as a demonstration of the group's ineffectualness. Although control mechanisms are sorely needed and desired, no one is willing to relinquish the rights of leadership and control to anyone else. The trainer's abdication has created a power gap, but no one is allowed to fill it.

2. Disenthrallment with the trainer proceeds rapidly. Group members see him as at best ineffectual, at worst damaging, to group progress. He is ignored and bullied almost simultaneously. His interventions are perceived by the counterdependents as an attempt to interrupt group progress; by the dependents, as weak and incorrect statements. His silences are regarded by the dependents as desertion; by the counterdependents as manipulation. Much of the group activity is to be understood as punishment of the trainer, for his failure to meet needs and expectations, for getting the group into an unpleasant situation, for being the worst kind of authority figure—a weak and incompetent one, or a manipulative, insincere one. Misunderstanding or ignoring his comments, implying that his observations are paranoid fantasies, demonstrations that the group is cracking up, references to him in the past tense as though he were no longer present—these are the punishments for his failure.

As, in the first subphase, the trainer's wisdom, power, and competence were overtly unquestioned, but secretly suspected; so, in the second subphase, the conviction that he is incompetent and helpless is clearly dramatized, but secretly doubted. Out of this secret doubt arises the belief in the trainer's omnipotence. None of the punishments meted out to the trainer are recognized as such by the group members; in fact, if the trainer suggests that the members feel a need to punish him, they are most likely to respond in injured tones or in tones of contempt that what is going on has nothing to do with him and that he had best stay out of it. The trainer is still too imposing and threatening to challenge directly. There is a secret hope that the chaos in the group is in fact part of the master plan, that he is really leading them in the direction they should be going. That he may really be helpless as they imply, or that the failure may be theirs rather than his, are frightening possibilities. For this reason subphase 2 differs very little in its fundamental dynamics from subphase 1. There is still the secret wish that the trainer will stop all the bedlam which has replaced polite uncertainty, by taking his proper role (so that dependent members can cooperate with him and counterdependent can rebel in the usual ways).

Subphase 2 thus brings the group to the brink of catastrophe. The trainer has consistently failed to meet the group's needs. Not daring to turn directly on him, the group members engage in mutually destructive behavior: in fact, the group threatens suicide as the most extreme expression of dependence. The need to punish the trainer is so strong, however, that his act of salvation would have to be magical indeed.

Subphase 3: Resolution-catharsis. No such magic is available to the trainer. Resolution of the group's difficulties at this point depends upon the presence in the group of other forces, which have until this time been inoperative, or ineffective. Only the degenerative aspects of the chain of events in subphases 1 and 2 have been presented up to this point and they are in fact the salient ones. But there has been a simultaneous, though less obvious, mobilization of constructive forces. First, within each of the warring subgroups bonds of mutual support have grown. The group member no longer feels helpless and isolated. Second, the trainer's role, seen as weak or manipulative in the dependence orientation, can also be perceived as permissive. Third, his interpretations, though openly ignored, have been secretly attended to. And, as the second and third points imply, some members of the group are less the prisoners of the dependence-counterdependence dilemma than others. These members, called the independents, have been relatively ineffective in the group for two reasons. First, they have not developed firm bonds with other members in either of the warring subgroups, because they have not identified with either cause. Typically, they have devoted their energies to an unsuccessful search for a compromise settlement of the disagreements in the group. Since their attitudes toward authority are less ambivalent than those of other members, they have accepted the alleged reason for disagreement in the group—for example, whether a chairman should be elected—at face value, and tried to mediate. Similarly, they have tended to accept the trainer's role and interpretations more nearly at face value. However, his interpretations have seemed inaccurate to them, since in fact the interpretations have applied much less to them than to the rest of the group.

Subphase 3 is the most crucial and fragile in group life up to this point. What occurs is a sudden shift in the whole basis of group action. It is truly a bridging phase; if it occurs at all, it is so rapid and mercurial that the end of subphase 2 appears to give way directly to the first subphase of Phase II. If it does not occur thus rapidly and dramatically, a halting and arduous process of vacillation between Phases I and II is likely to persist for a long period, the total group movement being very gradual.

To summarize the state of affairs at the beginning of subphase 3: 1. The group is polarized into two competing groups, each unable to gain or relinquish power. 2. Those group members who are uncommitted to either subgroup are ineffective in their attempts to resolve the conflict. 3. The trainer's contributions only serve to deepen the cleavage in the group.

As the group enters subphase 3, it is moving rapidly toward extinction: that is, splintering into two or three subgroups. The independents, who have until now been passive or ineffectual, become the only hope for survival, since they have thus far avoided polarization and stereotypic behavior. The imminence of dissolution forces them to recognize the fruitlessness of their attempts at mediation. For this reason, the trainer's hypothesis that fighting one another is off-target behavior is likely to be acted upon at this point. A group member may openly express the opinion that the trainer's presence and comments are holding the group back, suggest that "as an experiment" the trainer leaves the group "to see how things go without him." When the trainer is thus directly challenged, the whole atmosphere of the meeting changes. There is a sudden increase in alertness and tension. Previously, there had been much acting out of the wish that the trainer were absent, but at the same time a conviction that he was the *raison d'être* of the group's existence—that it would fall apart without him. Previously, absence of the trainer would have constituted desertion, or defeat, fulfillment of the members' worst fears as to their own inadequacy or the trainer's. But now leaving the group can have a different meaning. General agreement that the trainer should leave is rarely achieved. However, after a little further discussion it becomes clear that he is at liberty to leave, with the understanding that he wishes to be a member of the group, and will return if and when the group is willing to accept him.

The principal function of the symbolic removal of the trainer is in its effect of freeing the group to bring into awareness the hitherto carefully ignored feelings toward him as an authority figure, and toward the group

activity as an off-target dramatization of the ambivalence toward authority. The leadership provided by the independents (whom the group sees
as having no vested interest in power) leads to a new orientation toward
membership in the group. In the discussion that follows the exit of the
trainer, the dependents' assertion that the trainer deserted and the counterdependents' assertion that he was kicked out are soon replaced by
consideration of whether his behavior was "responsible" or "irresponsi-
ble." The power problem is resolved by being defined in terms of member
responsibilities, and the terms of the trainer's return to the group are
settled by the requirement that he behave as "just another member of the
group." This phrase is then explained as meaning that he should take
neither more nor less responsibility for what happens in the group than
any other member.

The above description of the process does not do justice to the excitement and involvement characteristic of this period. How much transfer-
able insight ambivalent members acquire from it is difficult to assess. At
least within the life of the group, later activity is rarely perceived in terms
of submission and rebellion.

An interesting parallel, which throws light on the order of events in
group development, is given in Freud's discussion of the myth of the
primal horde. In his version:

> These many individuals eventually banded themselves together, killed [the
> father], and cut him in pieces. . . . They then formed the totemistic commu-
> nity of brothers all with equal rights and united by the totem prohibitions
> which were to preserve and to expiate the memory of the murder (6, p. 112).

The horde's act, according to Freud, was soon distorted into an heroic
myth: instead of murder by the group, the myth held that the father had
been overthrown single-handed by one person, usually the youngest
son. In this attribution of the group act to one individual (the hero) Freud
saw the "emergence of the individual from group psychology." His
definition of a hero is ". . . a man who stands up manfully against his
father and in the end victoriously overthrows him" (8, p. 9). (The heroic
myth of Freud thus shares much in common with Sullivan's "delusion of
unique individuality.")

In the training group, the member who initiates the events leading to
the trainer's exit is sometimes referred to as a "hero" by the other members. Responsibility for the act is felt to be shared by the group, however,
and out of their experience comes the first strong sense of group solidarity
and involvement—a reversal of the original version, where the individual
emerges from the group. This turn of events clarifies Freud's remark
concerning the libidinal ties to the leader and to the other group members.
Libidinal ties toward the other group members cannot be adequately
developed until there is a resolution of the ties with the leader. In our

terms, those components of group life having to do with intimacy and interdependence cannot be dealt with until those components having to do with authority and dependence have been resolved.

Other aspects of subphase 3 may be understood by investigating the dramatic significance of the revolt. The event is always marked in group history as "a turning-point," "the time we became a group," "when I first got involved," etc. The mounting tension, followed by sometimes uproarious euphoria, cannot be entirely explained by the surface events. It may be that the revolt represents a realization of important fantasies individuals hold in all organizations, that the emotions involved are undercurrents wherever rebellious and submissive tendencies toward existing authorities must be controlled. These are the themes of some of our great dramas—*Antigone, Billy Budd, Hamlet,* and our most recent folk-tale, *The Caine Mutiny*. But the event is more than the presentation of a drama, or an acting-out of fantasies. For it can be argued that the moments of stress and catharsis, when emotions are labile and intense, are the times in the group life when there is readiness for change. Leighton's analysis of a minor revolution at a Japanese relocation camp is worth quoting in full on this point:

> While this [cathartic] situation is fraught with danger because of trends which may make the stress become worse before it gets better, there is also an opportunity for administrative action that is not likely to be found in more secure times. It is fairly well recognized in psychology that at periods of great emotional stir the individual human being can undergo far-reaching and permanent changes in his personality. It is as if the bone structure of his systems of belief and of his habitual patterns of behavior becomes soft, is fused into new shapes and hardens there when the period of tension is over. . . . Possibly the same can be true of whole groups of people, and there are historical examples of social changes and movements occurring when there was widespread emotional tension, usually some form of anxiety. The Crusades, parts of the Reformation, the French Revolution, the change in Zulu life in the reign of Chaca, the Meiji Restoration, the Mormon movement, the Russian Revolution, the rise of Fascism, and alterations in the social sentiments of the United States going on at present are all to some extent examples (12, p. 360).

Observers of industrial relations have made similar observations. When strikes result from hostile labor-management relations (as contrasted to straight wage demands), there is a fluidity of relationships and a wide repertoire of structural changes during this period not available before the strike act.[2]

---

[2]See A. Gouldner (10), W. F. Whyte, Jr. (22). Robert E. Park, writing in 1928, had considerable insight on some functions of revolution and change. See (14).

So it is, we believe, with the training group. But what are the new values and behavior patterns that emerge out of the emotional experience of Phase I? Principally, they are acceptance by each member of his full share of responsibility for what happens in the group. The outcome is autonomy for the group. After the events of subphase 3, there is no more attribution of magical powers to the trainer—either the dependent fantasy that he sees farther, knows better, is mysteriously guiding the group and protecting it from evil, or the very similar counterdependent fantasy that he is manipulating the group, exploiting it in his own interests, that the experience is one of "brain-washing." The criterion for evaluating a contribution is no longer who said it, but what is said. Thereafter, such power fantasies as the trainer himself may have present no different problem from the power fantasies of any other group member. At the same time, the illusion that there is a struggle for power in the group is suddenly dissipated, and the contributions of other members are evaluated in terms of their relevance to shared group goals.

Summary of Phase I

The very word development implies not only movement through time, but also a definite order of progression. The group must traverse subphase 1 to reach subphase 2, and subphase 3 before it can move into Phase II. At the same time, lower levels of development coexist with more advanced levels. Blocking and regression occur frequently, and the group may be "stuck" at a certain phase of development. It would, of course, be difficult to imagine a group remaining long in subphase 3—the situation is too tense to be permanent. But the group may founder for some time in subphase 2 with little movement. In short, groups do not inevitably develop through the resolution of the dependence phase to Phase II. This movement may be retarded indefinitely. Obviously much depends upon the trainer's role. In fact, the whole dependence modality may be submerged by certain styles of trainer behavior. The trainer has a certain range of choice as to whether dependency as a source of communication distortion is to be highlighted and made the subject of special experiential and conceptual consideration. The personality and training philosophy of the trainer determine his interest in introducing or avoiding explicit consideration of dependency.

There are other important forces in the group besides the trainer, and these may serve to facilitate or block the development that has been described as typical of Phase I. Occasionally there may be no strong independents capable of bringing about the barometric events that precipitate movement. Or the leaders of opposing subgroups may be the most assertive members of the group. In such cases the group may founder permanently in subphase 2. If a group has the misfortune to experience a "traumatic" event early in its existence—exceedingly schizoid behavior by some member during the first few meetings, for example—anxieties of other members may be aroused to such an extent that all culturally suspect behavior, particularly open expression of feelings, is strongly inhibited in subsequent meetings.

Table I summarizes the major events of Phase I, as it typically proceeds. This phase has dealt primarily with the resolution of dependence needs. It ends with acceptance of mutual responsibility for the fate of the group and a sense of solidarity, but the implications of shared responsibility have yet to be explored. This exploration is reserved for Phase II, which we have chosen to call the Interdependence Phase.

Phase II: Interdependence

The resolution of dependence problems marks the transfer of group attention (and inattention) to the problems of shared responsibility.

Sullivan's description of the change from childhood to the juvenile era seems pertinent here:

> The juvenile era is marked off from childhood by the appearance of an urgent need for compeers with whom to have one's existence. By "compeers" I mean people who are on our level, and have generically similar attitudes toward authoritative figures, activities and the like. This marks the beginning of the juvenile era, the great developments in which are the talents for cooperation, competition and compromise (20, pp. 17-18. Emphasis ours).

The remaining barriers to valid communication are those associated with orientations toward interdependence: i.e. intimacy, friendship, identification. While the distribution of power was the cardinal issue during Phase I, the distribution of affection occupies the group during Phase II.

Subphase 4: Enchantment-flight. At the outset of subphase 4, the group is happy, cohesive, relaxed. The atmosphere is one of "sweetness and light." Any slight increase in tension is instantly dissipated by joking and laughter. The fighting of Phase I is still fresh in the memory of the group, and the group's efforts are devoted to patching up differences, healing wounds, and maintaining a harmonious atmosphere. Typically, this is a time of merrymaking and group minstrelsy. Coffee and cake may be served at the meetings. Hours may be passed in organizing a group party. Poetry or songs commemorating the important events and persons in the group's history may be composed by individuals or, more commonly, as a group project. All decisions must be unanimous during this period, since everyone must be happy, but the issues on which decisions are made are mostly ones about which group members have no strong feelings. At first

Table I. Phase I. Dependence—Power Relations*

	SUBPHASE 1 DEPENDENCE-SUBMISSION	SUBPHASE 2 COUNTERDEPENDENCE	SUBPHASE 3 RESOLUTION
1. Emotional Modality	Dependence—Flight	Counterdependence — Flight. Off-target fighting among members. Distrust of staff member. Ambivalence.	Pairing. Intensive involvement in group task.
2. Content Themes	Discussion of interpersonal problems external to training groups.	Discussion of group organization; i.e. what degree of structuring devices is needed for "effective" group behavior?	Discussion and definition of trainer role.
3. Dominant Roles (Central Persons)	Assertive, aggressive members with rich previous organizational or social science experience.	Most assertive counterdependent and dependent members. Withdrawal of *less* assertive independents and dependents.	Assertive independents.
4. Group Structure	Organized mainly into multisubgroups based on members' past experiences.	Two tight subcliques consisting of leaders and members, of counterdependents and dependents.	Group unifies in pursuit of goal and develops internal authority system.
5. Group Activity	Self-oriented behavior reminiscent of most new social gatherings.	Search for consensus mechanism: Voting, setting up chairmen, search for "valid" content subjects.	Group members take over leadership roles formerly perceived as held by trainer.
6. Group movement facilitated by:	Staff member abnegation of traditional role of structuring situation, setting up rules of fair play, regulation of participation.	Disenthrallment with staff member coupled with absorption of uncertainty by most assertive counterdependent and dependent individuals. Subgroups form to ward off anxiety.	Revolt by assertive independents (catalysts) who fuse subgroups into unity by initiating and engineering trainer exit (barometric event).
7. Main Defenses	Projection Denigration of authority		Group moves into Phase II.

*Course terminates at the end of 17 weeks. It is not uncommon for groups to remain throughout the course in this phase.

the cathartic, healing function of these activities is clear; there is much spontaneity, playfulness, and pleasure. Soon the pleasures begin to wear thin.

The myth of mutual acceptance and universal harmony must eventually be recognized for what it is. From the beginning of this phase there are frequent evidences of underlying hostilities, unresolved issues in the group. But they are quickly, nervously smoothed over by laughter or misinterpretation. Subphase 4 begins with catharsis, but that is followed by the development of a rigid norm to which all members are forced to conform: "Nothing must be allowed to disturb our harmony in the future; we must avoid the mistakes of the painful past." Not that members have forgotten that the painful past was a necessary preliminary to the autonomous and (it is said) delightful present, though that fact is carefully overlooked. Rather, there is a dim realization that all members must have an experience somewhat analogous to the trainer's in subphase 3, before a mutually understood, accepted, and realistic definition of their own roles in the group can be arrived at.

Resistance of members to the requirement that harmony be maintained at all costs appears in subtle ways. In open group discussion the requirement is imperative: either the member does not dare to endanger harmony with the group or to disturb the *status quo* by denying that all problems have been solved. Much as members may dislike the tedious work of maintaining the appearance of harmony, the alternative is worse. The house of cards would come tumbling down, and the painful and exacting work of building something more substantial would have to begin. The flight from these problems takes a number of forms. Group members may say, "We've had our fighting and are now a group. Thus, further self-study is unnecessary." Very commonly, the possibility of any change may be prevented by not coming together as a total group at all. Thus the members may subgroup through an entire meeting. Those who would disturb the friendly subgroups are accused of "rocking the boat."

The solidarity and harmony become more and more illusory, but the group still clings to the illusion. This perseveration is in a way a consequence of the deprivation that members have experienced in maintaining the atmosphere of harmony. Maintaining it forces members to behave in ways alien to their own feelings; to go still further in group involvement would mean a complete loss of self. The group is therefore torn by a new ambivalence, which might be verbalized as follows: 1. "We all love one another and therefore we must maintain the solidarity of the group and give up whatever is necessary of our selfish desires." 2. "The group demands that I sacrifice my identity as a person; but the group is an evil mechanism which satisfies no dominant needs." As this subphase comes to a close, the happiness that marked its beginning is maintained only as a mask. The "innocent" splitting of the group into subgroups has gone so far that members will even walk around the meeting table to join in the conversation of a subgroup rather than speak across the table at the risk of bringing the whole group together. There is a certain uneasiness about the group; there is a feeling that "we should work together but cannot." There may be a tendency to regress to the orientation of subphase 1: group members would like the trainer to take over.

To recapitulate: subphase 4 begins with a happy sense of group belongingness. Individual identity is eclipsed by a "the group is bigger than all of us" sentiment. But this integration is short lived: it soon becomes perceived as a fake attempt to resolve interpersonal problems by denying their reality. In the later stages of this subphase, enchantment with the total group is replaced by enchantment with one's subgroup, and out of this breakdown of the group emerges a new organization based on the anxieties aroused out of this first, suffocating, involvement.

Subphase 5: Disenchantment-fight. This subphase is marked by a division into two subgroups—paralleling the experience of subphase 2—but this time based upon orientations toward the degree of intimacy required by group membership. Membership in the two subgroups is not necessarily the same as in subphase 2: for now the fragmentation occurs as a result of opposite and extreme attitudes toward the degree of intimacy desired in interpersonal relations. The counterpersonal members band together to resist further involvement. The overpersonal members band together in a demand for unconditional love. While these subgroups appear as divergent as possible, a common theme underlies them. For the one group, the only means seen for maintaining self-esteem is to avoid any real commitment to others; for the other group, the only way to maintain self-esteem is to obtain a commitment from others to forgive everything. The subgroups share in common the fear that intimacy breeds contempt.

This anxiety is reflected in many ways during subphase 6. For the first time openly disparaging remarks are made about the group. Invidious comparisons are made between it and other groups. Similarly, psychology and social science may be attacked. The inadequacy of the group as a basis for self-esteem is dramatized in many ways—from stating "I don't care what you think," to boredom, to absenteeism. The overpersonals insist that they are happy and comfortable, while the counterpersonals complain about the lack of group morale. Intellectualization by the overpersonals frequently takes on religious overtones concerning Christian love, consideration for others, etc. In the explanations of member behavior, the counterpersonal members account for all in terms of motives having nothing to do with the present group; the overpersonals explain all in terms of acceptance and rejection in the present group.

Subphase 5 belongs to the counterpersonals as subphase 4 belonged to the overpersonals. Subphase 4 might be caricatured as hiding in the womb of the group; subphase 5 as hiding out of sight of the group. It seems probable that both of these modalities serve to ward off anxieties associated with intimate interpersonal relations. A theme that links them together can be verbalized as follows: "If others really knew me, they would reject me." The overpersonal's formula for avoiding this rejection seems to be accepting all others so as to be protected by the others' guilt; the counterpersonal's way is by rejecting all others before they have a chance to reject him. Another way of characterizing the counterpersonal orientation is in the phrase, "I would lose my identity as a member of the group." The corresponding overpersonal orientation reads, "I have nothing to lose by identifying with the group." We can now look back on the past two subphases as countermeasures against loss of self-esteem; what Sullivan once referred to as the greatest inhibition to the understanding of what is distinctly human, "the overwhelming conviction of self-hood— this amounts to a delusion of unique individuality." The sharp swings and fluctuations that occurred between the enchantment and euphoria of subphase 4 and the disenchantment of subphase 5 can be seen as a struggle between the "institutionalization of complacency" on the one hand and anxiety associated with fantasy speculations about intimacy and involvement on the other. This dissociative behavior serves a purpose of its own: a generalized denial of the group and its meaning for individuals. For if the group is important and valid then it has to be taken seriously. If it can wallow in the enchantment of subphase 4, it is safe; if it can continually vilify the goals and objectives of the group, it is also safe. The disenchantment theme in subphase 5 is perhaps a less skillful and more desperate security provision with its elaborate wall of defenses than the "group mind" theme of subphase 4. What should be stressed is that both subphase defenses were created almost entirely on fantastic expectations about the consequences of group involvement. These defenses are homologous to anxiety as it is experienced by the individual; i.e., the state of "anxiety arises as a response to a situation of danger and which will be reproduced thenceforward whenever such a situation recurs" (7, p. 72). In sum, the past two subphases were marked by a conviction that further group involvement would be injurious to members' self-esteem.

Subphase 6: Consensual validation. In the groups of which we write, two forces combine to press the group toward a resolution of the interdependency problem. These are the approaching end of the training course, and the need to establish a method of evaluation (including course grades).

There are, of course, ways of denying or avoiding these realities. The group can agree to continue to meet after the course ends. It can extricate itself from evaluation activities by asking the trainer to perform the task, or by awarding a blanket grade. But turning this job over to the trainer is a regression to dependence; and refusal to discriminate and reward is a failure to resolve the problems of interdependence. If the group has developed in general as we have described, the reality of termination and evaluation cannot be denied, and these regressive modes of adaptation cannot be tolerated.

The characteristic defenses of the two subgroups at first fuse to prevent any movement toward the accomplishment of the evaluation and grading task. The counterpersonals resist evaluation as an invasion of privacy: they foresee catastrophe if members begin to say what they think of one another. The overpersonals resist grading since it involves discriminating among the group members. At the same time, all members have a stake in the outcome of evaluation and grading. In avoiding the task, members of each subgroup are perceived by members of the other as "rationalizing," and the group becomes involved in a vicious circle of mutual disparagement. In this process, the fear of loss of self-esteem through group involvement is near to being realized. As in subphase 3, it is the independents—in this case those whose self-esteem is not threatened by the prospect of intimacy—who restore members' confidence in the group. Sometimes all that is required to reverse the vicious circle quite dramatically is a request by an independent for assessment of his own role. Or it may be an expression of confidence in the group's ability to accomplish the task.

The activity that follows group commitment to the evaluation task does not conform to the expectations of the overpersonal or counterpersonal members. Its chief characteristic is the willingness and ability of group members to validate their self-concepts with other members. The fear of rejection fades when tested against reality. The tensions that developed as a result of these fears diminish in the light of actual discussion of member roles. At the same time, there is revulsion against "capsule evaluations" and "curbstone psychoanalysis." Instead, what ensues is a serious attempt by each group member to verbalize his private conceptual scheme for understanding human behavior—his own and that of others. Bringing these assumptions into explicit communication is the main work of subphase 6. This activity demands a high level of work and of communicative skill. Some of the values that appear to underlie the group's work during this subphase are as follows: 1. Members can accept one another's differences without associating "good" and "bad" with the differences. 2. Conflict exists but is over substantive issues rather than emotional issues. 3. Consensus is reached as a result of rational discussion rather than through a compulsive attempt at unanimity. 4. Members are aware of their own involvement, and of other aspects of group process, without being overwhelmed or alarmed. 5. Through the evaluation process, members take on greater personal meaning to each other. This facilitates communication and creates a deeper understanding of how the other person thinks, feels, behaves; it creates a series of personal expectations, as distinguished from the previous, more stereotyped, role expectations.

The above values, and some concomitant values, are of course very close to the authors' conception of a "good group." In actuality they are not always achieved by the end of the group life. The prospect of the death of the group, after much procrastination in the secret hope that it will be over before anything can be done, is likely to force the group into strenuous last-minute efforts to overcome the obstacles that have blocked its progress. As a result, the sixth subphase is too often hurried and incomplete. If the hurdles are not overcome in time, grading is likely to be an exercise that confirms members' worst suspicions about the group. And if role evaluation is attempted, either the initial evaluations contain so much hostile material as to block further efforts, or evaluations are so flowery and vacuous that no one, least of all the recipient, believes them.

In the resolution of interdependence problems, member-personalities count for even more than they do in the resolution of dependence problems. The trainer's behavior is crucial in determining the group's ability to resolve the dependence issue, but in the interdependence issue the group is, so to speak, only as strong as its weakest link. The exceedingly dependent group member can ride through Phase I with a fixed belief in the existence of a private relationship between himself and the trainer; but the person whose anxieties are intense under the threats associated with intimacy can immobilize the group. (*Table II* summarizes the major events of Phase II.)

CONCLUSIONS

Dependence and interdependence—power and love, authority and intimacy—are regarded as the central problems of group life. In most organizations and societies, the rules governing the distribution of authority and the degree of intimacy among members are prescribed. In the human relations training group, they are major areas of uncertainty. While the choice of these matters is the focus of group attention and experience rests to some extent with the trainer, his choice is predicated on the belief that they are the core of interpersonal experience. As such, the principal obstacles to valid interpersonal communication lie in rigidities of interpretation and response carried over from the anxious experiences with particular love or power figures into new situations in which they are inappropriate. The existence of such autisms complicates all discussion

TABLE II. Phase II. Interdependence—Personal Relations

	SUBPHASE 4—ENCHANTMENT	SUBPHASE 5—DISENCHANTMENT	SUBPHASE 6—CONSENSUAL VALIDATION
Emotional Modality	Pairing-Flight. Group becomes a respected icon beyond further analysis.	Fight-Flight. Anxiety reactions. Distrust and suspicion of various group members.	Pairing, understanding, acceptance.
Content Themes	Discussion of "group history," and generally salutary aspects of course, group, and membership.	Revival of content themes used in Subphase 1: What is a group? What are we doing here? What are the goals of the group? What do I have to give up—personally—to belong to this group? (How much intimacy and affection is required?) Invasion of privacy vs. "group giving." Setting up proper codes of social behavior.	Course grading system. Discussion and assessment of member roles.
Dominant Roles (Central Persons)	General distribution of participation for first time. Overpersonals have salience.	Most assertive counterpersonal and overpersonal individuals, with counterpersonals especially salient.	Assertive independents.
Group Structure	Solidarity, fusion. High degree of camaraderie and suggestibility. Le Bon's description of "group mind" would apply here.	Restructuring of membership into two competing predominant subgroups made up of individuals who share similar attitudes concerning degree of intimacy required in social interaction, i.e. the counterpersonal and overpersonal groups. The personal individuals remain uncommitted but act according to needs of situation.	Diminishing of ties based on personal orientation. Group structure now presumably appropriate to needs of situation based on predominantly substantive rather than emotional orientations. Consensus significantly easier on important issues.

TABLE II. (Continued)

	SUBPHASE 4— ENCHANTMENT	SUBPHASE 5— DISENCHANTMENT	SUBPHASE 6— CONSENSUAL VALIDATION
Group Activity	Laughter, joking, humor. Planning out-of-class activities such as parties. The institutionalization of happiness to be accomplished by "fun" activities. High rate of interaction and participation.	Disparagement of group in a variety of ways: high rate of absenteeism, tardiness, balkiness in initiating total group interaction, frequent statements concerning worthlessness of group, denial of importance of group. Occasional member asking for individual help finally rejected by the group.	Communication to others of self-system of interpersonal relations; i.e. making conscious to self, and others aware of, conceptual system one uses to predict consequences of personal behavior. Acceptance of group on reality terms.
Group Movement Facilitated by:	Independence and achievement attained by trainer-rejection and its concomitant, deriving consensually some effective means for authority and control. (Subphase 3 rebellion bridges gap between Subphases 2 and 4.)	Disenchantment of group as a result of *fantasied expectations of group life.* The perceived threat to self-esteem that further group involvement signifies creates schism of group according to amount of affection and-intimacy desired. The counterpersonal and overpersonal assertive individuals alleviate source of anxiety by disparaging or abnegating further group involvement. Subgroups form to ward off anxiety.	The external realities, group termination and the prescribed need for a course grading system, comprise the barometric event. Led by the personal individuals, the group tests reality and reduces autistic convictions concerning group involvement.
Main Defenses	Denial, isolation, intellectualization, and alienation.		

unduly and in some instances makes an exchange of meanings impossible.

Stating the training goal as the establishment of valid communication means that the relevance of the autistic response to authority and intimacy on the part of any member can be explicitly examined, and at least a provisional alternative formulated by him. Whether this makes a lasting change in the member's flexibility, or whether he will return to his more restricted formula when confronted with a new situation, we do not know, but we expect that it varies with the success of his group experience—particularly his success in understanding it.

We have attempted to portray what we believe to be the typical pattern of group development, and to show the relationship of member orientations and changes in member orientations to the major movements of the group. In this connection, we have emphasized the catalytic role of persons unconflicted with respect to one or the other of the dependence and interdependence areas. This power to move the group lies mainly in his freedom from anxiety-based reactions to problems of authority (or intimacy): he has the freedom to be creative in searching for a way to reduce tension.

We have also emphasized the "barometric event" or event capable of moving the group from one phase to the next. The major events of this kind are the removal of the trainer as part of the resolution of the dependence problem; and the evaluation-grading requirements at the termination of the course. Both these barometric events require a catalytic agent in the group to bring them about. That is to say, the trainer-exit can take place only at the moment when it is capable of symbolizing the attainment of group autonomy, and it requires a catalytic agent in the group to give it this meaning. And the grading assignment can move the group forward only if the catalytic agent can reverse the vicious circle of disparagement that precedes it.

Whether the incorporation of these barometric events into the training design merely makes our picture of group development a self-fulfilling prophecy, or whether, as we wish to believe, these elements make dramatically clear the major forward movements of the group, and open the gate for a flood of new understanding and communication, can only be decided on the basis of more, and more varied, experience.

The evolution from Phase I to Phase II represents not only a change in emphasis from power to affection, but also from role to personality. Phase I activity generally centers on broad role distinctions such as class, ethnic background, professional interests, etc.; Phase II activity involves a deeper concern with personality modalities, such as reaction to failure, warmth, retaliation, anxiety, etc. This development presents an interesting paradox. For the group in Phase I emerged out of a heterogeneous collectivity of individuals; the individual in Phase II emerged out of the group. This suggests that group therapy, where attention is focused on individual movement, begins at the least enabling time. It is possible that, before group members are able to help each other, the barriers to communication must be partially understood.

REFERENCES

1. Bion, W. R. "Experiences in Groups: I." *Hum. Relat.*, Vol. I, No. 3, pp. 314-320, 1948.

2. Bion, W. R. "Experiences in Groups: II." *Hum. Relat.*, Vol. I, No. 4, pp. 487-496, 1948.

5. Frenkel-Brunswik, E. "Intolerance of Ambiguity as an Emotional and Perceptual Personality Variable." In Bruner, J. S., and Krech, D. (eds.), *Perception and Personality*. Durham, N.C.: Duke Univ. Press, 1949 and 1950, p. 115.

6. Freud, Sigmund. *Group Psychology and the Analysis of the Ego*. Translated by J. Strachey. London: International Psycho-Analytical Press, 1922; New York: Liveright, 1949.

7. Freud, Sigmund. *The Problem of Anxiety*. Translated by H. A. Bunker. New York: Psychoanalytic Quarterly Press and W. W. Norton, 1936.

8. Freud, Sigmund. *Moses and Monotheism*. London: Hogarth Press, 1939; New York: Vintage Books, 1955.

10. Gouldner, Alvin. *Wildcat Strike*. Yellow Springs, Ohio: Antioch Press, 1954; London: Routledge & Kegan Paul, 1955.

12. Leighton, A. H. *The Governing of Men*. Princeton: Princeton Univ. Press, 1946.

14. Park, Robert E. "The Strike." *Society*. New York: Free Press of Glencoe, 1955.

16. Schutz, W. C. "Group Behavior Studies, I-III." Cambridge, Mass.: Harvard Univ., 1954 (mimeo).

17. Schutz, W. C. "What Makes Groups Productive?" *Hum. Relat.*, Vol. VIII, No. 4, p. 429, 1955.

19. Sullivan, H. S. "Tensions, Interpersonal and International." In Cantril, Hadley (ed.), *Tensions that Cause Wars*. Urbana, Ill.: Univ. of Illinois Press, 1950.

20. Sullivan, H. S. *Conceptions of Modern Psychiatry*. Washington D.C.: William Alanson White Psychiatric Foundation, 1940, 1945; London: Tavistock Publications, 1955.

22. Whyte, W. F., Jr. *Patterns for Industrial Peace*. New York: Harper, 1951.

Group Dynamics and the Individual

by Dorwin P. Cartwright and Ronald Lippitt

How should we think of the relation between individuals and groups? Few questions have stirred up so many issues of metaphysics, epistemology, and ethics. Do groups have the same reality as individuals? If so, what are the properties of groups? Can groups learn, have goals, be frustrated, develop, regress, begin and end? Or are these characteristics strictly attributable only to individuals? If groups exist, are they good or bad? How *should* an individual behave with respect to groups? How *should* groups treat their individual members? Such questions have puzzled man from the earliest days of recorded history.

In our present era of "behavioral science" we like to think that we can be "scientific" and proceed to study human behavior without having to take sides on these problems of speculative philosophy. Invariably, however, we are guided by certain assumptions about the reality or irreality of groups, about their observablity, and about their good or bad value.

Usually these preconceptions are integral parts of one's personal and scientific philosophy, and it is often hard to tell how much they derive from emotionally toned personal experiences with other people and how much from coldly rational and "scientific" considerations. In view of the fervor with which they are usually defended, one might suspect that most have a small basis at least in personally significant experiences. These preconceptions, moreover, have a tendency to assume a homogeneous polarization—either positive or negative.

Consider first the completely negative view. It consists of two major assertions: first, groups don't really exist. They are a product of distorted thought processes (often called "abstractions"). In fact, social prejudice consists precisely in acting as if groups, rather than individuals, were real.

From *International Journal of Group Psychotherapy*, January, 1957, 7(1), 86-102. Reprinted by permission.

Second, groups are bad. They demand blind loyalty, they make individuals regress, they reduce man to the lowest common denominator, and they produce what *Fortune* magazine has immortalized as "group-think."

In contrast to this completely negative conception of groups, there is the completely positive one. This syndrome, too, consists of two major assertions: first, groups really do exist. Their reality is demonstrated by the difference it makes to an individual whether he is accepted or rejected by a group and whether he is part of a healthy or sick group. Second, groups are good. They satisfy deep-seated needs of individuals for affiliation, affection, recognition, and self-esteem; they stimulate individuals to moral heights of altruism, loyalty, and self-sacrifice; they provide a means, through cooperative interaction, by which man can accomplish things unattainable through individual enterprise.

This completely positive preconception is the one attributed most commonly, it seems, to the so-called "group dynamics movement." Group dynamicists, it is said, have not only *reified* the group but also *idealized* it. They believe that everything should be done by and in groups—individual responsibility is bad, man-to-man supervision is bad, individual problem-solving is bad, and even individual therapy is bad. The only good things are committee meetings, group decisions, group problem-solving, and group therapy. "If you don't hold the group in such high affection," we were once asked, "why do you call your research organization the Research Center for Group Dynamics? And, if you are *for* groups and group dynamics, mustn't you therefore be *against* individuality, individual responsibility, and self-determination?"

FIVE PROPOSITIONS ABOUT GROUPS

This assumption that individuals and groups must necessarily have incompatible interests is made so frequently in one guise or another that it requires closer examination. Toward this end we propose five related assertions about individuals, groups, and group dynamics, which are intended to challenge the belief that individuals and groups must necessarily have incompatible or, for that matter, compatible interests.

1. Groups do exist; they must be dealt with by any man of practical affairs, or indeed by any child, and they must enter into any adequate account of human behavior. Most infants are born into a specific group. Little Johnny may be a welcome or unwelcome addition to the group. His presence may produce profound changes in the structure of the group and consequently in the feelings, attitudes, and behavior of various group members. He may create a triangle where none existed before or he may break up one which has existed. His development and adjustment for years to come may be deeply influenced by the nature of the group he

enters and by his particular position in it—whether, for example, he is a first or second child (a personal property which has no meaning apart from its reference to a specific group).

There is a wealth of research whose findings can be satisfactorily interpreted only by assuming the reality of groups. Recall the experiment of Lewin, Lippitt, and White (15) in which the level of aggression of an individual was shown to depend upon the social atmosphere and structure of the group he is in and not merely upon such personal traits as aggressiveness. By now there can be little question about the kinds of results reported from the Western Electric study (18) which make it clear that groups develop norms for the behavior of their members with the result that "good" group members adopt these norms as their *personal* values. Nor can one ignore the dramatic evidence of Lewin, Bavelas, and others (14) which shows that group decisions may produce changes in individual behavior much larger than those customarily found to result from attempts to modify the behavior of individuals *as* isolated individuals.

2. Groups are inevitable and ubiquitous. The biological nature of man, his capacity to use language, and the nature of his environment which has been built into its present form over thousands of years require that man exist in groups. This is not to say that groups must maintain the properties they now display, but we cannot conceive of a collection of human beings living in geographical proximity under conditions where it would be correct to assert that no groups exist and that there is no such thing as group membership.

3. Groups mobilize powerful forces which produce effects of the utmost importance to individuals. Consider two examples from rather different research settings. Seashore (22) has recently published an analysis of data from 5,871 employees of a large manufacturing company. An index of group cohesiveness, developed for each of 228 work groups, permitted a comparison of members working in high and in low cohesive groups. Here is one of his major findings: "Members of high cohesive groups exhibit less anxiety than members of low cohesive groups, using as measures of anxiety: (a) feeling 'jumpy' or 'nervous,' (b) feeling under pressure to achieve higher productivity (with actual productivity held constant), and (c) feeling a lack of support from the company" (p. 98). Seashore suggests two reasons for the relation between group cohesiveness and individual anxiety: "(1) that the cohesive group provides effective support for the individual in his encounters with anxiety-provoking aspects of his environment, thus allaying anxiety, and (2) that group membership offers direct satisfaction, and this satisfaction in membership has a generalized effect of anxiety-reduction" (p. 13).

Perhaps a more dramatic account of the powerful forces generated in groups can be derived from the publication by Stanton and Schwartz (24) of their studies of a mental hospital. They report, for example, how a patient may be thrown into an extreme state of excitement by disagree- ments between two staff members over the patient's care. Thus, two doctors may disagree about whether a female patient should be moved to another ward. As the disagreement progresses, the doctors may stop communicating relevant information to each other and start lining up allies in the medical and nursing staff. The patient, meanwhile, becomes increasingly restless until, at the height of the doctors' disagreement, she is in an acute state of excitement and must be secluded, put under sedation, and given special supervision. Presumably, successful efforts to improve the interpersonal relations and communications among mem- bers of the staff would improve the mental condition of such a patient.

In general, it is clear that events occurring in a group may have repercussions on members who are not directly involved in these events. A person's position in a group, moreover, may affect the way others behave toward him and such personal qualities as his levels of aspiration and self-esteem. Group membership itself may be a prized possession or an oppressive burden; tragedies of major proportions have resulted from the exclusion of individuals from groups, and equally profound conse- quences have stemmed from enforced membership in groups.

4. Groups may produce both good and bad consequences. The view that groups are completely good and the view that they are completely bad are both based on convincing evidence. *The only fault with either is its one-sidedness*. Research motivated by one or the other is likely to focus on different phenomena. As an antidote to such one-sidedness it is a good practice to ask research questions in pairs, one stressing positive aspects and one negative: What are the factors producing conformity? *and* what are the factors producing nonconformity? What brings about a break- down in communication? *and* what stimulates or maintains effective communication? An exclusive focus on pathologies or upon positive criteria leads to a seriously incomplete picture.

5. A correct understanding of group dynamics permits the possibility that desirable consequences from groups can be deliberately enhanced. Through a knowledge of group dynamics, groups can be made to serve better ends, for knowledge gives power to modify human beings and human behavior. At the same time, recognition of this fact produces some of the deepest conflicts within the behavioral scientist, for it raises the whole problem of social manipulation. Society must not close its eyes to Orwell's horrible picture of life in 1984, but it cannot accept the alternative that in ignorance there is safety.

To recapitulate our argument: groups exist; they are inevitable and ubiquitous; they mobilize powerful forces having profound effects upon individuals; these effects may be good or bad; and through a knowledge of group dynamics there lies the possibility of maximizing their good value.

A DILEMMA

Many thoughtful people today are alarmed over one feature of groups: the pressure toward conformity experienced by group members. Indeed, this single "bad" aspect is often taken as evidence that groups are bad in general. Let us examine the specific problem of conformity, then, in order to attain a better understanding of the general issue. Although contemporary concern is great, it is not new. More than one hundred years ago Alexis de Tocqueville wrote: "I know of no country in which there is so little independence of mind and real freedom of discussion as in America. . . . In America the majority raises formidable barriers around the liberty of opinion. . . . The master (majority) no longer says: 'You shall think as I do or you shall die'; but he says: 'You are free to think differently from me and to retain your life, your property, and all that you possess, but they will be useless to you, for you will never be chosen by your fellow citizens if you solicit their votes; and they will affect to scorn you if you ask for their esteem. You will remain among men, but you will be deprived of the rights of mankind. Your fellow creatures will shun you like an impure being; and even those who believe in your innocence will abandon you, lest they should be shunned in their turn'" (25, pp. 273-275).

Before too readily accepting such a view of groups as the whole story, let us invoke our dictum that research questions should be asked in pairs. Nearly everyone is convinced that individuals should not be blind conformers to group norms, that each group member should not be a carbon copy of every other member, but what is the other side of the coin? In considering why members of groups conform, perhaps we should also think of the consequences of the removal of individuals from group membership or the plight of the person who really does not belong to any group with clear-cut norms and values. The state of anomie, described by Durkheim, is also common today. It seems as if people who have no effective participation in groups with clear and strong value systems either crack up (as in alcoholism or suicide) or they seek out groups which will demand conformity. In discussing this process, Talcott Parsons writes: "In such a situation it is not surprising that large numbers of people should . . . be attracted to movements which can offer them membership in a group with a vigorous esprit de corps with submission to some strong authority and rigid system of belief, the individual thus finding a measure of escape from painful perplexities or from a situation of anomie" (17, pp. 128-129).

The British anthropologist, Adam Curle, has stressed the same problem when he suggested that in our society we need not four, but five freedoms, the fifth being freedom from that neurotic anxiety which springs from a man's isolation from his fellows and in turn, isolates him still further from them.

We seem, then, to face a dilemma: the individual needs social support for his values and social beliefs; he needs to be accepted as a valued member of some group which *he* values; failure to maintain such group membership produces anxiety and personal disorganization. But, on the other hand, group membership and group participation tend to cost the individual his individuality. If he is to receive support from others and, in turn, give support to others, he and they must hold in common some values and beliefs. Deviation from these undermines any possibility of group support and acceptance.

Is there an avenue of escape from this dilemma? Certainly, the issue is not so simple as we have described it. The need for social support for some values does not require conformity with respect to all values, beliefs, and behavior. Any individual is a member of several groups, and he may be a successful deviate in one while conforming to another (think of the visitor in a foreign country or of the psychologist at a convention of psychiatrists). Nor should the time dimension be ignored; a person may sustain his deviancy through a conviction that his fate is only temporary. These refinemnts of the issue are important and should be examined in great detail, but before we turn our attention to them, we must assert that we do *not* believe that the basic dilemma can be escaped. To avoid complete personal disorganization man must conform to at least a minimal set of values required for participation in the groups to which he belongs.

PRESSURES TO UNIFORMITY

Some better light may be cast on this problem if we refer to the findings of research on conformity. What do we know about the way it operates?

Cognitive Processes. Modern psychological research on conformity reflects the many different currents of contemporary psychology, but the major direction has been largely determined by the classic experiment of Sherif (23) on the development of social norms in perceiving autokinetic movement and by the more recent study of Asch (1) of pressures to conformity in perceiving unambiguous visual stimuli.

What does this line of investigation tell us about conformity? What has it revealed, for instance, about the conditions that set up pressures to conformity? Answers to this question have taken several forms, but nearly all point out that social interaction would be impossible if some beliefs and perceptions were not commonly shared by the participants. Speaking of the origin of such cognitive pressures to uniformity among group members, Asch says: "The individual comes to experience a world that he shares with others. He perceives that the surroundings include him, as well as others, and that he is in the same relation to the surroundings as others. He notes that he, as well as others, is converging upon the same object and responding to its identical properties. Joint action and mutual understanding require this relation of intelligibility and structural simplicity. In these terms the 'pull' toward the group becomes understandable" (1, p. 484).

Consistent with this interpretation of the origin of pressures to uniformity in a perceptual or judgmental situation are the findings that the major variables influencing tendencies to uniformity are (a) the quality of the social evidence (particularly the degree of unanimity of announced perceptions and the subject's evaluation of the trustworthiness of the other's judgments), (b) the quality of the direct perceptual evidence (particularly the clarity or ambiguity of the stimuli), (c) the magnitude of the discrepancy between the social and the perceptual evidence, and (d) the individual's self-confidence in the situation (as indicated either by experimental manipulations designed to affect self-confidence or by personality measurements).

The research in this tradition has been productive, but it has emphasized the individual and his cognitive problems and has considered the individual apart from any concrete and meaningful group membership. Presumably any trustworthy people adequately equipped with eyes and ears could serve to generate pressures to conformity in the subject, regardless of his specific relations to them. The result of this emphasis has been to ignore certain essential aspects of the conformity problem.

First, the origin of pressures to uniformity has been made to reside in the person whose conformity is being studied. Through eliminating experimentally any possibility that pressures might be exerted by others, it has been possible to study the conformity of people as if they existed in a world where they can see or hear others but not be reacted to by others. It is significant, indeed, that conformity does arise in the absence of direct attempts to bring it about. But this approach does not raise certain questions about the conditions which lead to *social* pressures to conformity. What makes some people try to get others to conform? What conditions lead to what forms of pressure on others to get them to conform? The concentration of attention on the conformer has diverted attention away from the others in the situation who may insist on conformity and make vigorous efforts to bring it about or may not exert any pressure at all on deviates.

A second consequence of this emphasis has been to ignore the broader social meaning of conformity. Is the individual's personal need for a social validation of his beliefs the only reason for conforming? What does deviation do to a person's acceptance by others? What does it do to his ability to influence others? Or, from the group's point of view, are there reasons to insist on certain common values, beliefs, and behavior? These questions are not asked or answered by an approach which limits itself to the cognitive problems of the individual.

Group Processes. The group dynamics orientation toward conformity emphasizes a broader range of determinants. Not denying the importance of the cognitive situation, we want to look more closely at the nature of the individual's relation to particular groups with particular properties. In formulating hypotheses about the origin of pressures to uniformity, two basic sources have been stressed. These have been stated most clearly by Festinger and his co-workers (5), who propose that when differences of opinion arise within a group, pressures to uniformity will arise (a) if the validity or "reality" of the opinion depends upon agreement with the group (essentially the same point as Asch's), or (b) if locomotion toward a group goal will be facilitated by uniformity within the group.

This emphasis upon the group, rather than simply upon the individual, leads one to expect a broader set of consequences from pressures to uniformity. Pressures to uniformity are seen as establishing: (a) a tendency on the part of each group member to change his own opinion to conform to that of the other group members, (b) a tendency to try to change the opinions of others, and (c) a tendency to redefine the boundaries of the group so as to exclude those holding deviate opinions. The relative magnitudes of these tendencies will depend on other conditions which need to be specified.

This general conception of the nature of the processes that produce conformity emerged from two early field studies conducted at the Research Center for Group Dynamics. It was also influenced to a considerable extent by the previous work of Newcomb (16) in which he studied the formation and change of social attitudes in a college community. The first field study, reported by Festinger, Schachter, and Back (7), traced the formation of social groups in a new student housing project. As each group developed, it displayed its own standards for its members. The extent of conformity to the standards of a particular group was found to be related directly to the degree of cohesiveness of that group as measured by sociometric choices. Moreover, those individuals who deviated from their own group's norms received fewer sociometric choices than those who conformed. A process of rejection for nonconformity had apparently set in. The second field study, reported by Coch and French (3), observed similar processes. This study was conducted in a textile factory and was concerned with conformity to production standards set by groups of workers. Here an individual worker's reaction to new work methods was found to depend upon the standards of his group and here, too, rejection for deviation was observed.

The next phase of this research consisted of a series of experiments with groups created in the laboratory. It was hoped thereby to be able to disentangle the complexity of variables that might exist in any field setting in order to understand better the operation of each. These experiments have been reported in various publications by Festinger, Back, Gerard, Hymovitch, Kelley, Raven, Schachter, and Thibaut (2, 6, 8, 9, 11, 20). We shall not attempt to describe these studies in detail, but draw upon them and other research in an effort to summarize the major conclusions.

First, a great deal of evidence has been accumulated to support the hypothesis that pressures to uniformity will be greater the more members want to remain in the group. In more attractive or cohesive groups, members attempt more to influence others and are willing to accept influence from others. Note that here pressures to conformity are high in the very conditions where satisfaction from group membership is also high.

Second, there is a close relation between attempts to change the deviate and tendencies to reject him. If persistent attempts to change the deviate fail to produce conformity, then communication appears to cease between the majority and the deviate, and rejection of the deviate sets in. These two processes, moreover, are more intense the more cohesive the group. One of the early studies which documented the process of rejection was conducted by Schachter (20) on college students. It has recently been replicated by Emerson (4) on high school students, who found essentially the same process at work, but he discovered that among his high school students efforts to influence others continued longer, there was a greater readiness on the part of the majority to change, and there was a lower level of rejection within a limited period of time. Yet another study, conducted in Holland, Sweden, France, Norway, Belgium, Germany, and England, found the same tendency to reject deviates in all of these countries. This study, reported by Schachter, et al. (21), is a landmark in cross-cultural research.

Third, there is the question of what determines whether or not pressures to uniformity will arise with respect to any particular opinion, attitude, and behavior. In most groups there are no pressures to uniformity concerning the color of necktie worn by the members. Differences of opinion about the age of the earth probably would not lead to rejection in a poker club, but they might do so in certain fundamentalist church groups. The concept of *relevance* seems to be required to account for such variations in pressures to uniformity. And, if we ask, "relevance for what?" we are forced again to look at the group and especially at the goals of the group.

Schachter (20) has demonstrated, for example, that deviation on a given issue will result much more readily in rejection when that issue is relevant to the group's goals than when it is irrelevant. And the principle of relevance seems to be necessary to account for the findings of a field study reported by Ross (19). Here attitudes of fraternity men toward restrictive admission policies were studied. Despite the fact that there was a consistent policy of exclusion in these fraternities, there was, surprisingly, little evidence for the existence of pressures toward uniformity of attitudes. When, however, a field experiment was conducted in which the distribution of actual opinions for each fraternity house was reported to a meeting of house members together with a discussion of the relevance of these opinions for fraternity policy, attitudes then tended to change to conform to the particular modal position of each house. Presumably the experimental treatment made uniformity of attitude instrumental to group locomotion where it had not been so before.

SOURCES OF HETEROGENEITY

We have seen that pressures to uniformity are stronger the more cohesive the group. Shall we conclude from this that strong, need-satisfying, cohesive groups must always produce uniformity on matters that are important to the group? We believe not. We cannot, however, cite much convincing evidence since research has focused to date primarily upon the sources of pressures to uniformity and has ignored the conditions which produce heterogeneity. Without suggesting, then, that we can give final answers, let us indicate some of the possible sources of heterogeneity.

Group Standards About Uniformity. It is important, first, to make a distinction between conformity and uniformity. A group might have a value that everyone should be as different from everyone else as possible. Conformity to this value, then, would result not in uniformity of behavior but in nonuniformity. Such a situation often arises in therapy groups or training groups where it is possible to establish norms which place a high value upon "being different" and upon tolerating deviant behavior. Conformity to this value is presumably greater the more cohesive the group and the more it is seen as relevant to the group's objectives. Unfortunately, very little is known about the origin and operation of group standards about conformity itself. We doubt that the pressure to uniformity which arises from the need for "social reality" and for group locomotion can simply be obliterated by invoking a group standard of tolerance, but a closer look at such processes as those of group decision-making will be required before a deep understanding of this problem can be achieved.

Freedom To Deviate. A rather different source of heterogeneity has been suggested by Kelley and Shapiro (12). They reason that the more an individual feels accepted by the other members of the group, the more ready he should be to deviate from the beliefs of the majority under conditions where objectively correct deviation would be in the group's best interest. They designed an experiment to test this hypothesis. The results, while not entirely clear because acceptance led to greater cohesiveness, tend to support this line of reasoning.

It has been suggested by some that those in positions of leadership are freer to deviate from group standards than are those of lesser status. Just the opposite conclusion has been drawn by others. Clearly, further research into group properties which generate freedom to deviate from majority pressures is needed.

Subgroup Formation. Festinger and Thibaut (8) have shown that lower group-wide pressures to uniformity of opinion result when members of a group perceive that the group is composed of persons differing in interest and knowledge. Under these conditions subgroups may easily develop with a resulting heterogeneity within the group as a whole though with uniformity within each subgroup. This conclusion is consistent with Asch's (1) finding that the presence of a partner for a deviate greatly strengthens his tendency to be independent. One might suspect that such processes, though achieving temporarily a greater heterogeneity, would result in a schismatic subgroup conflict.

Positions and Roles. A more integrative achievement of heterogeneity seems to arise through the process of role differentiation. Established groups are usually differentiated according to "positions" with special functions attached to each. The occupant of the position has certain behaviors prescribed for him by the others in the group. These role prescriptions differ, moreover, from one position to another, with the result that conformity to them produces heterogeneity within the group. A group function, which might otherwise be suppressed by pressures to uniformity, may be preserved by the establishment of a position whose responsibility is to perform the function.

Hall (10) has recently shown that social roles can be profitably conceived in the context of conformity to group pressures. He reasoned that pressures to uniformity of prescriptions concerning the behavior of the occupant of a position and pressures on the occupant to conform to these prescriptions should be greater the more cohesive the group. A study of the role of aircraft commander in bomber crews lends strong support to this conception.

In summary, it should be noted that in all but one of these suggested sources of heterogeneity we have assumed the process of conformity—to the norms of a subgroup, to a role, or to a group standard favoring heterogeneity. Even if the price of membership in a strong group be conformity, it need not follow that strong groups will suppress differences.

MORE THAN ONE GROUP

Thus far our analysis has proceeded as though the individual were a member of only one group. Actually we recognize that he is, and has been, a member of many groups. In one of our current research projects we are finding that older adolescents can name from twenty to forty "important groups and persons that influence my opinions and behavior in decision situations." Indeed, some personality theorists hold the personality should be viewed as an "internal society" made up of representations of the diverse group relationships which the individual now has and has had. According to this view, each individual has a unique internal society and makes his own personal synthesis of the values and behavior preferences generated by these affiliations.

The various memberships of an individual may relate to one another in various ways and produce various consequences for the individual. A past group may exert internal pressures toward conformity which are in conflict with a present group. Two contemporaneous groups may have expectations for the person which are incompatible. Or an individual may hold a temporary membership (the situation of a foreign student, for example) and be faced with current conformity pressures which if accepted will make it difficult to readjust when returning to his more permanent memberships.

This constant source of influence from other memberships toward deviancy of every member of every group requires that each group take measures to preserve its integrity. It should be noted, however, that particular deviancy pressures associated with a given member may be creative or destructive when evaluated in terms of the integrity and productivity of the group, and conformity pressures from the group may be supportive or disruptive of the integrity of the individual.

Unfortunately there has been little systematic research on these aspects of multiple group membership. We can indicate only two sets of observations concerning (a) the intrapersonal processes resulting from multiple membership demands, and (b) the effects on group processes of the deviancy pressures which arise from the multiple membership status of individual members.

Marginal Membership. Lewin (13), in his discussion of adolescence and of minority group membership, has analyzed some of the psychological effects on the person of being "between two groups" without a firm anchorage in either one. He says: "The transition from childhood to adulthood may be a rather sudden shift (for instance, in some of the primitive societies), or it may occur gradually in a setting where children and adults are not sharply separated groups. In the case of the so-called 'adolescent difficulties,' however, a third state of affairs is often prevalent: children and adults constitute two clearly defined groups; the adolescent does not wish any longer to belong to the children's group and, at the same time, knows that he is not really accepted in the adult group. He has a position similar to what is called in sociology the 'marginal man' . . . a person who stands on the boundary between two groups. He does not belong to either of them, or at least he is not sure of his belongingness in either of them" (p. 143). Lewin goes on to point out that there are characteristic maladjustive behavior patterns resulting from this unstable membership situation: high tension, shifts between extremes of behavior, high sensitivity, and rejection of low status members of both groups. This situation, rather than fostering strong individuality, makes belonging to closely knit, loyalty-demanding groups very attractive. Dependency and acceptance are a welcome relief. Probably most therapy groups have a number of members who are seeking relief from marginality.

Overlapping Membership. There is quite a different type of situation where the person does have a firm anchorage in two or more groups but where the group standards are not fully compatible. Usually the actual conflict arises when the person is physically present in one group but realizes that he also belongs to other groups to which he will return in the near or distant future. In this sense, the child moves between his family group and his school group every day. The member of a therapy group has some sort of time perspective of "going back" to a variety of other groups between each two meetings of the therapy group.

In their study of the adjustment of foreign students both in this country and after returning home, Watson and Lippitt (26) observed four different ways in which individuals cope with this problem of overlapping membership.

1. Some students solved the problem by "living in the present" at all times. When they were in the American culture all of their energy and attention was directed to being an acceptable member of this group. They avoided conflict within themselves by minimizing thought about and contact with the other group "back home." When they returned to the other group they used the same type of solution, quickly shifting behavior and ideas to fit back into the new, present group. Their behavior appeared

quite inconsistent, but it was a consistent approach to solving their problem of multiple membership.

2. Other individuals chose to keep their other membership the dominant one while in this country. They were defensive and rejective every time the present group seemed to promote values and to expect behavior which they felt might not be acceptable to the other group "back home." The strain of maintaining this orientation was relieved by turning every situation into a "black and white" comparison and adopting a consistently rejective posture toward the present, inferior group. This way of adjusting required a considerable amount of distorting of present and past realities, but the return to the other group was relatively easy.

3. Others reacted in a sharply contrasting way by identifying wholeheartedly with the present group and by rejecting the standards of the other group as incorrect or inferior at the points of conflict. They were, of course, accepted by the present group, but when they returned home they met rejection or felt alienated from the standards of the group (even when they felt accepted).

4. Some few individuals seemed to achieve a more difficult but also more creative solution. They attempted to regard membership in both groups as desirable. In order to succeed in this effort, they had to be more realistic about perceiving the inconsistencies between the group expectations and to struggle to make balanced judgments about the strong and weak points of each group. Besides taking this more objective approach to evaluation, these persons worked on problems of how the strengths of one group might be interpreted and utilized by the other group. They were taking roles of creative deviancy in both groups, but attempting to make their contributions in such a way as to be accepted as loyal and productive members. They found ways of using each group membership as a resource for contributing to the welfare of the other group. Some members of each group were, of course, threatened by this readiness and ability to question the present modal ways of doing things in the group.

Thus it seems that the existence of multiple group memberships creates difficult problems both for the person and for the group. But there are also potentialities and supports for the development of creative individuality in this situation, and there are potentialities for group growth and achievement in the fact that the members of any group are also members of other groups with different standards.

SOME CONCLUSIONS

Let us return now to the question raised at the beginning of this paper. How should we think of the relation between individuals and groups? If we accept the assumption that individuals and groups are both important social realities, we can then ask a pair of important questions. What kinds of effects do groups have on the emotional security and creative productivity of the individual? What kinds of effects do individuals have on the morale and creative productivity of the group? In answering these questions it is important to be alerted to both good and bad effects. Although the systematic evidence from research does not begin to provide full answers to these questions, we have found evidence which tends to support the following general statements.

Strong groups do exert strong influences on members toward conformity. These conformity pressures, however, may be directed toward uniformity of thinking and behavior, or they may foster heterogeneity.

Acceptance of these conformity pressures, toward uniformity or heterogeneity, may satisfy the emotional needs of some members and frustrate others. Similarly, it may support the potential creativity of some members and inhibit that of others.

From their experiences of multiple membership and their personal synthesis of these experiences, individuals do have opportunities to achieve significant bases of individuality.

Because each group is made up of members who are loyal members of other groups and have unique individual interests, each group must continuously cope with deviancy tendencies of the members. These tendencies may represent a source of creative improvement in the life of the group or a source of destructive disruption.

The resolution of these conflicting interests does not seem to be the strengthening of individuals and the weakening of groups, or the strengthening of groups and the weakening of individuals, but rather a strengthening of both by qualitative improvements in the nature of interdependence between integrated individuals and cohesive groups.

BIBLIOGRAPHY

1. Asch, S. E.: *Social Psychology*. New York: Prentice Hall, 1952.
2. Back, K. W.: Influence Through Social Communication. *J. Abn. & Soc. Psychol.*, 46: 9-23, 1951.
3. Coch, L. and French, J. R. P.: Overcoming Resistance to Change. *Hum. Relat.*, 1: 512-32, 1948.
4. Emerson, R. M.: Deviation and Rejection: An Experimental Replication. *Am. Sociol. Rev.*, 19: 688-93, 1954.
5. Festinger, L.: Informal Social Communication. *Psychol. Rev.*, 57: 271-92, 1950.
6. Festinger, L., Gerard, H. B., Hymovitch, B., Kelley, H. H., and Raven, B.: The Influence Process in the Presence of Extreme Deviates. *Hum. Relat.*, 5: 327-46, 1952.
7. Festinger, L., Schachter, S., and Back, K.: *Social Pressures in Informal Groups*. New York: Harper, 1950.

8. Festinger, L. and Thibaut, J.: Interpersonal Communication in Small Groups. *J. Abn. & Soc. Psychol.*, *46:* 92-99, 1951.

9. Gerard, H. B.: The Effect of Different Dimensions of Disagreement on the Communication Process in Small Groups. *Hum. Relat.*, *6:* 249-71, 1953.

10. Hall, R. L.: Social Influence on the Aircraft Commander's Role. *Am. Sociol. Rev.*, *20:* 292-99, 1955.

11. Kelley, H. H.: Communications in Experimentally Created Hierarchies. *Hum. Relat.*, *4:* 39-56, 1951.

12. Kelley, H. H. and Shapiro, M. M.: An Experiment on Conformity to Group Norms Where Conformity Is Detrimental to Group Achievement. *Am. Sociol. Rev.*, *19:* 667-77, 1954.

13. Lewin, K.: *Field Theory in Social Science*. New York: Harper, 1951.

14. Lewin, K.: Studies in Group Decision. In: *Group Dynamics: Research and Theory*, ed. D. Cartwright and A. Zander. Evanston: Row, Peterson, 1953.

15. Lewin, K., Lippitt, R., and White, R.: Patterns of Aggressive Behavior in Experimentally Created "Social Climates." *J. Soc. Psychol.*, *10:* 271-99, 1939.

16. Newcomb, T. M.: *Personality and Social Change*. New York: Dryden, 1943.

17. Parsons, T.: *Essays in Sociological Theory*. (Rev. ed.) Glencoe: Free Press, 1954.

18. Roethlisberger, F. J. and Dickson, W. J.: *Management and the Worker*. Cambridge: Harvard University Press, 1939.

19. Ross, I.: Group Standards Concerning the Admission of Jews. *Soc. Prob.*, *2:* 133-40, 1955.

20. Schachter, S.: Deviation, Rejection, and Communication. *J. Abn. & Soc. Psychol.*, *46:* 190-207, 1951.

21. Schachter, S., et al.: Cross-cultural Experiments on Threat and Rejection. *Hum. Relat.*, *7:* 403-39, 1954.

22. Seashore, S. E.: *Group Cohesiveness in the Industrial Group*. Ann Arbor: Institute for Social Research, 1954.

23. Sherif, M.: *The Psychology of Social Norms*. New York: Harper, 1936.

24. Stanton, A. H. and Schwartz, M. S.: *The Mental Hospital*. New York: Basic Books, 1954.

25. Tocqueville, A. de: *Democracy in America*, Vol. 1. New York: Alfred A. Knopf, 1945 (original publication, 1835).

26. Watson, J. and Lippitt, R.: *Learning Across Cultures*. Ann Arbor: Institute for Social Research, 1955.

Functional Roles of Group Members

by Kenneth D. Benne and Paul Sheats

THE RELATIVE NEGLECT OF MEMBER ROLES IN GROUP TRAINING

Efforts to improve group functioning through training have traditionally emphasized the training of group leadership. And frequently this training has been directed toward the improvement of the skills of the leader in transmitting information and in manipulating groups. Little direct attention seems to have been given to the training of group members in the membership roles required for effective group growth and production. The present discussion is based on the conviction that both effective group training and adequate research into the effectiveness of group training methods must give attention to the identification, analysis, and practice of leader *and* member roles, seen as co-relative aspects of over-all group growth and production.

Certain assumptions have undergirded the tendency to isolate the leadership role from membership roles and to neglect the latter in processes of group training. (1) "Leadership" has been identified with traits and qualities inherent within the "leader" personality. Such traits and qualities can be developed, it is assumed, in isolation from the functioning of members in a group setting. The present treatment sees the leadership role in terms of functions to be performed within a group in helping that group to grow and to work productively. No sharp distinction can be made between leadership and membership functions, between leader and member roles. Groups may operate with various degrees of diffusion of "leadership" functions among group members or of concentration of such functions in one member or a few members. Ideally, of course, the concept of leadership emphasized here is that of a multilaterally shared responsibility. In any event, effectiveness in the leader role is a matter of leader-memory relationship. And one side of a relationship cannot be

From *Journal of Social Issues*, 1948, 4(2), 41-49. Reprinted by permission.

effectively trained in isolation from the retraining of the other side of that relationship. (2) It has been assumed that the "leader" is uniquely responsible for the quality and amount of production by the group. The "leader" must see to it that the "right" group goals are set, that the group jobs get done, that members are "motivated" to participate. In this view, membership roles are of secondary importance. "Membership" is tacitly identified with "followership." The present discussion assumes that the quality and amount of group production is the "responsibility" of the group. The setting of goals and the marshalling of resources to move toward these goals is a group responsibility in which all members of a mature group come variously to share. The functions to be performed both in building and maintaining group-centered activity and in effective production by the group are primarily member roles. Leadership functions can be defined in terms of facilitating identification, acceptance, development and allocation of these group-required roles by the group. (3) There has frequently been a confusion between the roles which members enact within a group and the individual personalities of the group members. That there are relationships between the personality structures and needs of group members and the range and quality of group membership roles which members can learn to perform is not denied. On the contrary, the importance of studies designed to describe and explain and to increase our control of these relationships is affirmed. But, at the level of group functioning, member roles, relevant to group growth and accomplishment, must be clearly distinguished from the use of the group environment by individuals to satisfy individual and group-irrelevant needs, if clear diagnosis of member roles required by the group and adequate training of members to perform group-required roles are to be advanced. Neglect of this distinction has been associated traditionally with the neglect of the analysis of member roles in group growth and production.

A CLASSIFICATION OF MEMBER ROLES

The following analysis of functional member roles was developed in connection with the First National Training Laboratory in Group Development, 1947. It follows closely the analysis of participation functions used in coding the content of group records for research purposes. A similar analysis operated in faculty efforts to train group members in their functional roles during the course of the laboratory.[1]

---

[1] A somewhat different analysis of member-participations, in terms of categories used by interaction-observers in observation of group processes in the First National Training Laboratory, is described in the *Preliminary Report* of the laboratory, pages 122-132. The number of categories used by interaction-observers was "directed primarily by limitations of observer load."

The member roles identified in this analysis are classified into three broad groupings.

(1) Group task roles. Participant roles here are related to the task which the group is deciding to undertake or has undertaken. Their purpose is to facilitate and coordinate group effort in the selection and definition of a common problem and in the solution of that problem.

(2) Group building and maintenance roles. The roles in this category are oriented toward the functioning of the group as a group. They are designed to alter or maintain the group way of working, to strengthen, regulate and perpetuate the group as a group.

(3) Individual roles. This category does not classify member roles as such, since the "participations" denoted here are directed toward the satisfaction of the "participant's" individual needs. Their purpose is some individual goal which is not relevant either to the group task or to the functioning of the group as a group. Such participations are, of course, highly relevant to the problem of group training, insofar as such training is directed toward improving group maturity or group task efficiency.

GROUP TASK ROLES

The following analysis assumes that the task of the discussion group is to select, define and solve common problems. The roles are identified in relation to functions of facilitation and coordination of group problem-solving activities. Each member may, of course, enact more than one role in any given unit of participation and a wide range of roles in successive participations. Any or all of these roles may be played at times by the group "leader" as well as by various members.

a. The *initiator-contributor* suggests or proposes to the group new ideas or a changed way of regarding the group problem or goal. The novelty proposed may take the form of suggestions of a new group goal or a new definition of the problem. It may take the form of a suggested solution or some way of handling a difficulty that the group has encountered. Or it may take the form of a proposed new procedure for the group, a new way of organizing the group for the task ahead.

b. The *information seeker* asks for clarification of suggestions made in terms of their factual adequacy, for authoritative information and facts pertinent to the problem being discussed.

c. The *opinion seeker* asks not primarily for the facts of the case but for a clarification of the values pertinent to what the group is undertaking or of values involved in a suggestion made or in alternative suggestions.

d. The *information giver* offers facts or generalizations which are "authoritative" or relates his own experience pertinently to the group problem.

e. The *opinion giver* states his belief or opinion pertinently to a suggestion made or to alternative suggestions. The emphasis is on his proposal of what should become the group's view of pertinent values, not primarily upon relevant facts or information.

f. The *elaborator* spells out suggestions in terms of examples or developed meanings, offers a rationale for suggestions previously made, and tries to deduce how an idea or suggestion would work out if adopted by the group.

g. The *coordinator* shows or clarifies the relationships among various ideas and suggestions, tries to pull ideas and suggestions together, or tries to coordinate the activities of various members or subgroups.

h. The *orienter* defines the position of the group with respect to its goals by summarizing what has occurred, points to departures from agreed upon directions or goals, or raises questions about the direction which the group discussion is taking.

i. The *evaluator-critic* subjects the accomplishment of the group to some standard or set of standards of group-functioning in the context of the group task. Thus, he may evaluate or question the "practicality," the "logic," the "facts" or the "procedure" of a suggestion or of some unit of group discussion.

j. The *energizer* prods the group to action or decision, attempts to stimulate or arouse the group to "greater" or "higher quality" activity.

k. The *procedural technician* expedites group movement by doing things for the group—performing routine tasks, e.g., distributing materials, or manipulating objects for the group, e.g., rearranging the seating or running the recording machine, etc.

l. The *recorder* writes down suggestions, makes a record of group decisions, or writes down the product of discussion. The recorder role is the "group memory."

GROUP BUILDING AND MAINTENANCE ROLES

Here the analysis of member-functions is oriented to those participations which have for their purpose the building of group-centered attitudes and orientation among the members of a group or the maintenance and perpetuation of such group-centered behavior. A given contribution may involve several roles and a member or the "leader" may perform various roles in successive contributions.

a. The *encourager* praises, agrees with and accepts the contribution of others. He indicates warmth and solidarity in his attitude toward other group members, offers commendation and praise and in various ways indicates understanding and acceptance of other points of view, ideas and suggestions.

b. The *harmonizer* mediates the differences between other members, attempts to reconcile disagreements, relieves tension in conflict situations through jesting or pouring oil on the troubled waters, etc.

c. The *compromiser* operates from within a conflict in which his idea or position is involved. He may offer compromise by yielding status, admitting his error, by disciplining himself to maintain group harmony, or by "coming half-way" in moving along with the group.

d. The *gate-keeper and expediter* attempts to keep communication channels open by encouraging or facilitating the participation of others ("we haven't got the ideas of Mr. X yet," etc.) or by proposing regulation of the flow of communication ("why don't we limit the length of our contributions so that everyone will have a chance to contribute?" etc.).

e. The *standard setter* or *ego ideal* expresses standards for the group to attempt to achieve in its functioning or applies standards in evaluating the quality of group process.

f. The *group-observer and commentator* keeps records of various aspects of group process and feeds such data with proposed interpretations into the group's evaluation of its own procedures.

g. The *follower* goes along with the movement of the group, more or less passively accepting the ideas of others, serving as an audience in group discussion and decision.

INDIVIDUAL ROLES

Attempts by "members" of a group to satisfy individual needs which are irrelevant to the group task and are non-oriented or negatively oriented to group building and maintenance set problems of group and member training. A high incidence of "individual-centered" as opposed to "group-centered" participation in a group always calls for self-diagnosis of the group. The diagnosis may reveal one or several of a number of conditions—low level of skill-training among members, including the group leader; the prevalence of "authoritarian" and "laissez-faire" points of view toward group functioning in the group; a low level of group maturity, discipline and morale; an inappropriately chosen and inadequately defined group task; etc. Whatever the diagnosis, it is in this setting that the training needs of the group are to be discovered and group training efforts to meet these needs are to be defined. The outright "suppression" of "individual roles" will deprive the group of data needed for really adequate self-diagnosis and therapy.

(a) The *aggressor* may work in many ways—deflating the status of others, expressing disapproval of the values, acts or feelings of others, attacking the group or the problem it is working on, joking aggressively, showing envy toward another's contribution by trying to take credit for it, etc.

(b) The *blocker* tends to be negativistic and stubbornly resistant, disagreeing and opposing without or beyond "reason" and attempting to maintain or bring back an issue after the group has rejected or by-passed it.

(c) The *recognition-seeker* works in various ways to call attention to himself, whether through boasting, reporting on personal achievements, acting in unusual ways, struggling to prevent his being placed in an "inferior" position, etc.

(d) The *self-confessor* uses the audience opportunity which the group setting provides to express personal, non-group-oriented "feeling," "insight," "ideology," etc.

(e) The *playboy* makes a display of his lack of involvement in the group's processes. This may take the form of cynicism, nonchalance, horseplay and other more or less studied forms of "out-of-field" behavior.

(f) The *dominator* tries to assert authority or superiority in manipulating the group or certain members of the group. This domination may take the form of flattery, of asserting a superior status or right to attention, giving directions authoritatively, interrupting the contribution of others, etc.

(g) The *help-seeker* attempts to call forth "sympathy" response from other group members or from the whole group, whether through expressions of insecurity, personal confusion or depreciation of himself beyond "reason."

(h) The *special interest pleader* speaks for the "small business man," the "grass roots" community, the "housewife," "labor," etc., usually cloaking his own prejudices or biases in the stereotype which best fits his individual need.

THE PROBLEM OF MEMBER ROLE-REQUIREDNESS

Identification of group task roles and of group building and maintenance roles which do actually function in processes of group discussion raises but does not answer the further question of what roles are required for "optimum" group growth and productivity. Certainly the discovery and validation of answers to this question have a high priority in any advancing science of group training and development. No attempt will be made here to review the bearing of the analyzed data from the First National Training Laboratory in Group Development on this point.

It may be useful in this discussion, however, to comment on two conditions which effective work on the problem of role-requiredness must meet. First, an answer to the problem of optimum task role requirements must be projected against a scheme of the process of group production. Groups in different stages of an act of problem selection and solution will have different role requirements. For example, a group early in the stages of problem selection which is attempting to lay out a range of possible problems to be worked on, will probably have relatively less need for the roles of "evaluator-critic," "energizer" and "coordinator" than a group which has selected and discussed its problem and is shaping to decision. The combination and balance of task role requirements are a function of the group's stage of progress with respect to its task. Second, the group building role requirements of a group are a function of its stage of development—its level of group maturity. For example, a "young" group will probably require less of the role of the "standard setter" than a mature group. Too high a level of aspiration may frustrate a "young" group where a more mature group will be able to take the same level of aspiration in its stride. Again the role of "group observer and commentator" must be carefully adapted to the level of maturity of the group. Probably the distinction between "group" and "individual" roles can be drawn much more sharply in a relatively mature group than in a "young" group.

Meanwhile, group trainers cannot wait for a fully developed science of group training before they undertake to diagnose the role requirements of the groups with which they work and help these groups to share in such diagnosis. Each group which is attempting to improve the quality of its functioning as a group must be helped to diagnose its role requirements and must attempt to train members to fill the required roles effectively. This describes one of the principal objectives of training of group members.

THE PROBLEM OF ROLE FLEXIBILITY

The previous group experience of members, where this experience has included little conscious attention to the variety of roles involved in effective group production and development, has frequently stereotyped the member into a limited range of roles. These he plays in all group discussions whether or not the group situation requires them. Some members see themselves primarily as "evaluator-critics" and play this role in and out of season. Others may play the roles of "encourager" or of "energizer" or of "information giver" with only small sensitivity to the role requirements of a given group situation. The development of skill and insight in diagnosing role requirements has already been mentioned as an objective of group member training. An equally important objective is the development of role flexibility, of skill and security in a wide range of member roles, on the part of all group members.

A science of group training, as it develops, must be concerned with the relationships between the personality structures of group members and the character and range of member roles which various personality structures support and permit. A science of group training must seek to discover and accept the limitations which group training per se encounters in altering personality structures in the service of greater role flexibility on the part of all members of a group. Even though we recognize the importance of this caution, the objective of developing role flexibility remains an important objective of group member training.

METHODS OF GROUP MEMBER TRAINING

The objectives in training group members have been identified. Some of the kinds of resistances encountered in training group members to diagnose the role requirements of a group situation and to acquire skill in a variety of member roles have been suggested. Before analyzing briefly the methods used for group member training in the First National Training Laboratory, a few additional comments on resistances to member training may be useful. The problem of group training is actually a problem of re-training. Members of a training group have had other group experiences. They bring to the training experience attitudes toward group work, more or less conscious skills for dealing with leaders and other members, and a more or less highly developed rationale of group processes. These may or may not support processes of democratic operation in the training group. Where they do not, they function as resistances to re-training. Again, trainees are inclined to make little or no distinction between the roles they perform in a group and their personalities. Criticism of the role a group member plays is perceived as criticism of "himself." Methods must be found to reduce ego-defensiveness toward criticism of member roles. Finally, training groups must be helped to make a distinction between group feeling and group productivity. Groups which attain a state of good group feeling often perceive attempts to diagnose and criticize their level of productivity as threats to this feeling of group warmth and solidarity.

(1) Each Basic Skill Training group in the Laboratory used self-observation and diagnosis of its own growth and development as a primary means of member training.

(a) Sensitization to the variety of roles involved in and required by group functioning began during the introduction of members to the group. In one BST group, this early sensitization to member role variety and role requiredness began with the "leader's" summarizing, as part of his introduction of himself to the group, certain of the member roles in which he was usually cast by groups and other roles which he found it difficult to play, even when needed by the group. He asked the group's help in criticizing and improving his skill in those roles where he felt weakest. Other members followed suit. Various members showed widely different degrees of sensitivity to the operation of member roles in groups and to the degree of their own proficiency in different roles. This introduction procedure gave the group a partial listing of member roles for later use and supplementation, initial self-assessments of member strengths and weaknesses and diagnostic material concerning the degree of group self-sophistication among the members. The training job had come to be seen by most members as a re-training job.

(b) A description of the use of training observers in group self-evaluation sessions may be found in Jenkins.[2] At this point, only the central importance which self-evaluation sessions played in member training needs to be stressed. Research observers fed observational data concerning group functioning into periodic discussions by the group of its strengths and weaknesses as a group. Much of these data concerned role requirements for the job the group had been attempting, which roles had been present, which roles had probably been needed. "Individual" roles were identified and interpreted in an objective and non-blaming manner. Out of these discussions, group members came to identify various kinds of member roles, to relate role requiredness to stages in group production and in group growth and to assess the range of roles each was able to play well when required. Out of these discussions came group decisions concerning the supplying of needed roles in the next session. Member commitments concerning behavior in future sessions also came out of these evaluations. These took the form both of silent commitments and of public commitments in which the help of the group was requested.

(c) Recordings of segments of the group's discussion were used by most Basic Skill Training groups. Groups listened to themselves, diagnosed the member and leader functions involved and assessed the adequacy of them.

(2) Role-played sessions in each group, although they were pointed content-wise to the skills of the change-agent, offered important material

---

[2]Jenkins, David H., "Feedback and Group Self-Evaluation," *The Journal of Social Issues*, Vol. IV, No. 2, Spring, 1948.

for the diagnosis of member roles and of role-requiredness. These sessions offered an important supplement to group self-diagnosis and evaluation. It is easier for members to get perspective on their participation in a role-played episode of group process than it is on their own participation in a "real" group. The former is not perceived as "real." The role is more easily disengaged for purposes of analysis and evaluation from the person playing the role. Ego-defensiveness toward the role as enacted is reduced. Role-playing sessions also provided practice opportunity to members in a variety of roles.

(3) Practice by group members of the role of *observer-commentator* is especially valuable in developing skill in diagnosing member roles and in assessing the role requirements of a group situation. In several groups, each member in turn served as observer, supplementing the work of the research observers in evaluation sessions. Such members worked more or less closely with the anecdotal observer for the group on skill-problems encountered. Practice opportunity in the *observer-commentator* role was also provided in clinic group meetings in the afternoon.

SUMMARY

Training in group membership roles requires the identification and analysis of various member roles actually enacted in group processes. It involves further the analysis of group situations in terms of roles required in relation both to a schema of group production and to a conception of group growth and development. A group's self-observation and self-evaluation of its own processes provide useful content and practice opportunity in member training. Practice in enacting a wider range of required roles and in role flexibility can come out of member commitment to such practice with help from the group in evaluating and improving the required skills. Member training is typically re-training and resistances to re-training can be reduced by creating a non-blaming and objective atmosphere in group self-evaluation and by using role-playing of group processes for diagnosis and practice. The training objectives of developing skill in the diagnosis of group role requirements and developing role flexibility among members also indicate important research areas for a science of group training.

How To Diagnose Group Problems

by Leland P. Bradford, Dorothy Stock, and Murray Horwitz

A group has two things in common with a machine or with any organism anywhere.

1. *It has something to do.*
2. *It must be kept in running order to do it.*

These twin functions require continual attention. Groups show their concern for the first—their specific jobs, goals, activities—by establishing procedures, rules of order, expected leadership responsibilities. But sometimes the rules a group sets up for itself fail to take into account its maintenance needs. When this happens the group finds itself bogging down.

The importance of the maintenance function is immediately recognized in other situations. Airliners require the services of maintenance crews as well as navigators. An automobile, a sewing machine, a typewriter, or a whistling peanut wagon that has no care paid to its upkeep soon begins to break down.

We can't, of course, carry the analogy too far. Among the important ways in which groups differ from machines, consider this: A new machine has its peak of efficiency at the beginning of its life. A new group, on the other hand, is likely to be more inept and less efficient at the beginning than it is later. If it is healthy, a group grows and changes, becoming more cohesive, more productive, more capable of helping its individual members in specific ways. The problem of maintenance, therefore, is inseparable from the process of growth.

This article will analyze the causes and symptoms of some common problems that interfere with group growth and productivity, and describe some methods of diagnosis.

From *Adult Leadership*, December, 1953, 2(7), 12-19. Reprinted by permission.

GROUP PROBLEMS

Three of the most common group problems are:

1. Conflict or fight
2. Apathy and nonparticipation
3. Inadequate decision-making.

Fight—we don't necessarily mean a heavyweight bout. Fight here means disagreement, argumentation, the nasty crack, the tense atmosphere, conflict.

Some ways in which fight can be expressed are:

a) members are impatient with one another

b) ideas are attacked before they are completely expressed

c) members take sides and refuse to compromise

d) members disagree on plans or suggestions

e) comments and suggestions are made with a great deal of vehemence

f) members attack one another on a personal level in subtle ways

g) members insist that the group doesn't have the know-how or experience to get anywhere

h) members feel the group can't get ahead because it is too large or too small

i) members disagree with the leader's suggestions

j) members accuse one another of not understanding the real point

k) members hear distorted fragments of other members' contributions.

The following are several possible reasons for such fight behavior:

1. *The group has been given an impossible job and members are frustrated because they feel unable to meet the demands made of them.* This frequently happens when the group is a committee of a larger organization. Perhaps the committee has a job which is impossible because it doesn't have enough members. Or perhaps the job is impossible because it is ambiguous—the task for the committee has not been clearly defined by the larger group. (Under these circumstances the committee has no way of knowing to what extent alternative plans are appropriate or will be acceptable to the larger group.) For whatever reason, an impossible task can easily produce frustration and tension among the members of a group, and this may be expressed in bickering and attack.

2. *The main concern of members is to find status in the group.* Although the group is ostensibly working on some task, the task is being used by the members as a means of jockeying for power, establishing alignments and cliques, or trying to suppress certain individuals or cliques. Under such circumstances certain members may oppose one another stubbornly on some issue for reasons which have nothing to do with the issue. Or there may be a lot of attack on a personal level which is intended to deflate and reduce the prestige of another member. This kind of power struggle may involve the leader. If it does, the attack will include him, perhaps in the form of refusing to understand or to follow his suggestions (if members can show that the leader is not a good leader, then he should be deposed).

3. *Members are loyal to outside groups of conflicting interests.* This can happen when the members of a committee are each representing some outside organization. They have an interest in getting a job done within the committee but they also have a loyalty to their own organization. This situation creates conflict within each individual so that he doesn't know whether he should behave as a member of this committee or as a member of another group. His behavior may be inconsistent and rigid and his inner confusion may burst out as irritation or stubbornness. His loyalty to his own organization may make him feel that he has to protect its interests carefully, keep the others from putting something over on him, be careful not to give more than he gets. This may lead to a refusal to cooperate, expressions of passive resistance, etc.

4. *Members feel involved and are working hard on a problem.* Members may frequently express impatience, irritation, or disagreement because they have a real stake in the issue being discussed. They fight for a certain plan because it is important to them—and this fight may take the form of real irritation with others because they can't "see" or won't go along with a suggestion which—to the member—is obviously the best one. As long as there is a clearly-understood goal and continuing movement on a problem, this kind of fight contributes to good problem-solving.

These are not intended to be *all* the possible reasons for fight behavior, but they are some, and they are quite different from one another. The obvious question arises: How can a member or leader tell which diagnosis is appropriate to a specific situation? If the fourth situation obtains, then fight is operating in the service of work and should not worry a group. If fight is interfering with getting things done on the work task, as it is in the other three situations, then it is important to know which description fits the group so that the underlying causes can be attacked.

The solution to this diagnostic problem lies in the need to understand the context in which the symptom has occurred. That is, one cannot understand fight, or any other symptom, by looking at the symptom only. It is necessary to broaden one's view and look at the syndrome—all the others things which are going on in the group at the same time.

Let's re-examine our four descriptions of symptoms, this time in terms of possible diagnoses:

If

—every suggestion made seems impossible for practical reasons,

—some members feel the committee is too small,

—everyone seems to feel pushed for time,

—members are impatient with one another,

—members insist the group doesn't have the know-how or experience to get anywhere,

—each member has a different idea of what the committee is supposed to do,

—whenever a suggestion is made, at least one member feels it won't satisfy the larger organization,

Then

—the group may have been given an impossible job and members are frustrated because they feel unable to meet the demands made of them, or the task is not clear or is disturbing.

If

—ideas are attacked before they are completely expressed,

—members take sides and refuse to compromise,

—there is no movement toward a solution of the problem,

—the group keeps getting stuck on inconsequential points,

—members attack one another on a personal level in subtle ways,

—there are subtle attacks on the leadership,

—there is no concern with finding a goal or sticking to the point,

—there is much clique formation,

Then

—the main concern of members may be in finding status in the group. The main interest is not in the problem. The problem is merely being used as a vehicle for expressing interpersonal concerns.

If

—the goal is stated in very general, non-operational terms,

—members take sides and refuse to compromise,

—each member is pushing his own plan,

—suggestions don't build on previous suggestions, each member seeming to start again from the beginning,

—members disagree on plans or suggestions,

—members don't listen to one another, each waiting for a chance to say something,

Then

—each member is probably operating from a unique, unshared point of view, perhaps because the members are loyal to different outside groups with conflicting interests.

If

—there is a goal which members understand and agree on.

—most comments are relevant to the problem,

—members frequently disagree with one another over suggestions,

—comments and suggestions are made with a great deal of vehemence,

—there are occasional expressions of warmth,

—members are frequently impatient with one another,

—there is general movement toward some solution of the problem,

Then

—probably, members feel involved and are working hard on a problem. The fight being expressed is constructive rather than destructive in character and reflects real interest on the part of members.

Apathy—An apathetic membership is a frequent ailment of groups. Groups may suffer in different degrees from this disease. In some cases members may show complete indifference to the group task, and give evidences of marked boredom. In others, apathy may take the form of a lack of genuine enthusiasm for the job, a failure to mobilize much energy, lack of persistence, satisfaction with poor work.

Some ways in which apathy may be expressed:

a) frequent yawns, people dozing off

b) members lose the point of the discussion

c) low level of participation

d) conversation drags

e) members come late; are frequently absent

f) slouching and restlessness

g) overquick decisions

h) failure to follow through on decisions

i) ready suggestions for adjournment

j) failure to consider necessary arrangements for the next meeting

k) reluctance to assume any further responsibility.

A commonly held idea is that people require inspirational leadership in order to maintain a high level of interest and morale and to overcome apathy. An outgrowth of this belief is the prescription of pep talks which, unfortunately, have only momentary effects, if any, and become less and less effective the more often they are used. To overcome or prevent apathy, we must treat the causes rather than the symptoms.

Here are some of the common reasons for apathy:

1. *The problem upon which the group is working does not seem important to the members, or it may seem less important than some other problem on which they would prefer to be working.* The problem may be important to someone. Perhaps to some outside part, perhaps to the total organization of which the group is a part, perhaps to the group leader, or even to a minority of the members. But it fails to arouse positive feelings or "involvement" on the part of the apathetic members.

Sometimes problems will be considered because of tradition. Again, members may find it difficult to express themselves freely enough to call for reconsideration of an unsatisfactory group goal. Sometimes, in organizational settings, problems are assigned, and the members haven't enough information to judge why the problem is important, except that "somebody upstairs" thinks it is. Again, the problem may be important to the leader or to some dominant member, and the group is coerced by these individuals into working on the problem as if it were really its own. In all of these cases the members will feel that they have had no part in initiating the problem, but that it has been imposed upon them. The basic feature of such imposed, "meaningless" tasks is that they are not related to the present needs of the members.

2. *The problem may seem important to members, but there are reasons which lead them to avoid attempting to solve the problem.* If members both desire to achieve the goal and fear attempting to achieve it, they are placed in a situation of conflict which may lead to tension, fatigue, apathy. Where subordinates feel they will be punished for mistakes, they will avoid taking action, hoping to shift responsibility to someone higher up the line of organizational authority. Similar fears, and similar desires to avoid working on particular problems, may stem from hostile feelings to other individuals, or to subgroups within the group. Sometimes the group atmosphere is such that members avoid exposing themselves to attack or ridicule, and feel insecure, self-conscious or embarrassed about presenting their ideas.

3. *The group may have inadequate procedures for solving the problem.* Inadequacies in procedure arise from a variety of sources. There may be lack of knowledge about the steps which are necessary to reach the goal. There may be poor communication among members within the group based on a failure to develop mutual understanding. There may be a poor coordination of effort so that contributions to the discussion are made in a disorganized, haphazard way, with a failure of one contribution to build upon previous ones. Members may not have the habit of collecting facts against which to test decisions, so that decisions turn out to be unrealistic and unrealizable.

4. *Members may feel powerless about influencing final decisions.* Although none of the apathy-producing conditions described above exists, it is possible that any decisions they arrive at are "meaningless." If the decisions will have no practical effects, the activity of problem-solving becomes only an academic exercise. Examples of this may be found in committees within an organization which are assigned some job, where members feel that their recommendations will get lost somewhere up the line. Or, perhaps they may feel that the top personnel in the organization are pretending to be "democratic," and are only making a show of getting participation, but will in all likelihood ignore their suggestions. In such cases groups tend to operate ritualistically, going through the required motions, without involvement.

The same effect may occur if within the group there is a domineering leader, who is recognized by other members as making all the decisions. Again it is pointless for the members to invest their emotional energy in attempting to create solutions to their problem. Apathy may also arise because individual members are passed by while a smoothly functioning subgroup forces quick decisions, not giving the slower members opportunity to make decisions. Status differences within the group will frequently have the same effect. People with lower status may find it difficult to get an opportunity to be heard by other members, with the result that they come to feel that their contributions will have little effect upon the outcome.

5. *A prolonged and deep fight among a few members has dominated the group.* Frequently two or three dominant and talkative members of a group will compete with one another or with the leader so much that every activity in the group is overshadowed by the conflict. Less dominant members who feel inadequate to help solve the conflict become apathetic and withdraw from participation.

In considering these five types of causes for apathy, it seems clear we have to direct our attention to underlying conditions, rather than symptoms. Measures which are taken directed at the symptom itself—pep-talks, for example, may be completely off the mark. It should also be borne in mind that while a single explanation may largely account for the apathetic behavior, this is not necessarily the case. Any of the suggested reasons may apply, in any combination, and in varying degrees. To determine whether a given reason applies to a particular group situation, it is sometimes helpful to look for the set of symptoms, the syndrome— which may be associated with each cause. Not all the symptoms under each set need be present to indicate that the disease is of a given type, but if several can be observed, it is probably a good bet that the particular diagnosis applies.

If

—questions may be raised about what's really our job, what do *they* want us to do,

—members fail to follow through on decisions,

—there is no expectation that members will contribute responsibly, and confused, irrelevant statements are allowed to go by without question,

—members wonder about the reason for working on this problem,

—suggestions are made that we work on something else,

—the attitude is expressed that we should just decide on anything, the decision doesn't really matter,

—members seem to be waiting for a respectable amount of time to pass before referring the decision to the leader, or to a committee,

—members are inattentive, seem to get lost and not to have heard parts of the preceding discussion,

—suggestions frequently "plop," are not taken up and built on by others,

—no one will volunteer for additional work,

Then

—the group goal may seem unimportant to the members.

If

—there are long delays in getting started, much irrelevant preliminary conversation,

—the group shows embarrassment or reluctance in discussing the problem at hand,

—members emphasize the consequences of making wrong decisions, imagine dire consequences which have little reference to ascertainable facts,

—members make suggestions apologetically, are over-tentative, and hedge their contributions with many *if*'s and *but*'s.

—solutions proposed are frequently attacked as unrealistic,

—suggestions are made that someone else ought to make the decision— the leader, an outside expert, or some qualified person outside the group,

—members insist that we haven't enough information or ability to make a decision, and appear to demand an unrealistically high level of competence,

—the group has a standard of cautiousness in action,

—numerous alternative proposals are suggested, with the group apparently unable to select among them,

Then

—members probably fear working toward the group goal.

If

—no one is able to suggest the first step in getting started toward the goal,

—members seem to be unable to stay on a given point, and each person seems to start on a new tack,

—members appear to talk past, to misunderstand one another, and the same points are made over and over,

—the group appears to be unable to develop adequate summaries, or restatements of points of agreement,

—there is little evaluation of the possible consequences of decisions reached, and little attention is given to fact-finding or use of special resources,

—members continually shift into related, but off-target, tasks,

—complaints are made that the group's job is an impossible one,

—subgroups continually form around the table, with private discussions held off to the side,

—there is no follow-through on decisions or disagreement in the group about what the decisions really were,

—complaints are made that you can't decide things in a group anyway, and the leader or somebody else should do the job,

Then

—the group may have inadequate problem-solving procedures.

If

—the view is expressed that someone else with more power in the organization should be present in the meeting, that it is difficult to communicate with him at a distance,

—unrealistic decisions are made, and there is an absence of sense of responsibility for evaluating consequences of decisions,

—the position is taken that the decision doesn't really matter because the leader or someone outside the group isn't really going to listen to what we say,

—there is a tendency to ignore reaching consensus among members, the important thing being to get the leader to understand and listen,

—the discussion is oriented toward power relations, either within the group, jockeying to win over the leader, or outside the group, with interest directed toward questions about who really counts in the organization,

—doubts are voiced about whether we're just wasting our efforts in working on this program,

—members leave the meeting feeling they had good ideas which they didn't seem to be able to get across,

Then

—members feel powerless about influencing final decisions.

If

—two or three members dominate all discussion, but never agree,

—conflict between strong members comes out no matter what is discussed,

—dominant members occasionally appeal to others for support, but otherwise control conversation,

—decisions are made by only two or three members,

Then

—a conflict among a few members is creating apathy in the others.

Inadequate Decision-Making—getting satisfactory decisions made is often a major struggle in the group.[1] Here is a list of common symptoms of inefficient decision-making.

If

—the group swings between making too rapid decisions and having difficulty in deciding anything,

---

[1]These problems are discussed in detail by R. Blake and L. P. Bradford in "Decisions . . . Decisions . . . Decisions!," *Adult Leadership*, 1953, 2 (7).

—the group almost makes the decision but at the last minute retreats,

—group members call for definition and redefinition of minute points,

—the discussion wanders into abstraction,

Then

—there has been premature calling for a decision, or the decision is too difficult, or the group is low in cohesiveness and lacks faith in itself.

If

—the group has lack of clarity as to what the decision is,

—there is disagreement as to where consensus is,

—a decision is apparently made but challenged at the end,

—group members refuse responsibility,

—there is continued effort to leave decision-making to leader, subgroup or outside source,

Then

—the decision area may be threatening to the group, either because of unclear consequences, fear of reaction of other groups, or fear of failure for the individuals.

IMPROVING GROUP EFFICIENCY

Today guided missiles have a feedback mechanism built into them that continuously collects information about the position of the target in relation to the flight of the missile. When the collected information indicates a shift of the target or a discrepancy in the arc of flight of the missile, the feedback mechanism corrects the flight of the missile.

Most houses with central heating today have a small feedback mechanism, called a thermostat. When the information collected by it indicates the temperature is below a certain point, the mechanism signals the furnace to turn itself on. When information collected by the thermostat indicates that the temperature is too high, it signals the furnace to stop.

Groups need to build in feedback mechanisms to help in their own steering. Such a process of feedback calls for collecting information on the discrepancy between what the group wants to do (its target) and what it is doing (reaching its target) so that it can make corrections in its direction.

DIAGNOSIS AND FEEDBACK

Human beings, and therefore groups, not only need continuous self-correction in direction but also (and here they differ from machines) need to learn or grow or improve. Collecting adequate data and using this information to make decisions about doing things differently is one of the major ways of learning.

There are three basic parts to the process of changing group behavior:

1. Collecting information
2. Reporting the information to the group
3. Making diagnoses and decisions for change.

WHO SHOULD DIAGNOSE?

If a member of a group strives to improve his own behavior in the group so that he can make more useful contributions, he will need to make his own personal observations and diagnoses about the group and about his behavior in it. Each member has this individual responsibility.

If the group as a whole is to make decisions about changing its procedures or processes, then the entire group must assume responsibilty for collaborative diagnoses of its difficulties and its effectiveness. If the leader takes over this function, he continues to direct and dominate the group—leading them like sheep. If only the leader analyzes group difficulties and acts upon them, only he learns. Similar problems arise if diagnosis is left to any group member; he may too readily use this job to steer the group in the direction he desires.

Each member and the leader may guide and encourage the group toward diagnosis, but the responsibility for self-steering and the opportunities to learn and to grow must remain with the group if it is to improve its operational effectiveness.

COLLECTING INFORMATION

While analysis and evaluation of information and decision about what to do should be carried out by the total group, the collecting of information may be delegated. A number of patterns of delegation are possible.

1. The leader, serving also as observer, can report to the group certain pertinent observations he has made about problems and difficulties of group operation. However, although the leader may have more experience with groups, to add the function of observer to his leadership responsibilities complicates his job and also tends to create greater dependency upon him.

    But when the group is unfamiliar with the process of observation, the leader may play an informal observer role for a few meetings, gradually getting other group members to assume this function.

2. The group may appoint one of its members, perhaps on a rotating

basis, to serve as group observer, with the task of noting the manner in which the group works. While a group loses a member as far as work on its task is concerned, it can gain in the growth and improvement of the group.

Frequently there is a leader-team made up of a discussion leader and observer. The leader and observer work together in behalf of the group, one helping to guide the group and making procedural suggestions, the other watching how it works.

When a leader-team is formed, it makes possible team planning for each meeting. Between meetings the leader-observer team can look back at the past meeting from two vantage points, and look forward to the next meeting.

3. A third method calls for all group members to be as sensitive as they can, while participating actively, to the particular problems the group faces. Although in mature groups members may raise a question about group procedures or maintenance at any time as a normal contribution to the discussion, in new groups the leader may start a discussion looking at how the group has worked and what its problems are. This may occur at some time during the discussion, when the group has bogged down, or during the last fifteen minutes to half an hour as an evaluation of the entire meeting.

WHAT INFORMATION TO COLLECT?

Because of the many group problems and the many causes of these problems there is a wide range of information that a group may need at different points in time. General questions such as these may help get started:

1. What is our goal? Are we "on" or "off the beam"?
2. Where are we in our discussion? At the point of analyzing the problem? Suggesting solutions? Testing ideas?
3. How fast are we moving? Are we bogged down?
4. Are we using the best methods of work?
5. Are all of us working or just a few?
6. Are we making any improvement in our ability to work together?

In any observation of a group more can be seen than can possibly be used for steering, corrective or growth purposes. The following questions may help guide an observer in collecting data about a group.

1. What basic problems does the group seem to have for which information is needed?
2. What is the most important or pertinent information? What information will lead the group into stray paths?
3. What is the essential minimum of material the group needs?

METHODS OF OBSERVATION

Just as there are many areas of information about group behavior, so there are many possible guides and scales for observation. Frequently groups develop such scales to fit their particular needs. Three techniques of observation are given, each useful for collecting a different kind of information.

1. Who Talks to Whom

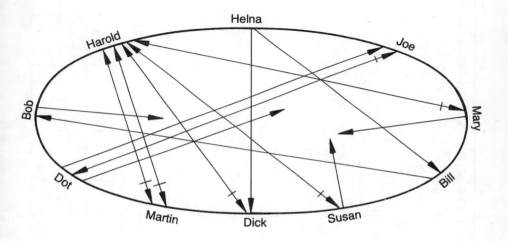

The number of lines made by the observer on this form indicates the number of statements made in a fifteen-minute period—20. Four of these were made to the group as a whole, and so the arrows go only to the middle of the circle. Those with arrows at each end of a line show that the statement made by one person to another was responded to by the recipient.

We see that one person, Harold, had more statements directed toward him than did anyone else and that he responded or participated more than anyone else. The short lines drawn at the head of one of the pair of arrows indicates who initiated the remark. Harold, the leader, in other words had remarks directed at him calling for response from four other people.

2. Who Makes What Kinds of Contributions[2]

Member No.	1	2	3	4	5	6	7	8	9	10
1. Encourages										
2. Agrees, accepts										
3. Arbitrates										
4. Proposes action										
5. Asks suggestion										
6. Gives opinion										
7. Asks opinion										
8. Gives information										
9. Seeks information										
10. Poses problem										
11. Defines position										
12. Asks position										
13. Routine direction										
14. Depreciates self										
15. Autocratic manner										
16. Disagrees										
17. Self-assertion										
18. Active aggression										
19. Passive aggression										
20. Out-of-field										

This record makes possible the quick rating not only of who talked, but the type of contribution. Individuals in the group are given numbers which are listed at the top of the columns. At the end of a time period it is possible to note the frequency and type of participation by each member.

3. What Happened in the Group

1. What was the general atmosphere in the group?

Formal_____	Informal_____
Competitive_____	Cooperative_____
Hostile_____	Supportive_____
Inhibited_____	Permissive_____
Comments:	

---

[2]Based upon observation categories discussed in *Interaction Process Analysis* by Robert F. Bales. Cambridge, Mass.: Addison-Wesley Press, 1950.

2. Quantity and quality of work accomplished

Accomplishment:	High_____	Low_____
Quality of Production:	High_____	Low_____
Goals:	Clear_____	Vague_____
Methods:	Clear_____	Vague_____
	Flexible_____	Inflexible_____

Comments:

3. Leader behavior

Attentive to group needs_____
Supported others_____
Concerned only with topic_____   Took sides_____
Dominated group_____   Helped group_____
Comments:

4. Participation

Most people talked_____   Only few talked_____
Members involved_____   Members apathetic_____
Group united_____   Group divided_____
Comments:

This form can be used as a checklist by an observer to sum up his observations, or it can be filled out by all group members to start an evaluation discussion. Forms 1 and 2 can be used only by a full-time observer.

REPORTING INFORMATION TO THE GROUP

The second step is feeding back pertinent information to the entire group. Whether the information is collected and reported by the leader or by the observer, it is very easy to hurt the group rather than help it. The following cautions are particularly pertinent in reporting to the group.

1. Be sensitive to what information the group is ready to use—what will be most helpful to the group now, rather than what was the most interesting point observed.

2. Don't "avalanche" the group with information. If too much information is given it can't be used. Select only two or three observations which will stimulate thinking and discussion. Let the group ask for more information as it needs it.

3. Don't praise the group too much. Learning doesn't take place by being told only when we are "on the beam." Mentioning accomplishments is desirable as it helps difficulties get honestly faced.

4. Don't punish or preach or judge. The observer can't play the role of God. He says, "It was interesting that participation was less widespread today than yesterday." He doesn't say, "Some of you dominated the discussion today."

5. It is easier to discuss role behavior than people's behavior. "What role did the group need filled at that time," rather than, "That behavior is bad."

6. Go lightly on personality clashes. It is usually better to discuss what helped and what hindered the whole group.

EVALUATING INFORMATION AND DECIDING ABOUT CHANGE

The third stage is diagnosis from the information reported and the consideration of what the group and its members will do differently in the future. Usually this has a number of steps.

1. The members assess the observations, relate them to their experiences, test to see whether they agree with the report.

2. The group examines the reasons. What caused a thing to happen? Could we have recognized it earlier?

3. The group moves to a decision of what to do. What can be done in future similar circumstances? What can individual members do earlier to help? What methods or procedures should be changed? What new directions sought?

This stage is the crucial one if the group is to benefit from its feedback activities. Unless the members are able to gain new insights into the functioning of the group, and are able to find new ways of behaving, the group will not improve its processes and continue in its growth and development.

It is very easy for the time of the discussion to be consumed by the first two steps in this procedure. The leader, as well as the members, needs to be sensitive to this danger and encourage the group to move into the third step of decision. Although the decisions which are made may be quite simple, agreement on future action sets up common expectations for the next meeting and gives a point to the evaluation.

Improving Decision-Making with Groups

by Gordon L. Lippitt

One of the basic problems facing organization leaders is the need to improve decision-making in the groups with which they work. Groups come together for a variety of purposes. In most instances, however, they are brought together to reach some decision or conclusion, or to solve a problem. In the experience of many of us, frequently a group is not an effective decision-making instrument. Many a leader has felt frustrated in trying to achieve effective votes, unanimity, or consensus with group members. Moreover, in some cases, it might be that the decision should not be made by a group of people.

Let us look first at some of the conditions that make group-decision-making the most appropriate means to solve a problem:

1. *Groups should be used for decision-making when they can contribute to the solution of the problem.* A group may be used effectively for decision-making when the type of decision to be reached is one in which there is a quantitative need for various points of view and opinions. This might be especially true where there is a complex problem that has no easy solution within the resources of a single individual.

Similarly, inasmuch as people tend to carry out decisions in which they share, a decision might best be made in a group when the people comprising it will be the ones who will carry out what is decided. Thus, a leader or administrator will find it extremely worthwhile to involve in the process of making the decision those who will ultimately implement it.

In addition, of course, a decision should be reached by the group if it is directly affected by it. If a club, committee, or work unit of an organization is going to be affected by the decision, it is strategic and important that the leader of that group involve its members in the decision-making function.

From *Y Work with Youth*, April 1958, 1-3. Reprinted by permission.

This does not mean, however, that there are not many instances where, due to the pressure of time, type of decision, or deferred area of responsibility, an individual may most appropriately make a decision. In other words, there is a place for individual as well as group decision-making in most organizational situations.

2. *Group decision-making can be valuable if the group members have learned to work together effectively.* One of the major reasons for ineffective group decision-making is that the group members have not learned to work together effectively as a unit. If this is the case, the leader might want to spend some time on improving the efficiency of the work group rather than to jump into too hasty decision-making. A group of persons does not spring into mature group action just because its members happen to be in the same room at the same time. A group of persons may need to deal with some of the emotional problems of its members' interpersonal relationships before it can reach decisions effectively. Group action is a complex thing. Decision-making, at its best, depends on the kind of working relationship in which disagreement, creativity, and shared responsibility can flourish. With such an atmosphere established, the group is ready to reach decisions effectively.

3. *Group decision-making is most appropriate where shared leadership is practiced.* A group of persons brought together in a decision-making situation will not function at maximum efficiency if its members are "rubber-stamp" or "yes" men for an administrator or leader. In such a situation a leader is merely communicating to the group his own desires.

If the leader of a group is interested both in assuming his own responsibility for chairmanship in the decision-making process and in developing the membership of the group so that the functions of leadership are shared, his attitude will go a long way toward achieving effective decision-making.

In addition, the group will need to maintain its working relationship by having its members contribute to harmonizing, compromising, and gate-keeping functions. A leader may, of course, perform all of these functions himself; but if he does, he will tend to run the risk of losing the interest and involvement of the members in the decision-making process. Conversely, and without abdicating his own responsibilities, the leader can build the kind of group atmosphere in which these functions can be shared through the spontaneous responsibility of its members.

4. *To reach group decisions, a group will need to have appropriate procedures for the particular problem or situation.* We are all familiar with the use of parliamentary procedure in some group situations. There have been a number of research studies showing that in many cases it is not the most appropriate tool for group action. In fact, in many settings it is only a way

by which the leader can keep control of the group. In most of the situations in which group action is taken, there is need for parliamentary procedure.

This is not to say, however, that in certain situations where there is a legislative body, a need for historical record, and a large decision-making body, *Robert's Rules of Order* are not the most appropriate. Too, there are some situations in which a group will not be using parliamentary procedure but will decide an issue or a decision by a vote; or it might develop some procedure such as majority or two-thirds rule. However, such a creation of a minority group frequently poses problems later on unless, of course, the group members show an unusual degree of maturity, or the decision to be made is so inconsequential that no one really cares who wins.

To get away from *Robert's Rules* or dependence upon the vote-taking situation, there has been a great deal of talk about trying to get "unanimous" group decision. As laudable as this might be in group-decision-making, it is extremely difficult. People being as complex as they are, it is extremely unlikely that one can get unanimous decisions very frequently in group decision-making: in many cases, it would take a great deal of time and an extraordinary amount of patience for a group to be able to reach unanimity.

It is the opinion of this author that there is a difference between unanimous decision-making and a "consensus" decision. In a consensus type of decision, the members of the group agree on the *next steps*, but those who are not in agreement with the decision reserve the right to have the tentative decision tested and evaluated for later assessment. In other words, certain members of the group will agree that on a "provisional try" or a "first-time" basis we could try out a particular alternative; *but* they want to put in certain evaluative means for testing whether or not the feelings of the majority are the most appropriate for group action. In a very real sense, this is different from compromise. In a compromise situation, the decision is taken from two opposing points of view and becomes something quite different from either of them. In the consensus type of decision, individuals in the group might be saying that they are "not sure" of the best decision, but realizing the need for action, they will build in some commitment to an action step that will be assessed later.

FACTORS WHICH FACILITATE GROUP DECISION-MAKING

In looking at some of the factors that improve group decision-making, one could make long lists of dimensions which affect any group situation. This list, however, will focus on some of the specific factors relating to the decision-making phase of group action.

1. *A clear definition of the problem*. If the problem is ambiguous and the group is unable to understand it, the decision-making process will be greatly impeded. In many cases, a problem is so general that the group is unable to come to grips with it. A problem should be defined clearly, the limits of the group responsibility should be set, and any clarification relative to the problem should be encouraged.

2. *A clear understanding as to who has the responsibility for the decision*. When a group is asked to assume responsibility for a decision, it should have an understanding as to its freedom to act and the degree of its responsibility.

3. *Effective communication for idea production*. In group decision-making, it is important to get the ideas of the group out in the open. Too often the group will seize on the first solution or suggestion to solve a problem. This too-early evaluation of an idea can frequently block effective decision-making. In the idea-production phase of decision-making, such methods as brainstorming and encouraging the group not to associate ideas with people are valuable.

4. *Appropriate size of group for decision-making*. If a group is too large for decision-making, it should use sub-groups in trying to reach a decision. Frequently, a group gets "bogged down" because of its size.

5. *A means for effective testing of different alternatives relative to the problem*. If a decision is to be made effectively by a group, it should have some means of getting data about the effects of the different alternatives it is considering. To ask a group to make a decision without adequate data is unfair and ineffective. It might be that a group needs to postpone making a decision until it can get further data to enable it to make the most appropriate decision.

6. *A need for building in commitment to the decision*. To achieve effective decision-making, a group needs to realize that the reaching of the actual decision is only one step in the process: the implementation of the decision and the carrying out of the action are the important parts. A group needs to build into its planning some responsibility, and the delegation of it, for the carrying out of the action. Frequently, failure to pin down responsibility causes a decision to become ineffective and necessitates further meetings which result in certain frustration and apathy on the part of group members.

7. *Honest commitment of the leader to the group decision-making process*. A leader should be interested in the process and not in a predetermined idea or opinion of his own. This does not mean, however, that the leader, or any other status person, does not have the right to make a contribution;

although for him to do so too early is a mistake. If the group members feel he has a particular solution, they will tend to react to it and not be so creative in suggesting new ideas.

8. *A need for agreement on the procedures and methods for decision-making prior to deliberation on the issue.* On issues which are particularly controversial and cause a "split" in the group, decision-making will become a real problem. It is valuable to have the group spend some time at the beginning of the meeting to reach agreement on the methods and procedures it will use in reaching its decision. If it can come to an agreement on the criteria and standards it will use, it will have established the basis of agreement for later decision-making. The point between the emergence of a problem and reaching a decision on it is not the shortest distance between two points. It is extremely valuable for a group to take the time to prepare itself for effective decision-making so that it does not get into the situation of making a hasty decision before there is a readiness for group action.

SUMMARY

Effective group decision-making is possible. The use of the consensus method over voting or unanimity is realistic, but it is not easy. Careful attention to the decision-making process, mature group membership, and democratic leadership combine to contribute maximally to those situations where groups can meet most effectively their obligation in solving problems.

The Case of the Hidden Agenda

by Leland P. Bradford

The main reason for people's coming together and forming a group is that there is a publicly stated, agreed-on task to be accomplished. This is the surface, or public, agenda. It may be a program, a task, an objective. But below the surface there are quite apt to be hidden agendas which the group probably does not openly recognize. Individual members often have these private agendas.

It would seem that if the task is clear and the leader competent there could be no reason why the group should not proceed logically and calmly to an intelligent conclusion.

Yet, as we know too well, groups do not always work logically nor react intelligently. They wrangle over inconsequential points while the main issue is neglected, make decisions that would ill become a ten-year-old, or forget all patterns of logical thinking as they tortuously twist their way through masses of muddled thinking.

Before our judgment of groups becomes too severe, however, we need to realize that groups are working simultaneously and continuously on two levels. One level is formally labelled. Whether confused or clear, simple or difficult, this is the obvious, advertised purpose for which the group meets. It represents the acknowledged task facing the group: to nominate a slate of officers for the local PTA, to plan a meeting or conference, to gain understanding of child behavior, or to study the Declaration of Independence. It is the open and acknowledged agenda for the group.

Unlabelled, private and covered, but deeply felt and very much the concern of the group, is another level. Here are all of the conflicting

From *Adult Leadership*, September, 1952, 1(4), 3-7. Reprinted by permission.

motives, desires, aspirations and emotional reactions held by the group members, subgroups or the group as a whole that cannot be fitted legitimately into the accepted group task. Here are all of the problems which, for a variety of reasons, cannot be laid on top of the table.

Appropriately, these are called hidden agendas.

□   □   □   □   □

An assistant superintendent of schools believed that many of the teachers in her city needed further training. The superintendent accepted her idea and suggested that such training be started either by conducting a two-day training institute on Fridays and Saturdays or by having hour-and-a-half meetings once a week for ten weeks. Either plan placed the training period on the teachers' own time.

At a meeting the principals agreed at once on the value of such training and appeared at first to like both of the alternative plans. However, difficulties then arose. Some wanted one plan, some the other. All the teachers could not meet at the same time. Hidden agendas were never mentioned. Many of the principals resented being given only two choices. Others suspected that the superintendent believed their schools were backward. They thought that the training program was really aimed at showing up their schools.

Two of the principals were younger; they felt they were better liked by the superintendent and they wanted to support him in anything he wanted. Two other principals had a number of older teachers who they knew would object seriously to the whole idea.

The situation was further complicated by the assistant superintendent who was new to her job and not entirely accepted by the principals. At the meeting she made the weight of the superintendent too obvious. She implied that she thought the system was behind the times. The principals hoped secretly that something would happen to eliminate the entire idea, so they delayed matters, waiting for a miracle.

These were only some of the hidden agendas. They are sufficient to indicate why any decision was difficult and action almost impossible. The group was working on private agendas and hence moved illogically on its surface task.

□   □   □   □   □

Each agenda level affects the other. When a group is proceeding successfully on its surface agenda with a sense of accomplishment and group unity, it is evident that major hidden agendas have either been settled, are being handled as the surface agenda is being worked on, or have been temporarily put to sleep. Let the group reach a crisis on its surface agenda and run into difficulties, however, and somnolent hidden agendas come awake.

Groups can work hard on either or both agendas. A group frequently spends endless time getting nowhere on its surface agenda, seemingly running away from its task, and yet, at the end, gives the impression of a hard-working group. Often group members leave a meeting saying, "Well, we got somewhere at last." Yet, if asked where they got, they would have mentioned some relatively trivial decisions on the surface level. What they were really saying was that some very important hidden agenda had been solved.

A group may have been working hard without visible movement on its appointed task. Suddenly it starts to move efficiently on its surface task and in a short time brings it to an adequate conclusion. The group had to clear its hidden agenda out of its way before it could go to work on its obvious job.

A high school faculty committee met to decide what to do about the coming retirement of the head of the English Department. The meeting meandered in a curious fashion. Under the rather easy leadership of the chairman, each committee member seemingly felt impelled to make two kinds of statements in one sentence—such as:

"I certainly want to have us give a fine present to Miss X, but I do worry what kind of precedent we are setting."

"If any one deserves a fine ceremony, Miss X does. However, I wonder how much the teachers can afford to give."

"Miss X herself wouldn't want us to do anything for her, but we really shouldn't let her feeling stand in the way of doing something nice for her."

After these statements were expressed in a number of ways, there seemed to be a sudden group feeling that something had been completed. At a certain point, the group dropped all hesitancies and methodically, objectively and quickly analyzed its task, determined how to collect information about what Miss X would want most, what the rest of the teachers would most like to give her, how the ceremony of presentation could be dignified, and how to keep it all at a cost that was neither too niggardly nor too profligate.

To the observer it appeared that here was a group hidden agenda that needed to be handled—the opportunity for each group member to express in a legitimate fashion certain hostilities he felt toward Miss X, or thought that other teachers felt. If the leader had moved too fast to a decision or had tried to prevent these expressions, the hidden agenda would probably come out in a less adequate solution to the group task. Committees under circumstances of that sort have bought presents that were obviously inappropriate or unwanted by the recipient.

LET'S NOT JUDGE HIDDEN AGENDAS

Hidden agendas are neither better nor worse than surface agendas. Rather they represent all of the individual and group problems that differ from the surface group job and therefore may get in the way of the orderly solving of the surface agenda. They may be conscious or unconscious for the member or for the group. They are not to be blamed or damned.

Burying them does little good. Pretending that they, like country cousins, are unrelated to the group is equally ineffective. They are important, because they concern the group, and something needs to be done about them. The answer may be to solve them or to shelve them.

Groups, fortunately, can work on both agenda levels at the same time. What is needed is improvement in effective ways of working on hidden agendas as well as on the surface agenda. The first step toward greater effectiveness is to recognize the kinds and sources of hidden agendas.

TYPES OF HIDDEN AGENDAS

Hidden agendas can be held by:

1. Group members
2. The leader
3. The group itself.

Each of these, in turn, can be divided in terms of the cause of the hidden agenda held and the person or group unit to which its actions are directed.

The hidden agendas held by various individuals in a group grow out of a number of causes. Some hidden agendas deal with the group task.

The Individual and the Group Task

While the group may be struggling for an acceptable solution to its problem, some members may have brought answers in their hip-pockets. Obviously a hip-pocket answer is usually not acceptable to a group because it implies that one individual stands to gain, somehow, more than the rest, and because it implies that the individual, by himself, is much more competent than the group. So the individuals with hip-pocket answers wait until they judge the time is appropriate for them to have just thought of a good idea. If their minds are pretty well closed to any other solution but their own, and if they are intent on watching the group discussion to find the best time to enter their solution, they are probably not the best contributing members of the group. Their hidden agendas are definitely affecting the group.

In back of some group members stand invisible companions. They, with the particular group member, belong to some other group and they are present to make certain their representative fights for the special interest of their group. The fact that these invisible companions are present only in the mind of the group member makes them no less effective in controlling his behavior in the present group.

So some group members are torn by divided loyalties. They are members of two groups at the same time. So long as the groups follow the same path, there is no conflict. Let the paths divide and the individual must try to bring them together or be forced to choose between them. The individual may change from a flexible, cooperative group member to one who is more tense as he tries to push the group toward a point to which it doesn't particularly want to go. To the group which doesn't know of the hidden conflict of divided loyalties, the behavior of the individual may seem suddenly incomprehensible.

A community group, composed of representatives of various organizations and agencies, that meets to work on a problem of importance to all present, usually presents a clear picture of divided loyalties and invisible companions. In the mind of each member is a picture of the group he represents and their wishes. In essence, he is participating as a member of the present committee with interest in its program, but he is speaking the words and thoughts of another committee. His two purposes sometimes get in each other's way.

As a group moves toward the solution of its task, it may suddenly threaten some group member and make him fearful. Perhaps a staff group is about to make a decision that threatens to bring criticism to the job area of one individual. Perhaps a group is approaching a decision that makes one group member fear he will have difficulty in defending his colleagues in another group. Perhaps the class discussion, in high school or college, is approaching the point beyond which the group member has studied. Perhaps the group discussion of intellectual ideas is beginning to challenge certain long-held beliefs of a group member—beliefs he doesn't want to re-examine. For differing reasons these individuals would hesitate to state their fears. Nevertheless, these fears are going to become dominant hidden forces causing members to try to change the group's direction, irrespective of the logic or desirability of the path the group is taking.

Sometimes group members have hidden agendas directed against group procedures that limit their freedom to dominate the group. When proposals are made for better group organization of time and resources (buzz groups, subgroups, blackboard recording, limitations on time), it is frequently the person who manipulates and monopolizes the group who is most distressed and who feels too much attention is being paid to group procedures.

The Individual and His Place in the Group

Having entered into a group, each individual is concerned with his place in the group and his relationships to the other group members. He wants to know what is expected of him and the limitations on his actions. The depth and intensity of his concern will vary with the importance of the group to him.

No one wants to be excluded and everyone wants to bask in the sunlight of the group respect. Some need to be liked more than do others, and some need to have more power to influence the group. Certain individuals have more need for protection against dominance and aggression and the need for greater dependency on others.

In any group there is a struggle for power and position which continues until a temporary equilibrium of influence structure has been reached. As individuals leave the group, as new members enter or as a crisis develops, the equilibrium may be disturbed and the power struggle renewed and sometimes intensified.

One of the best times to observe the force of these hidden agendas is during the opening period of a group or its first few meetings. Tension is present in the group—hesitancies and watchful waitings—opening gambits by some who aspire to influence or power. Each individual figuratively has sensitive feelers out, probing the atmosphere, the group behavior, and the actions of others so that he can answer satisfactorily questions concerning the degree of security and protection against attack. He wants to know what is expected of him and how his contribution will fit into the group; who will fight for power in the group; who is likely to compete with him; whom does he feel closest to when issues arise; and what can be expected of the leaders. Here are the basic problems the group is struggling with as it starts its history. The fumbling, stiff beginnings of many groups are more readily understood when seen against the background of the crucial hidden agendas of getting acquainted and moving as a group.

Leadership obviously affects the way in which the struggle for position and influence develops and the effectiveness of its solution. The highly dominant leader who so controls the group that members answer only his questions, merely pushes the struggle for position farther underground, delays its solution, and makes possible the emergence of a few secondary group dominators. He maintains the tension of insecurity among members because the group has had little chance to form as a group. He has tried to keep it a collection of individuals responsive to him.

The weak leader, who gives the group no help in its problem of group formation, merely serves to encourage one or two overly dominant individuals either to take over the group and immobilize it by fear of aggression or to use the group as a battlefield as the two competing leaders fight it out. In either case the normal process of group formation is distorted and handicapped.

Obviously, even after the initial effort of the group to develop as a group is well under way (and it should be emphasized that this process never ends), interpersonal struggles on the hidden agenda level can continue or develop and have their effect upon the way the group works and the quality of its products.

The Individual and the Leader

Each individual possibly has a special set of hidden agendas concerning the leader.

He may compete with the leader for influence on the group. Obviously he cannot state his purpose—he may not even be aware of it. He would have to make denial if it were brought up. But his hidden agenda comes through in a variety of indirect ways. He may challenge what the leader has said at some point. (There is a definite but not always easily recognizable difference between the legitimate member challenge of a mistake by the leader, and the challenge that has for its purpose the destruction of the leader.) Usually the competing member waits until he senses the group is reluctant to follow the leader, and so his challenge is more likely to gain group support. By directing questions at various other group members, he may try to direct discussion back to himself, and so, for a while, control the group. By suggesting acceptable solutions to group impasses, or by making procedural suggestions, he may try to prove himself more important to the group than is the leader. He is usually content that the designated leader retain the title so long as the group is largely influenced and controlled by himself.

He may, as another type of hidden agenda, feel generally hostile to all leaders. This hostility, usually unconscious, probably has grown out of childhood experiences with his father, school teachers, church leaders, etc. One difference between attack on leadership growing out of such hostility toward leadership and attack growing out of desire to take over leadership is that hostility to leadership does not always lead the individual to desire to dominate the group himself. He may be more concerned with attacking leadership wherever found.

On the other hand, childhood experiences lead some individuals generally to seek to be dependent on leadership. For these people there is greater satisfaction when they can find and cling to a person who assumes leadership responsibilities. Their hidden agenda is to maintain the comfortable state of dependence and their group contributions are affected by the degree of attack upon the leader and the extent of group acceptance of the leader.

On the conscious level, individuals may have certain hidden agendas in relation to the leader. If he is seen as likely to make possible the acceptance of a solution favorable to them, they will support him. He may equally well be rejected if the individuals feel he endangers the solution desired by them.

Most people have no great hostility toward leadership or overwhelming need to compete for leadership. Furthermore, the hidden agendas toward leadership are seldom clear-cut. A number may be present, to greater or lesser degrees, in any one individual.

Also group members rightly need to criticize and endeavor to change the leadership in its direction because of the mistakes of omission or commission the leader may be making. Since criticisms do not necessarily indicate indulging hostility toward the leader, this article would be failing of its purpose if it made people feel guilty every time they differed from the group leader.

The Leader and His Hidden Agendas

Even the leader has his hidden agendas. One may be merely the desire, which he nobly or prudently inhibits, to cut the throat of an obstreperous individual. Another, and unfortunately too frequently present when the role of leader should be that of helping the group work out its decisions, may be a hip-pocket solution which he inserts when he thinks the group has reached an impasse and is ready to accept his solution.

On the deeper, and usually unconscious level, his hidden agenda may be that of maintaining his leadership at any cost. The position of influence and power is pleasing, and he will resist relinquishing it. One of the hardest tasks facing any leader of a continuing group is to allow it to grow up and to be less dependent on him. In little ways, as so frequently parents do, he maintains his control over the group.

On the other hand, other individuals may tend to want to give away their leadership at the same time they seek it. Usually this ambivalence grows out of a feeling of guilt about wanting to be leader.

Of course, many leaders have neither hidden agenda. They may be willing to accept leadership when the group requires it, be pleased by their opportunity to serve and to have recognition, but glad to release the leadership and pass it on. Where groups have grown in ability and maturity to a point where every member is playing a leader role in some way in the group, pressures toward maintaining the leader role are greatly reduced.

Group Hidden Agendas

Once a group has begun to form (when there is some expectation that it will meet more than once and when there is felt to be some common concern of the group as a whole), it shows many characteristics common to individuals. Its most fundamental trait seems to be a will to survive. No matter how much at war parts of the group may be with other parts, there is usually a movement of the group itself that can be explained only on the basis of an urge for survival. A group under attack, either from a source outside the group or from one of its own members, will move to resist this attack, whether or not it is a logical criticism of the group's operation. A group with absent members will show signs of depression and worry. Somehow the fact that these members are absent seems an attack on the group—as if the members, if they really valued the group, would find some way of attending. When new members come into a group, there is a period in which the group exudes a sense of tension until it knows whether the new members will disrupt the group. When one member moves too fast and too far, causing potential splits in the group, a quiet resistant movement grows within the group.

A group is fearful of conflict when the conflict promises to destroy the group, even though it permits and encourages conflict among members, against the leader, against an outside force, as a means of escape from its job. The difference lies in whether the conflict threatens the basic group being. Warfare is tolerated—is even fun—until it threatens the basic survival of the group.

The group may have hidden agendas about its task. If the task is seen as too difficult; if it suggests consequences that might be harmful to the group; if it has been pressed on the group by some outside group or individual who is disliked by the group; if it is solely the leader's task—the group's hidden agenda may be to slow down on the task. While this is never brought out on the surface, the group has many ways of running away from its job. One pattern of flight may be that of endless discussion over unimportant details, another, through listing on the blackboard endless lists that could better be done by one person later. Escape into discussion of principles or into esoteric arguments is very common. Anecdotal periods that delay work are found in many groups.

Groups develop hidden agendas about a given group member or leader. Where someone has been overly aggressive, the group may center its hostility upon that individual. Under tension from sources that cannot be adequately attacked, a group may "scapegoat" one of its own members. Thus groups distort the pattern of work on the task level to fit the many hidden agendas present.

Groups can readily develop hidden agendas concerning the leader. If he is too dominant, the hidden agenda reaction may take the form of passive resistance. If he takes sides on crucial issues or leaves the group with no security about his fairness, active revolt may take place. Frequently a group is obviously following the leadership of one of its members, while it permits the designated leader to go through the empty forms of leadership.

What To Do About Hidden Agendas

The problem of handling hidden agendas in such a way that they do not block group productivity or lead to group failure and disintegration faces every leader.

Pretending these agendas are not present, ruling the group with an iron hand, and forcing it to stay "on the beam" have been relatively unsuccessful. Usually a leader who acts in this way comes out with an apathetic endorsement of his own plan, with no responsibility upon the part of the members to carry it out, with much conflict and aggression in the group, or with many efforts of the group to run away from its job.

Effective leadership, however, can do much to help the group bring together its work on both its surface and hidden levels. The leader who recognizes that his function is basically to help the group at its points of need, rather than to direct the group or pull it along, reluctantly, after him, can do much with the problem of hidden agendas. His approach of service to the group should tend to make him more sensitive to group needs and more diagnostic about group problems.

Such a leader can observe the following suggestive points:

1. Look for hidden agendas that are present. Recognition of the possibility of hidden agendas on individual and group levels is the first step in diagnosis of group difficulty. Diagnosis is the necessary first step before intelligent action can be taken.

2. Remember that the group is continuously working on two levels at once. Consequently it may not move so fast on the surface task as the leader might wish.

3. Sometimes the leader can make it easier for a group to bring its hidden agenda to the surface. The leader may say, for example: "I wonder if we have said all we feel about the issue. Maybe we should take time to go around the table so that any further thoughts can be opened up."

4. When hidden agendas can be laid on the table and talked about, they are easier to handle. *But many hidden agendas would hurt the group more if they were talked about openly.* A leader or group member needs to be sensitive to this point and should try to recognize what a group can and cannot face at a given point.

5. Don't scold or pressure the group because it has hidden agendas. They are present and legitimate and need to be worked on as much as the surface task.

6. Help the group to remove feelings of guilt about hidden agendas. As groups are aided to bring out into the open some of the hidden agendas and treat them legitimately, there will be a lessening of feelings of guilt about them and a tendency to lay more of them on the table. The leader might say: "We certainly could expect that each of us might see

things somewhat differently and we certainly shouldn't feel guilty about wanting different things accomplished. That is all part of the many differences that make up a group."

7. Help the group work out methods of solving their hidden agendas just as they develop methods of handling their surface agenda. Such methods may vary, but basically they call for opening up the problem, collecting as many relevant data as possible, and seeking a solution based on such data. Obviously, data relating to the individual's feelings and problems are as important as more logical data. In the last analysis, problem-solving methods are needed for solving hidden agendas.

8. Help the group evaluate its progress in handling hidden agendas. Each experience should indicate better ways of more openly handling future hidden agendas. As groups grow in maturity and strength, the number of hidden agendas that remain hidden is definitely reduced. Short evaluation sessions, either the last fifteen minutes of a group meeting, or one meeting out of a series of meetings, can be very profitable to a group. In such sessions a group can look back to see how many more problems it was able to talk freely about and how much more confidence the group had in its members.

Stereotypes and the Growth of Groups

by Herbert A. Thelen and Watson Dickerman

Varied social mechanisms differ in the explicitness of their policies of operation. In an association which operates according to a constitution, bylaws, and parliamentary procedure, policies of operation are comparatively explicit. In an informal group, such as a club or discussion group, policies of operation are much less explicit. Members do have concepts, frequently at a stereotypic level, about policies of operation—how the leader is to be chosen, how decisions are to be made, how status among the members is to be determined. But these concepts differ considerably from member to member, and often conflicts, which reduce the group's productivity, result. These conflicts are the more difficult to reconcile because the members of the group do not realize that they are the direct result of the varying concepts which the members hold about the group's operational policies. Or, if they realize this, they assume that each one's concepts about these policies are within his area of freedom of belief and, thus, nobody's business but his own.

GROUPS IN ACTION

What are these stereotypes about the operation of groups and how are they related to the stages by which a group grows in productivity? Groups which were in operation for three weeks at the 1948 session of the National Training Laboratory in Group Development serve to illustrate stereotypes at various stages of group growth. We shall try to describe both the phases in the development of these groups and the stereotypes about policies of operation which accompanied these phases. Our data are the sound recordings of the discussions of the eight groups at different

From *Educational Leadership*, February, 1949, 6(5), 309-316. Reprinted by permission.

stages in their development and the daily written records of the observer in each group.

In the light of what happened in these eight groups at the NTLGD, a group may perhaps be seen as going through four phases as it grows in ability to operate efficiently. *In the first phase various members of the group quickly attempt to establish their customary places in the leadership hierarchy.* In effect, this may be thought of as an attempt to establish the "peck order" of the group. *Next comes a period of frustration and conflict brought about by the leader's steadfast rejection of the concept of peck order and the authoritarian atmosphere in which the concept of peck order is rooted. The third phase sees the development of cohesiveness among the members of the group, accompanied by a certain amount of complacency and smugness.* This third phase seems to be characterized by a determination to achieve and maintain harmony at all costs. Insofar as this effort is successful, it results in an atmosphere of deceptive "sweetness and light," which, nevertheless, is sufficiently permissive to enable the members to assess their own positions, modes of interaction, and attitudes in the group. This phase is unstable because it is unrealistic, and it gives way to a fourth phase. *In the fourth phase the members retain the group-centeredness and sensitivities which characterized the third phase, but they develop also a sense of purpose and urgency which make the group potentially an effective social instrument.*

We turn now to an effort to identify some of the stereotypes about policies of operation which seem to characterize these four phases of the growth of our groups.

Phase One — Individually Centered

- Every group needs a strong, expert leader.
- Good group membership consists of active, oral participation; those who do not talk are not good group members.
- The group is wasting its time unless it is absorbing information or doing something active—listening to lectures, receiving bibliographies, making long lists on the blackboard, role playing, working in subcommittees, passing resolutions.
- The group cannot become cohesive or efficient until each member has certain "necessary" information about the other members—occupation, title, job responsibilities, age, education, family, hobbies.
- The group's observer makes his assessment of the group's process by using his intuition. He gives the members interesting information about themselves.
- Any expression of feeling, particularly of aggression or hostility, is bad. It upsets the group and should be squelched.

- The chief function of the leader is to manipulate the group toward the goals which he knows are appropriate for it because of his competence and authority.

- Each member sees the other members primarily as individuals rather than as parts of a group. Each must be dealt with individually through the kinds of appeals which are persuasive for him.

Phase Two – Frustration and Conflict Among Stereotypes

The stereotypic conflicts which characterize this phase are perceived quite differently by the members of the group at the beginning of the phase and at its end. At the beginning the leader is seen as a frustrating figure because he has refused to fit the stereotypes which characterized Phase One. This results in the direction of a good deal of hostility against him, which may be expressed quite overtly. By the end of Phase Two, this and other stereotypic conflicts are seen as simply the verbalization of the ambivalences of members of the group. In other words, they are seen as representing unsolved problems which plague all of us but which we manage to repress if our group has a strong leader who is willing to act as such. These conflicts seem to the writers to pose some of the most fundamental problems that individuals have to solve before they can become secure as members of a group. Typical stereotypic conflicts which characterize Phase Two follow:

- We must have a leader who is strong to the point of being dominating and autocratic *versus* We must have a leader who is permissive to the point of being laissez-faire.

- Our troubles of operation would disappear if only the leader would tell us the theory of group dynamics *versus* Our troubles can disappear only when we have acquired skill in formulating a theory about and assessing the operations of our group.

- Democratic group process requires a strong leader who is subject to criticism and recall by the group at any time *versus* Democratic group process requires a chairman whose primary job is to conciliate interpersonal conflicts among the active members of the group.

- Efforts to assess our own group processes are an invasion of the sacredness of individual personalities *versus* Assessment of group process is a sounder starting point for intelligent group action than is attention to motivations and attitudes of individual members of the group.

- Our basic problem is that members do not take enough initiative and responsibility *versus* Members who exhibit initiative and willingness to assume responsibility are competing with the leader.

- A decision by majority vote is binding on all members of the group *versus* No individual should be coerced into going along with what he thinks is wrong.

- Leadership is a role vested in a single competent member of the group *versus* Leadership is a complex function which should be distributed among all members of a group.

The first problem, which runs through most of these conflicts, appears to be the notion that the answer must be either A or B. Such thinking is most fruitless when neither A nor B is satisfactory. Members of a group must learn to ask, "Under what conditions is this policy wise?" rather than, "What policy is wise under all conditions?" The latter alternative is, of course, a legitimate question. But its answer would require appraisal of each of the alternative policies, followed by identification of the essential criteria for answering the first question. The answer to the second would be: any policy is wise if it satisfies this list of criteria; and the list of criteria would then have to be given.

It seems likely that the members of a group must reorient their ideas about how knowledge should be formulated. The notion that a set of generalizations about psychological phenomena can be given is less tenable than the notion that the legitimate content of psychological knowledge is only description and rationale for a set of procedures by which appropriate policy can be determined in a given situation. We are asserting, in effect, that content knowledge in the area of group dynamics consists not of generalizations about psychological phenomena *per se*. Rather, it consists of generalizations about how to proceed in determining right conduct. Generalizations of the first kind enter into generalizations of the second kind only insofar as they help us to speculate about whether or not a suggested method of procedure will have the consequences required by the criteria.

A second major problem which a group faces, in the light of the conflicts which have been described, is how to ask the right kinds of questions—those which will lead to fruitful answers.

For example, an important question is: What is the relationship between an individual's rights and his duties to society? An unfruitful way to get at this relationship is to ask: What are the rights of individuals? The question might better be phrased: What are the characteristics of individual participation which most facilitate those types of interaction through which both the individual and his society can develop in desirable directions? The change in wording makes a *sine qua non* of neither the inalienable rights of individuals nor the demands of society. Instead, it focuses attention on the kinds of individual action which can contribute most both to his own individual growth and to a healthy society.

A third problem is partly one of insight of the group's goal and the steps necessary to reach it, and partly one of skill in communicating such insight to one another. Many of the conflicts arose because members of the group felt forced to take untenable positions—for example, on the nature of good leadership or the characteristics of democratic group process. When one has taken an untenable position, he is vulnerable to attack and is likely to become defensive because even he can see that his position is weak.

By the development of insight about goals and of skill in their communication, could each member's responses have contributed to the sequential solution of the problems the group was trying to solve rather than frittering away the group's time and strength on inconsequential flank skirmishes? For example, it may be that these destructive side battles could have been avoided if the members had seen the group's goal in terms of a series of sub-goals, each of which was to be reached through group action. One such sub-goal might be the existence of enough permissiveness so that members could alleviate their anxieties rather than project them into stereotypic conflicts. Another might be orientation in the methodology of action research so that members would acquire more know-how about solving problems. Another might be the acquisition of skill in making group decisions. Surmounting each of these sub-goals would carry the group forward progressively toward the final goal instead of encouraging endless and fruitless stereotypic conflicts.

Phase Three – Attempted Consolidation of Group Harmony

During this phase, the group's major purpose appears to be to avoid conflict of the sort that was so debilitating during the second period. This requires the development of skill in playing supportive roles, conciliating roles, integrating roles. It also requires the members to become more responsive to subtle cues and to take more responsibility for indicating agreement or disagreement with tentative notions, rather than flat rejections or acceptances of proposed solutions. Perhaps the major pitfall to be avoided at this point is that of glossing over significant differences for the sake of apparent harmony.

During the third period, then, we find the following stereotypes dominant:

- The goal of the group is cohesiveness, not productivity.
- Group-centered behavior is essentially a kind of polite behavior which avoids upsetting the group. Each individual must curb his impulses in such a way that conflict does not become open.
- The leader is essentially a laissez-faire chairman.
- Planning or steering committees should be used to make concrete proposals for the group's consideration.

- A person who is silent must be brought into the discussion so we can tell whether he is unhappy.
- Our most important goal is satisfaction for each individual in the group. We must work at this objectively and with considerable self-assessment. The self-assessment, however, must not reveal apparent individual weaknesses but rather the difficulties of a normal individual who is struggling with difficult problems.
- Our leader may be seen as a fairly worthy person to have brought us to this pleasant position but, nevertheless, we will divide the job of chairmanship among ourselves.

During this third phase there is a marked increase in the sense of individual responsibility for satisfying group needs. One might see the preceding period of frustration as one in which every individual became highly involved emotionally in the group's process; in it, it is no longer possible to sit back to judge or to be amused. On the other hand, the desire to avoid further bitterness and conflict acts as a strong disciplining influence and stimulates the development of skill which the members did not previously possess—those skills which allow a person to participate and yet avoid conflict. The former leader is now reinstated, not as a leader but as a resource person; and the group discussion shows fairly clearly that it is rejecting the concept of leadership as a personal role in favor of the concept of leadership as one aspect of good group membership—a function which is shared by all.

In a very real sense, the test of whether the preceding experiences of the members of the group have resulted in understanding may well be whether they move out of this stage in which "we all love one another with qualifications" but in which also significant skills are developing, to a later stage in which the group becomes a social instrument geared for action, directed outward toward improvement of its environment rather than inward toward the adjustment of members to the present environment. Until this moving on to a later stage takes place, it is as if the group were operating with some elements of phantasy, primarily in regard to its own goals. This phantasy is perilously close to the institutionalization of complacency on the one hand and to fear of ideational and other conflicts associated with solving action problems on the other.

It is probable that the only way in which this socially reinforced complacency can be broken down is through each individual's objective self-assessment. This will enable him to realize that if this period is too prolonged it will become an obstacle to any further growth on his part. It is necessary, then, for skills to be developed in a new functional area— skills which will enable each individual to realize his own needs for action in the group as distinguished from skills required for the individual to realize his needs for position and security. Along with this, at the conceptual level, must come the understanding that security is not a sufficient goal in itself, but is the necessary condition for effective action.

Phase Four — Individual Self-Assessment, Flexibility of Group Processes, and Emphasis upon Productivity in Problem-Solving

We present the apparent stereotypes of this fourth phase with somewhat less confidence than those of the other phases because most of our groups did not go on into the social action stage. They did not actually tackle problems of adjusting their own environment. One had the feeling that the Laboratory ended with the groups in the middle of a phase, with things yet to happen. It is quite possible, also, that even if there had been time for this fourth phase to develop completely, other still more mature phases may lie beyond it. There are, however, a number of impressions that most of the observers seemed to concur in, which suggest directions such as those described in the preceding paragraph and require the development of skills beyond those required in the third phase.

The two most obvious characteristics of this fourth phase are the attainment by the members of much greater objectivity with regard to individual roles in the group, and the attainment of much greater ease in making decisions and much more flexibility in controlling group processes. For a third characteristic of the fourth phase, namely, participation as a group in problem-solving activities designed to change or modify the social scene through direct impact on it rather than merely through the changed attitudes and skills of individuals, we have less evidence than expectation. But there is some reason to believe that readiness for this kind of activity is developing.

Another difficulty encountered in trying to describe the stereotypes which govern this fourth phase is that stereotypic thinking was much less frequent, and in many of the group members there was a definite feeling of revulsion whenever anyone attempted to produce a capsule evaluation as to whether the chairman were behaving in a "democratic" manner or not. It is as if the conceptualization had been driven down into a much deeper level, whose complexity made verbalization difficult. Permissiveness had developed at the level of individual thinking; that is, individuals were now free to theorize about these processes in their own way.

It is the introduction of this element which takes the method of control out of the laissez-faire area in which there is considerable permissiveness of specific behaviors but very little permissiveness of conceptualization and thinking about behaviors. It is because of the deeper, more personalized conceptualizations that frustration and impasse due to conflict can be avoided in a climate having this second sort of permissiveness.

The stereotypes that we can identify, then, in the fourth phase, should probably be thought of not as verbalizations whose relation to operation is vague and conflicting in the minds of members, but rather as principles of operation which have developed inductively and more or less consciously as by-products of the individual's attempt to meet his own needs in the group. Among these notions are:

- Each individual has a personality of his own which is different from that of other group members and is not to be judged as either good or bad.

- The nature of this personality determines the efficiency and ease with which individuals will be able to play different roles in the group.

- If a member of a group is to grow in ability to participate in the group, other members must help him by demonstrating their expectation that he will grow and their approval of his growing ability to formulate perceptions about group process.

- This, in turn, means that all individual perceptions and differences among them have to be treated as realities. It also means that we cannot assume that any one individual's perceptions are the "right" ones.

- Contributions of each individual must be assumed to be relevant to the problem under consideration. It is up to the group to find out what the relevance is. Only thus can the goal directions of each individual be continually woven into the goal direction of the group as a whole.

- Although the deeper meanings of each individual's contribution cannot be taken for granted, enough rapport has developed that the members know about what to expect from each individual. It is only when these expectations are violated by the introduction of novel and threatening elements into the situation that a serious problem arises.

- The question of "What is our purpose at this point? What is the problem we are trying to solve?" is recognized as one of the most helpful questions that can be asked instead of one of the most obstructing questions which should, at all costs, be avoided and resented.

- In a sense, every member is expected to play all roles at appropriate times. The question of which roles should be formally structured by the group and assigned to particular individuals and for what periods of time remains unanswered. The members seem to feel that the answer lies in analysis of what roles are needed by the group for the solution of the problems at hand and of the interests and needs of individuals for playing these roles.

- The place of ethics, as a source of guidance for the group, lies in making easier the formulation of criteria for success in particular situations. It does not, in itself, provide the policies for running the group.

A HYPOTHESIS PROPOSED

The identification of the four phases of group growth which have been discussed amounts to stating a hypothesis about the course of group growth: Beginning with individual needs for finding security and activity in a social environment, we proceed first to emotional involvement of the individuals with one another, and second to the development of a group as a rather limited universe of interaction among individuals and as the source of individual security. We then find that security of position in the group loses its significance except that as the group attempts to solve problems it structures its activities in such a way that each individual can play a role which may be described as successful or not in terms of whether the group successfully solved the problem it had set itself.

It is not our contention that these four phases develop in sequential order. We have attempted to identify some of the stereotypes which seem to us to represent the perceptions of the members of these groups at different stages in the development into groups. We do not claim that this particular course of development of stereotypes about policies of operation would be found in all groups under all conditions. We do feel that identification of the members' stereotypes about policies of operation would help many groups in their growth as individually satisfying social milieux and as effective social action instruments.

The Group as a Growing Organism

by Jack R. Gibb and Lorraine M. Gibb

Some groups seem to grow. They appear healthy. Members are proud of the group and what it is achieving. They feel a sense of accomplishment and fulfillment in doing things with the group. Thus, it comes to play an increasingly significant part in their lives.

Some groups appear to stagnate. They seem sick. Members may speak defensively about belonging or perhaps not even mention their membership. They may wonder if the organization is ever really going to amount to much or if it will ever accomplish its aims. The group seems to be deteriorating and appears unworthy of the concern it would take to maintain active membership.

What distinguishes sick from healthy groups is a significant question for most of us. Groups are important elements in the structure of our culture. Each of us belongs to several groups which we value to different degrees. Some groups grow, becoming, in a sense, actualized. Other groups progress slowly or fail to develop in one or more meaningful dimensions. Therapy groups can provide a setting for therapy and remedial help or can be useless to the members. Classroom groups can be environments where growth and learning is easy, or they can be of little help, and actually inhibit such growth. Families, regardless of such variables as economic welfare or presence or absence of father, can foster healthy growth in parents and children, or they can be festering grounds for juvenile delinquency, neurotic habits, or unhappiness.

This is an earlier and abridged version of an article, "Humanistic Elements in Group Growth," published in J. F. T. Bugental (Ed.), *Challenges of Humanistic Psychology*. Copyright 1967 by McGraw-Hill, Inc. Used with permission of the authors and McGraw-Hill Book Company.

How can I, as a member of such a group, make a difference in the growth rate and actualization of the groups to which I belong? Our research provides some significant information on these questions.[1]

In our research on group growth, we have obtained a revealing and even inspiring view of man as he might become and occasional glimpses of groups in peak experiences of sustained creativity and trust, i.e., group actualization. These group experiences have most often, but not always, come when (a) groups have been in sensitivity training in semi-weekly sessions for eight or nine consecutive months, (b) when groups have been in around-the-clock "marathon" sessions for thirty or forty hours with little or no sleep, or (c) when groups have been in twelve-hour sessions daily for twelve or thirteen consecutive days. In our experience, this optimal growth occurs most frequently in groups which have no professional leader present, and in which emergent and interdependent strength is maximized.

Under these conditions, groups are qualitatively different from the groups usually meeting in the natural setting. The groups attain and often maintain states of creativity, depth of communication, and trust that are impressive and memorable, both to those participating and to those observing.

Our impression is that man's capacity for creativity, happiness, and personal growth is greatly underrated, both by himself and by scientists who study man. Behavioral scientists in evaluating potential have looked at persons and groups in the natural setting and judged what they might become. It is as if, in wishing to determine how well men could hit golf balls, we had lined up fifty average adult males on a golf tee, had each hit two balls, measured the distance, and concluded that the average man's driving potential was thirty yards. After practice and effort, the average man could hit the ball perhaps 155 yards. However, after applying new theory to the instruction process, the average person could possibly be trained to hit the ball 255 yards. The above analogy is relevant to the testing of the group's capability for creative growth. There is a qualitative difference between the average management team in the usual organizational setting and the same group after the kind of training that is now possible. This significant fact has led to a new look at human potential in persons and groups, to new organizational theories, and to new theories of individual and group development.

---

[1]Since 1951 the authors have conducted a series of experimental and field studies designed to investigate longitudinal changes in small groups, particularly as these changes are associated with the arousal and maintenance of defensive or productive behavior. These studies were mainly financed by a series of grants from the Group Psychology Branch of the Office of Naval Research.

Groups form the fabric of the society in which we live. Although the number of formal memberships that individuals hold varies greatly, it is probably true that all healthy persons are members to some extent in a number of relevant groups. In fact, it seems valid that membership itself is health producing.

What produces growth? When are groups sick and should be discontinued? When do groups have potential for growth and should be fostered? These questions are of concern both to the individual person who makes decisions about the organizations to which he will belong and to community organizers.

Coaches have the problem of using group variables to produce relationships that lead to the effectiveness of teams as teams. The vast difference in results between various athletic clubs is due, not only to training method and coach recruiting, but also to significant variables of team growth.

Staff, line, assembly crew, and other units of industrial and manufacturing operations can be observed from the standpoint of group performance and health. These observations are often camouflaged in such pseudo-questions as span of control, but are increasingly looked on by modern management as problems of group growth. There is clear evidence that healthy groups with appropriate development, effective decision making, and team formation require very little of the classical functions of management such as supervision, delegation, and motivation.

Parents are faced with the group health problem in planning family size, instituting family councils, and encouraging or discouraging total family activities. The father can look at the family as a series of relationships between him and each of the other members in turn, or he can look at the family as a group. This perceptual stance makes a great deal of difference in family growth and child rearing.

All managers and people with special responsibilities have the option of looking at their systems as groups. Knowledge of system effectiveness is relevant to the building of management theory.

Our research indicates four significant dimensions upon which groups differ. These dimensions are interdependent. As yet we have no clear comprehension of the interdependence, but we do have some convincing evidence of the relevance of each of these factors in group growth, health or actualization.

1. Groups differ in degree of *reciprocal trust* among members.
2. Groups differ in the *validity, depth and quality of the feedback system*.
3. Groups differ in the degree of *directionality toward group determined goals*.

4. Groups differ in the degree of *real interdependence in the system*. A schematic picture of these four variables is given in Table 1.

Let's take each one of these factors and look at them in some detail.

THE FORMATION OF TRUST

Trust is the pacemaker variable in group growth. From it stem all the other significant variables. That is, to the extent that trust develops, people are able to communicate genuine feelings and perceptions on relevant issues to all members of the system; they are able to communicate with themselves and others to form consensual goals; and they can be truly interdependent. Each of the four growth variables is dependent upon the prior variable in the hierarchy. Feedback is dependent upon trust. Goal formation is dependent upon feedback and trust. Interdependence is dependent upon goal formation, feedback, and trust formation.

As is indicated in Table 1 the four factors in group growth are related to parallel factors in personal growth. There is some agreement among psychologists on the criteria of mental health in personal growth.[2] There is considerably less agreement among group scientists on the criteria of group health. The schema outlined here provides a framework for analyzing group actualization.

Table 1.
Personal and Group Growth

Key Areas of Social Behavior	Directions of Personal Growth	Directions of Group Growth
Climate (Membership)	Acceptance of self Acceptance of others	Climate of trust Climate of support
Data Flow (Decision making)	Awareness (input) Openness (output)	Valid feedback system Consensual decision making
Goal formation (Productivity)	Goal integration in self Self-determination Self-assessment	Goal integration in group Group determination and assessment of goals
Control (Organization)	Interdependence (Inner, emergent control and value system)	Interdependence (Inner, emergent control and norm system)

[2]See a helpful analysis of contemporary agreement and disagreement on criteria of personal growth in *Current Concepts of Positive Mental Health*, by Marie Johoda, a report by the Joint Commission on Mental Illness and Health, published by Basic Books, Inc., in 1958.

The most impressive dynamic of most group life in its early stages is the presence of fear. Fear grows out of distrust. We tend to fear events, people, and stimuli for which we feel we have no adequate response. Many factors in the new or immature group increase the normal residual fear that all people share. Great uncertainty increases fear, and individuals have many ways of trying to reduce this uncertainty.

Some of these efforts to lessen uncertainty are unsuccessful, while others are fairly effective. Even if the ambiguity in one's own perceptual world is reduced, this gets shattered when individuals realize that growth in them and in the group can only come with ambiguity, tension, conflict, and unfreezing. They cannot become safe from their fears by building their own perceptual worlds into safe and predictable categories. Growth turns out to be something more.

The group in its early stages will attempt to cling to and create fragile structural stabilities to reduce fear. These apparently secure structures turn out to be made of sand. A group may assign a timekeeper so one person won't monopolize the group, appoint a chairman, or decide in what order people will speak. This supposedly "rules in" order and control and "rules out" chaos and threatening situations.

Another way of handling fear and distrust is caution. People can be self-protective and cautious in many ways. Some chatter about familiar and safe topics. Some stay within protective and familiar roles, and some hide behind masks.

A person is also being self-protective by engaging in a variety of unconscious and partially conscious delaying tactics: semantics quibbles, legalistic arguments, displaced discussions of minor issues, and over-elaborateness of plans. All are ways of keeping the group from making direct movements toward unknown and feared vistas.

For some people, moving quickly lessens fear by reducing the tension and turmoil of decision making in depth. "Let's do anything," "Let's get something done," "We are wasting time," and other impatient expressions aimed at speeding up direct movement are common in early groups. Later observations show that these frantic demands for movement are fear based.

Politeness and formality are early indications of fear. Politeness prevents retaliation, keeps people at a safe distance, avoids the facing of members that would reveal intimidating negative feelings, discourages the other person from giving you negative feedback, and in general serves the unanalyzed needs of the fearful person.

The early group is sometimes work addicted. The group can avoid fearsome confrontation, interpersonal conflict and exposure by hard, safe work upon a seemingly legitimate task. Groups can make long lists, engage in routine tasks, and attempt to look busy to themselves and others, in order to avoid depth relationships.

People who are afraid distrust the motivations of other members, particularly those who are authority and power seekers. Mistrusting people tend to step in and try to control the situation in order to prevent those whom they fear from exerting prior influence. This is often done in subtle ways. The individual may nominate a less-feared person to be chairman. This apparently cleanly motivated act can hopefully be seen as selfless and group oriented rather than as a disguised manipulation for control.

Fearful people often have concern about inclusion. They want to be sure to be in an appropriate group, to be paired with someone safe, strong or of high status. Belonging to the most "popular" church in town, joining only clubs or organizations that are considered "in," and choosing socially acceptable friends are all methods used by the distrusting person.

Thus, fear and distrust are the manner of behavior in the early stages of group development. As groups grow, these fears gradually become reduced. Trust grows. People learn to tolerate greater degrees of ambiguity. They become more spontaneous and less cautious. Members make allowances for greater differences, both in themselves and others.

One significant sign of growth on the trust dimension is a greater degree of acceptance of non-conformity. People are allowed to hold a wider variety of opinions. They are permitted to be themselves—to dress differently, to be unpredictable, and perhaps even to be disloyal. The boundaries of acceptance of conformity widen. Whereas in the early stages of development the group boxes in or punishes persons who deviate from the group norms, in the later stages, non-conformists are encouraged. Radical ideas are used to test reality or to create new solutions. Deviation is perhaps even welcomed as a creative contribution to possible group productivity.

As trust grows, people are able to eliminate much of the structure. They enjoy informality and are able to function and satisfy work demands with spontaneous organization. There is an easy expression of "I feel this way" on the assumption that other members will permit the voicing of individualistic feelings. People spontaneously say and feel "We." The use of "you" in referring to the group is a sign of membership denial.

The problem of trust formation is the problem of attaining membership. One achieves genuine belonging by trusting himself and the group. As the group grows, fear decreases and trust increases. Thus, group actualization is a process of attaining increasingly higher levels of trust.

COMMUNICATION AND DECISION MAKING

In the early stages of group development, the customary fear and distrust make it difficult for a valid feedback system to occur, for people to talk honestly with each other, and for the group to integrate these feelings and perception data into appropriate decisions for the group.

The processes of ambiguity, strategy, facade building, and games-manship mentioned in the earler paragraph as resulting from fears, also tend to reduce the effectiveness of the communication system. These processes are the dominant method of entry into the unhealthy group.

With the presence of fear and the lack of trust, there is little encour-agement for open exploration of one's own inner world of motivations and attitudes. Because of this lack of agreement, people give off mixed messages. There is a difference between facial expression and verbal content, between tone of voice and what one says, between what one has courage enough to say in a sub-group and what one says publicly in the total group, and between what one says the first time and what one says when challenged to repeat or clarify the message. Thus, differences further increase the distortion of data.

In low trust a great number of concealing skills develop. People become adept at consciously or unconsciously withholding feelings. Especially in situations of unequal power or supposed power difference, the weaker person, the person lower in the hierarchy, or the person with the lowest status may deliberately treat a disliked person with great friendliness in order to cover their real negative feelings. Secretaries may develop complicated strategies for seeming busy.

Another source of distortion occurs because of the inadequate methods of problem solving. In its early stages, the group seldom ade-quately or clearly defines the problem. Consequently, many feelings and opinions are expressed which are unrelated to the problem issue. Mem-bers recognize these irrelevant opinions, particularly in other members, but often lack the mechanisms for helping the group to define the prob-lem or work through the interpersonal relations which breed unrelated behavior and speech.

The concept of the hidden agenda is significant here. Each of us comes into the group situation with a variety of motivations, most of which are hidden from and unavailable to the person himself.

A sign of ill health is the magnitude of the difference between the level of frankness in the group and the level of frankness outside of the group when members in sub-groups are talking about the total group or absent members. When the trust level is low, it is difficult or impossible for people to talk honestly or openly about deep concerns. As fear reduces and trust grows, a functional communications system emerges in the group. People learn to express direct feelings and unite them into decision making and effective work.

Effective groups, with development, are able to develop consensual decision making about significant problems that the group faces. This is the payoff of data processing and the feedback system of the group. Unhealthy groups are those in which communication in depth is blocked. Group actualization is a process of learning synthesized ways of exploring hitherto unguessed depths of relationships among members who care and trust.

GOAL FORMATION AND PRODUCTIVITY

Group health is related to the integration of group goals. Unhealthy groups are unable to decide what they want to be or do. Lacking an adequate system of communication, members may not know that they, as a group, are not doing what they want to do. The difficulties in goal formation arise rather directly from partial data processing which in turn grows out of fear and distrust. When members distrust the motivations of other members, it is difficult to share goals in a meaningful way.

Sometimes, people are not clearly aware of what they would like to do. This absence of a distinct purpose in the minds of the individual members works against the kind of data sharing that makes for appropriate growth. The problem that the group faces is to somehow create out of the available data, a satisfying goal that would adequately include the real goals of the members and that would be more fulfilling than any of the half-verbalized goals that the individuals have.

One of the early errors that groups make is to force the expression of a few goals that come "off the top of the head," separate these into some alternatives, and then vote on the goal. This process necessitates a compromise so that participants often feel that they are now doing something less satisfying than they would have done alone. They say that they are going along to satisfy others, to appear flexible, to avoid being seen as stubborn or rebellious, and to please authorities. In our early research, we found a high "reservation score" in early stages of group growth. That is, members who were seen by the rest of the group as consenting were found, when data was later gathered by better means such as depth interviews, to have a number of unverbalized, non-public reservations about the decisions that were made by the group.

One error made by unhealthy groups is the attempt to impose control mechanisms and to verbalize public goals before the group has worked through its fears and data-processing problems. Verbal, anxious, or dominant people are prone to do this. These members take on roles that they have inherited socially from other authority models and try to persuade or push goals upon the other members. For various reasons, weak, disinterested, or non-verbal individuals often go along with these coercive members. Members may be withdrawn, apathetic, and will show a low commitment to verbalize any goals. Participants may or may not be aware of the relationship between their apathy and the manner of goal attainment.

This analysis forces a look at the dynamics of apathy. One of the first tasks in training groups or in teams in natural situations is to work on the problem of learning to examine motivations of individuals. This may be a lengthy task, using long dormant skills and feelings. Well-intentioned group members and administrators, in order to get things going on an efficient basis, will often push hard to get people to accept undigested goals. The members rely on a few specific people who get things going and rush in to set goals. Vague or explicit resentments are difficult to verbalize. Irritations occur because people don't really understand the dynamics of persuasion-apathy, and attack members for reasons rather unrelated to the behavior that is producing the problem. It's like fighting the fever without treating the disease.

The apparent reverse of apathy is a condition of frenetic work at tasks that the group uses to respond to duty motivations, loyalty to the organization, compulsive needs, and the desire to prove to themselves and others that they can work hard. This busy work can easily be misunderstood and seen as productive or creative work.

There are other motivational and goal-forming errors which have to do with the processes of goal building themselves. Over-aspiration, for instance, can create vague and distant goals which are relatively unattainable and provide little immediate reward value, thus frustrating the group. The need to make quick decisions often leads people to decide upon goals before the goals have been thought through and worked out at a deep level. Decision making problems make it difficult to arrive at commitments to goals.

When a group of people have worked through the fear, trust, and data flow problems to a degree where they can communicate in high trust or to "speak the truth in love," then it is possible to work to a reasonable consensus on major problems of goal formation and decision making.

Group growth moves toward greater functional relationship of the goal statement to the activities of the group, and a greater creative working level because people are doing what they want to do and know that they all want to do it. The creative work potential of a well-motivated group is true interdependence.

The members integrate tasks, groups, and individual goals. We are assuming that all people are achievement motivated and that work, when self-determined, is intrinsically satisfying. In order for personal and group needs to be met, the group must select a task and make some kind of visible progress toward accomplishing it. In effective groups, esprit de corps, individual satisfaction over group achievement, and commitment to the group are vital. There are also a number of personal and individualistic goals. Group members must feel some sense of belonging, fulfillment, self-worth, influence, and whatever kinds of goals that are presently important to the individuals. As a high trust and a valid communication system develop, it becomes possible to mesh these needs in satisfying ways without undue group pressures to conform for the sake of conformity. The creation of this state of affairs gives people a sense of freedom, within interdependence.

CONTROL SYSTEMS AND ORGANIZATION

Most all of us in the process of socialization develop authority and influence problems that stem from our early relations with our parents and teachers. When a group of people meets in the early stages, problems of mutual influence become immediately visible to the observer and to the more sensitive members. Distrust, distorted communication, and imposed or ambiguous goals tend to make these authority feelings more severe and limit growth.

A sense of powerlessness or impotence is a dominant characteristic of the early life of groups. Because people seldom listen, because the group has a difficult time finding a satisfying direction, and for a number of other reasons explored above, individuals in the group feel that it is very difficult to influence other individuals or "the group." Both the quiet and the talkative people have these feelings.

A recent study indicated that, in general, members of the early groups thought that unusually restrained people were either stupid, disinterested, afraid, or lazy! Another factor that leads to the feeling of powerlessness is the tendency of people, especially under the early fear and distrust stages, to be suspicious of the motivations of other people. Thus, our study indicated that quiet members thought that the aggressive members were insecure, manipulative, domineering and showing off their knowledge! It is also true that some of the non-initiators saw the initiators as helpful, full of ideas, and courageous. Some of the talkative members saw quiet individuals as good listeners, flexible and courteous. As people trust and communicate better, the initiators are more apt to be seen as wanting to help, and the quiet members are more apt to be seen as receptive listeners. Ironically, in early stages the same behavior is viewed as dominance, manipulation, or disinterested resistance.

Because of the mechanisms described earlier, this resistance is camouflaged and not easily seen except by the sophisticated observer or by the suspicious initiator. Highly resistant people in atmospheres of distrust tend to become even more polite, passive, or withdrawn, covering their opposition in a multitude of ingenious ways. Except in extreme instances, people are not likely to express resentment in more directly rebellious behavior. The resistance will often be displaced and show itself in arguments about minor issues and semantic quibbling about definitions of terms used by the verbal initiators or the high power people.

Sometimes the opposition may be conscious and take the form of strategies like appointing committees, parliamentary maneuvers, calling for a summary, or an apparently innocent or useful list-making in order to prevent an impending decision that is being pushed by a person who is thought to be seeking power.

As indicated above, the frequent rejection of the expert is a case in point. People have so often associated the expert with undue influence that he is resisted. The expert may also be opposed because of jealousy, a feeling of inadequacy in the face of his knowledge, suspicion of attributed power due to his apparent wisdom, and his wishes to talk intellectual talk and the group's wish to get acquainted, play, or wield influence.

When people are afraid and feel powerless to influence their own important development or goal setting, they try to sway the group in a number of ways. People may not wish to admit to themselves or to the other members of the group that they do desire to influence, because this unrelieved need for power, as such, is looked down on in our aspiring-to-be-democratic society. Direct influence efforts are fairly easy to deal with, but camouflaged or devious attempts are more difficult for the group to examine and handle. Covered strategies are used by individuals with varying degrees of consciousness. Some may deliberately try to use strategies and manipulative gimmicks. Others may unconsciously use tricky means of getting their way.

Some indirect methods of influence are often masks both to the influencer and influencee. Advice giving is a common form in the early group. In the framework of our Madison Avenue culture this has the impact of persuasion or even coercion if the person who expresses the advice is a high status model for the members.

Desires to influence are apparently characteristic of all of us. These needs are only troublesome when they are covered up and are thus difficult for the group to handle, when they become overpowering because of fear and anxiety on the part of others, and then are denied by the influencer. The wish to influence and be influenced is a productive and creative one and necessary for group growth.

Groups in early development seem unmanageable. This gives rise to the feeling that special procedures are necessary to control the group. The organization tries rules, regulations, appointed leaders, span of control, parliamentary procedure, channels of communication, tight organization, and "articles" of war to formally control the behavior of people in the group. It seems to members that it would be unthinkable for the group to operate without strong formal leadership and regulations. Tight controls arise which tend to be self-deceiving. People resist the rules by various forms of displaced rebellion, apathy, or by a kind of unimaginative obedience. Conflict, spontaneity, and vigorous interplay are all productive in a high trust and high feedback situation. These factors, however, produce disruptions and unproductive organizations in a low trust and low feedback condition.

Permissiveness, another uncertain concept, may be many things. In low trust and low communication groups, it may be a kind of unrelated, undigestable disorder in which people look like they are doing what they want to do but, in fact, are responding to impulse, play, and resistance. Permissiveness in high trust, high feedback groups can be exciting, spontaneous, and an integration of creative effort in the group. Opponents of permissiveness think about the low trust type while the advocates of permissiveness think about the high trust kind that occurs in the relatively well-developed group.

As the group develops in this dimension, many changes are seen to occur. The conflict of influence and power becomes visible. The desires to influence are faced and examined. The need of a legitimate influence process is recognized. The group begins to develop adequate propping mechanisms.

When the group realizes that as the problems of distrust, poor communication, and unresolved goal formation become apparent, they must be faced in order for control mechanisms to develop. Artificial controls cannot camouflage the problems. The only sure way to group development is to wipe out these barriers to growth.

Because of low trust and low communication, groups have invented mechanisms for solving the problems on these four dimensions. A legal system of formal laws has been invented to solve the fear and distrust problem. Membership requirements such as college entrance examinations and racial and religious codes for housing, clubs, and jobs have been passed.

A great many mechanisms have been produced to solve the low communication, poor data flow problems: parliamentary procedures which guarantee minimal opportunity for people to talk, formal rules for making decisions by majority vote. Company newspapers, written memoranda, multiple copy systems, and many tools of the communications and public relations profession have arisen to improve poor communications.

All these mechanisms are control systems which arise due to recognition of membership, decision, and motivation problems. Mechanisms to handle control problems of course are also used. Rules of way, bargaining contracts, codes of gentlemen, punishments for nonconformity, formal job prescriptions, and tables of organizations, are all examples of mechanisms produced to control the influence problem. In general, it seems clear that as groups grow the necessity for these formal control systems disappear.

One of the clearest kinds of growth is the ability to transform conflict into creative problem solving which makes group activity exciting and fun. Conflicts will occur in living and in active and creative people. The production or unearthing of difference can be revealing. Difference on vital issues indicates some disparities, which will be reduced to a minimum when data is free flowing. Resolving the conflict, by finding alternatives that are creative solutions rather than deadening compromises, can be a productive process. The motivation to build something new can come from the dissatisfaction revealed by the discord. When conflict does exist, the best way to handle it is to look at it and resolve it. The mature group is able to do this. A process analysis of the way the conflict arose and was solved is potentially meaningful, and is likely to be cathartic. The aftermath of conflict can also be productive. People can learn about themselves, about the group, and about the reality of the world by the way that they as individuals or as a group have handled the discord.

Groups are often unhealthy and add little to the lives of their members. They might well be discontinued or certainly changed. Grouping can become a fetish, and preserved long beyond their day. As we have seen, signs of ill health include undue fear and distrust, inadequate and distorted communication, undigested and dysfunctional goal systems, and unresolved dependency problems.

Groups *can* be healthy. Groups can be creative, fulfilling, and satisfying to all of their members. We have seen groups that can be appropriately described as actualizing. Such groups develop a high degree of trust, valid communication in depth, a consensual goal system, and a genuine interdependence. Our research has shown promising data that provide a way for therapists, parents, managers, and teachers to aid in the process of creating groups which are in themselves healthy organisms, and provide a climate for member growth and fulfillment. It is such groups that can provide the framework for a better world.

Applying a Group Development Model to Managing a Class*

by Eric H. Neilsen

This paper presents a model of group development that provides useful clues for managing a class during a typical course in organizational behavior. My assumption is that classes, like all groups, go through a developmental process. The process may be more apparent in courses or training programs that are highly process oriented, but its elements can be found in every teaching effort. This ubiquitousness has important implications for what students are capable of learning and for how a teacher can act.

The model to be presented was originally derived by two of my colleagues, Suresh Srivastva and Steven Obert, to describe the developmental process in any task group (Srivastva, Obert and Neilsen, 1977). I have revised and elaborated it slightly to fit the special case of classes in organizational behavior. After reviewing the assumptions behind their model, the format of this paper will be to describe the basic outlines of each of its several stages and then comment on what each stage implies for the task of managing a class.

Assumptions Underlying the Model

Every group needs a common language and a common body of meanings in order to get a task done. This includes not only task-related concepts such as resources and technology but also person-related concepts such as roles, statuses, and relational identities.

---

*Developed from a workshop presented at the 4th Annual Organizational Behavior Teaching Conference held at the University of Toronto, May 15-18, 1977.

From *The Teaching of Organization Behavior*, 1977, 11(4), 9-16. Reprinted by permission.

117

Since all individual experience is in some degree unique, this common set of meanings has to be built up over time through members' interactions. Such interaction resocializes each member so that he sees the world in a similar enough fashion to his colleagues to engage in joint activities. Presocialization in similar institutions and common selection criteria help to a certain extent but some resocialization always needs to occur.

The resocialization process parallels that of primary socialization in the family. The first issue is that of individual identity and centers around the basic question "Who do others perceive me to be, and who must I become to gain membership in this group?" Just as the child initially has no sense of self and gains this sense from other family members' responses to his behavior, the new group member does not know who he is in the context of the group and must find this out through other members' reactions to his behavior. In this process, tensions arise over differences between the identity the new member is developing in the group and the identities he has already established in other groups. The struggle is to change as little as possible, while still establishing a viable image in other members' eyes.

When the group is new and everyone is engaged in this self-identification process, issues such as the following become important: quality, quantity, and style of participation, fairness and equity in membership, norms and standards of personal behavior, physical comfort, one's own share of task responsibility, and the costs and benefits of membership. This is basically a process of *inclusion*.

The second issue is the complement of the first and deals with the member's perception of other's identities. The focal question is "Who is the other in relation to me in the context of the group, and who must he become to be a full group member?" Self-definition is an interactive process. In order for my identity to be viable, I not only need to know who I am to you, but you must know who you are to me. The basic process involved here is one of *influence*. Issues that members become preoccupied with in relation to it are: others' conformity to norms and rules, acceptance and expulsion, cooperation with or resistance to group authority, and equitability and fairness.

The final question is "Who are we (self and other)—what is our relationship—in the context of the group?" As particular members interact more with each other than with others, they take on an identity as a dyad or clique in the eyes of the rest of the group. This is the *intimacy* process. It involves expressions of closeness or distance, jealousy, warmth, love, hate, friendship, emnity, etc.

All three processes—inclusion, influence, intimacy—are tightly interwoven in group life and the answers to each question are always being revamped as their solutions interact. But in line with Schutz (1958),

Srivastva and Obert argue that the central concern of a group in its development shifts from one process to another in a fixed sequence; from inclusion to influence to intimacy.

Working through these general issues, moreover, causes the group to focus on a series of basic dilemmas, reminiscent of Erikson's (1968) stage-based dilemmas of individual development, whose resolutions (or the lack thereof) cause the group to progress and regress along the path of member socialization. Each stage is marked by particular structural characteristics, behaviors, and relationships with the group authority figure. The dilemmas and their attendant structural and behavioral characteristics are outlined in Figure 1.

THE MODEL

Stage One: Safety vs. Anxiety

Behavior centers around expressions of anxiety over efforts to establish an acceptable identity and/or efforts to protect the self and gain safety by avoiding exploration of what membership requires. The focal question is "Who must I be to gain membership in this group?"

Structurally, the group looks like a collection of isolated individuals, seeking contact with others but preoccupied with their own identities, hoping to find a niche with minimal redefinition of the self.

In this context, the leader has the only clearly differentiated identity. He/she becomes the reference point for others to use in establishing their own identities. Interaction focuses on this person. Dependency is high. Attributions of omnipotence develop. People play dumb, asking questions when they already know the answers, hoping to seduce the leader into doing the whole group task himself so that they can focus on establishing their personal identities.

The group's environment becomes a scapegoat for anxiety over feeling dependent on the leader. Members complain about the lighting, ventilation, seating, aesthetics, texts, etc. The leader is the representative of the organization but too powerful to be attacked. Consequently, the organization becomes the target.

Intermember relations are initially superficial. Background data are exchanged. The focus is on the self. Energy is expended on providing information about the self, not to gain information about the other. Members compete by showing off in order to get the leader's attention. Members do not listen much to each other. Only things which are most relevant to the listener appear to be heard or understood.

There is a lot of activity for activity's sake. But this apparent enthusiasm for the task is really a way to cope with anxiety, since members continuously violate the rules and procedures they have just set up. Discussion of goals and procedures is self-oriented rather than intended to clarify a common task. Member-to-member

Stage	Structure of Group	Basic Issues	Salient Behavioral Patterns
1	Each man for himself	Inclusion	Safety vs. Anxiety — Later forms of safety vs. anxiety
2	Dyadic relationship	INC — INF	Earlier forms of similarity vs. dissimilarity / Similarity vs. Dissimilarity — Later forms of similarity vs. dissimilarity
3	Coalition and clique formation	Influence	Earlier forms of support vs. panic / Support vs. Panic — Later forms of support vs. panic
4	Spread effect: Enlarging membership to entire group	INF — INT	Earlier forms of concern vs. isolation / Concern vs. Isolation — Later forms of concern vs. isolation
5	Goal-directed task group formation	Intimacy	Earlier forms of interdependence vs. withdrawal / Inter-dependence vs. withdrawal

(Adapted from Srivastva, et al., *op. cit.*)

Figure 1: Five observable stages of group development

feedback on task performance is low and is designed to enhance the self rather than help the other. When not overenthusiastically involved with the task, members are busy running away from it in order to avoid exploring the requirements of group membership.

Different teachers, of course, are likely to handle a situation such as this in different ways. The primary value of the model is simply to suggest that such a state exists at the beginning of the course. It may help to explain why certain tactics have proven to be effective or it may call into question other tactics that on the surface have appeared appropriate but have never really worked. The following suggestions make sense both in terms of the model and my experience.

Implications

Present your course objectives and yourself in ways that are congruent with member needs and expectations.

This proposition follows from the notion that the class members will only hear what they experience as relevant to themselves. The course initially has to be sold in terms of the perspectives they bring with them. For instance, I may be intrigued with using the class as a vehicle for generating personal insights, while they may be preoccupied with how the course fits into a business curriculum that is costing them quite a bit of money.

Particular tactics include putting the institutional objectives on the line first, referring to useful outputs that previous classes have reported, stating objectives in terms that make sense to class members' spouses and business colleagues. In this way one can protect students' external identities so that they will feel freer to experiment with new ones in class.

The same principle holds true for presenting oneself. For instance, I introduce those aspects of my experience that have positive value in the students' worlds. I may be proud of my academic accomplishments, but they tend to be more interested in my consulting experience.

Be direct and unconditional in stating your course requirements.

This follows from the idea that members need to see the instructor as omnipotent. This does not imply that one should be rigid or unwilling to change, but students want something hard to lean against and if they need clarity on an issue they will push for it. Throwing course requirements, grading procedures and deadlines up for general discussion, only invites long and frustrating discourses and may raise anxiety rather than lower it.

Establish a logical procedure for dealing with nonteaching matters and avoid dwelling on them in class.

The environment, physical and administrative, is an ideal scapegoat for students in dealing with anxiety over gaining membership in the class. It does not talk back, and in universities, it is typically handled by lower status people. Not only is it easy for students to scapegoat but it is also easy for an instructor to be seduced into being overly responsive to students' complaints about it in order to gain acceptance for himself. Environmental problems should be resolved by the people who have that administrative responsibility, and if this happens to be the instructor, they should be dealt with outside of class.

Focus on your teaching style as opposed to course content during your early classes.

If one buys into the notions that students engage in activity for activity's sake during the early classes, and that they rely on you to do most of the work, this, coupled with the fact that their anxiety interferes with their active listening, means that they are not likely to learn a great deal of course content during this period. The classes need be no less rich in learning, however, only learning of a different sort. You, as the teacher are the powerful other and, while the content of what you say may not be heard, how you say it is likely to come across loud and clear. Use these early classes to model the kind of behavior you would like the class to engage in. For instance, if you value personal introspection or complex analysis, the class may be unable to engage in either activity, but you can begin to teach them that process by modeling it yourself. Another reason why it is important not to rely heavily on students to carry the class is that the people who dive in with you on the first demonstration represent potential scapegoats who students find safer to attack than the teacher.

Stage Two: Similarity vs. Dissimilarity

This stage is transitional between preoccupation with inclusion and preoccupation with influence. While still concerned with their own identities, members start to turn toward definition of the other.

Exploration of the other is begun but only in the context of the degree of similarity or difference from the self. The central question becomes "If I am who the others say I am, then is the other like or unlike me?"

Structurally, the group forms into supportive dyadic relationships based on personal similarities. Individuals tend to form dyads with those who best conform to the identity that is being established for them in the group.

Members begin to show concern and interest for those who appear to be most like themselves. Sharing starts superficially with background data but proceeds to fuller explorations of interests, skills, and values. Listening becomes more active but only with similar others. The dissimilar other is not actively rejected but simply ignored.

Task involvement is similar to the first stage. But there is a stronger negative attitude to show the leader that he indeed cannot do the task alone. Feedback oriented toward helping others occurs within dyads but not outside them. Norms begin to be stated and tested. Members begin to test the boundaries of their influence.

The relationship with the leader shifts toward counterdependency. Members now have enough security to be passively aggressive but not enough to confront the leader openly, e.g., assignments not quite done, instructions slightly misinterpreted to avoid tough issues, hands not raised voluntarily, complaints in hallways about work overload.

The group's relationship with the environment is now likely to involve direct hostility. Members no longer complain to the leader but confront the environment directly, e.g., demands for warmer classroom, faster case processing, more flexible time schedules.

Movement from the first to the second stage of group development, or from any stage to another, is never guaranteed. Some teachers are quite capable of keeping the class in a highly dependent state throughout most of the term. In highly technical courses where students are truly dependent on the teacher for acquiring certain information, a certain degree of emotional dependency may be desirable. Following Bion (1961) one can argue that this emotional mode enhances accomplishment of such tasks.

But in most organizational behavior courses, the integration of conceptual material with personal experience is an important aspect of the learning process. This demands active participation on the part of the students which also breaks the dependency. In the first few sessions the demand for class participation leads to a lot of conceptually irrelevant contributions, such as requests for clarifications of what the teacher really wants or showoff statements that are off the subject. Luckily there are usually a few honest attempts to respond to the issue and even some very insightful contributions, but these are in the minority.

As people get used to the classroom and start to develop greater awareness of what the teacher wants, a potential conflict develops. Friendships are beginning to form which, depending on student values, can lead to the dilemma of whether to respond to the spirit of the teacher's demands and thereby risk failure in the eyes of their friends or, alternatively, to reject the teacher's demands and signal their friends to do likewise. The latter tactic is an attempt both to influence the other and to be included in a friendship network, and this represents the onset of the second stage.

Implications

Legitimize friendships that are forming by assigning tasks and encouraging dialogue among friends during class.

While the friendships that begin to form in a class after the first few sessions can provide the basic motivation and support for counterdependent behavior, they paradoxically represent important vehicles for overcoming it. By recognizing friendships and delegating risky tasks to them, such as making presentations and engaging in helpful feedback, the teacher is implicitly recognizing peoples' need for support in these endeavors and sanctioning its development. This reduces the threat of dependence on the teacher alone which allows counterdependent emotions to be held in check while people attempt to respond to the teacher's demands.

I typically rely on friendship networks that I see developing in my classes as the key vehicles for preparing, presenting, and critiquing presentations early on in the course. The same results presumably might be achieved through assigned study groups, task force teams, or classwide learning organizations. The trick is to get people to find support in each other for responding positively to task demands. To do this, the instructor needs to find ways of openly inviting and appreciating interdependent efforts, so that not only the content of students' performance but also an emotionally comfortable way of performing is rewarded.

Deal with attacks on your leadership by relating the content of complaints to task demands.

With all the emotional involvement we have in our classes, it is often easy for us to read students' questions about subject matter as personal attacks, even when this is not the case. This "paranoia" has some basis in reality (which makes knowing how to respond to it all the more difficult), since the theory of group development suggests that there is an element in every student's thinking that supports or at least condones veiled antagonism toward the teacher early in the course.

In one sense there is no quick resolution to counterdependent behavior. A very negative response to students' comments early in the course, even if the latter are indeed attacks, can lead to very poor teacher-class relationships. Even the most appreciative students would agree that a harsh defense is unwarranted, presumably because they too are feeling the emotional strains of being dependent on the teacher for establishing their identities in the group.

The teacher is seen as too powerful to be entitled to emotional self-defense. He is obliged to understand this dynamic and to curb his own emotions even when it hurts. Unless this is a class in group process where emotional interactions are pertinent subject matter, the best a teacher can do is take students' questions about the material at their face value and discuss the content implications. Trying to discuss counterdependence openly when it occurs, perhaps even using a theory such as the one being presented here, is extremely difficult in a class of any size.

Make a special effort to present material that heightens the immediate experience of the learning process.

While this may read like a precept for effective teaching in general, I find it especially germane to the early-to-middle part of the course. The intent is to reduce anxiety by channeling energy into intrinsically reward-ing material that makes trusting the teacher worthwhile. Around a third of the way through the course, I try to introduce some of the most interesting ideas I have that can be presented in ways which require little conceptual dexterity, e.g., demonstrations, movies, lectures that do not require repeated explanation and back tracking. The insights that are raised are rarely as poignant as in the later classes, but people are given the chance to engage more immediately in exploring their relevance to "real life" and thereby consensually validate the importance of the course material. This, in turn, heightens motivation to master the more con-ceptually complex material.

Stage Three: Support vs. Panic

The dominant issue is influence.

Attention moves to the dissimilar other. The central question is "Given that I am who I appear to be, who must the other be or become to support my identity as a member of this group?"

Structurally, dyads are no longer essential for supporting one's identity. The task now is to get others to accept one's identity as it has unfolded in the context of the dyad. For instance, if A and B agree that A is an expert on a particular issue, then both will work together to get the rest of the group to support this defini-tion of A.

Relationships with the leader become less counterdependent. Members begin to willingly accept responsibility for particular tasks, e.g., project reports, plan-ning committees, case presentations. The leader is confronted with realistic tests of his or her skills, and a fuller picture of the teacher's qualities is developed.

Relationships with the environment remain confrontive, but there is now less hostility for its own sake. Substantive issues are tackled and the group's real influence and responsibilities to the larger system are clarified, e.g., students gain permission to use extra rooms for projects, accept the fact that it is too late to recruit more women for the class, agree to follow case distribution procedures.

Intermember relations are characterized by heavy and active confrontation. Members experience support when their influence attempts are effective and panic when they fail. The choice to take on greater responsibilities for the group's tasks leads to clarification of roles and expectations and much negotiation, e.g., "Do we trust you to be our planning committee?" "Do you have the right to assign me to coffee duty?" "Are you more effective than I am in making presentations?" Clearer rewards and punishments are created for sanctioning group norms. The norms themselves are clarified. The group begins to develop an integrated set of work rules. More active listening and more helpful feedback develop to influence the dissimilar other. The group begins to become an operating entity.

I find that the atmosphere in my classes usually reaches a fairly stable plateau, be it good or bad, about a third of the way through the course. My routines are pretty well understood and certain people have emerged in predictable roles, e.g., clique leaders, devil's advocate, and outright deviants. Three kinds of events tell me that we have reached this third stage. First, those students who habitually wander off the topic, or are ill prepared, are confronted by other students either through requests to get to the point or through cutting critiques of their work. Second, lively debates arise among members of different cliques, indicating that people are now willing to address the dissimilar other. Third, people start to ask me what I personally think about particular issues. I often feel a little threatened when this happens since I have been so busy "getting others to think" that I have not thought about where I stand beyond my teaching notes. I also find, however, that this is the time when the class seems to have become a group.

Implications

Invite feedback on your own performance and on course content.

In most teaching programs where students have an opportunity to evaluate the instructors and course material, the rating sessions usually come at the end of the course. While this may be helpful to the teacher for future classes, it does not improve that class at that point in time. McCaskey (1976) describes an approach for collecting and utilizing feedback on an ongoing basis and I find that this is a point in the group's development where such feedback can occur. Counterdependency has decreased sufficiently so that students can provide undistorted and helpful feedback.

Structure debates among particular subgroups that are known to the class to have different viewpoints.

This is simply a matter of coopting the developmental energy of the class in the service of the learning task.

Set aside time to discuss your own work.

Since the class is now becoming interested in you as an individual and is in the mood to evaluate the ideas with the criteria you have taught them to use, you now have an opportunity to get some helpful feedback on matters that are pertinent to your own professional and research interests. If you present this material early in the course, you may get responses that are more related to your relationship with the class than to its content. If you present it too late, it may interfere with the other developmental issues or the class's attempt to gain closure on what it has learned.

Assign responsibility for later sessions to particular teams that are interested in subjects not included in the syllabus.

I frequently leave a session or two open toward the end of the course. This middle period is when the class can decide what should be presented in these sessions and it is when particular cliques will have the energy to take responsibility for preparing them. Engaging in such planning activities also provides opportunities for clarifying people's interests and the criteria for effective performance.

Stage Four: Concern vs. Isolation

This is another transitional stage; the group moves from issues of influence to those of intimacy. As issues of influence and responsibility become resolved, attention turns to a fuller exploration of what it means to be a member of a particular clique or dyad within the larger group.

The focal question is "Who are we—our dyad, clique—in the context of the larger group?"

Group structure exhibits a spread effect. The members of one clique begin to reach out to those of another to explore how their own clique is perceived and what life is like in the other. Since personal identities and influence have already been established, subgroups are no longer necessary for maintaining them. Members feel free to reach out to many other individuals in the larger group, e.g., what's it like to be a woman in this class? How does this course relate to your experience in the armed service? Is so-and-so the real brains behind your study group?

The authority figure is accepted more and more as just another member of the group. This person is allowed to pursue personal interests in the context of the larger group task, to ask more intimate questions and be responded to openly.

The group becomes more confident in its relations with the environment. Sometimes there is a desire to render greater service to it: "Let's write up this exercise for the rest of the school." At other times there is a desire to exploit the environment in legitimate ways: "Let's start our own company."

Intermember relations shift from issues of influence to interdependency. Concern arises for making meaningful space for dissimilar others, e.g., the idiosyncratic styles of particular members are no longer ridiculed, and the values of deviant members are accepted on their own merits. Such differences are accepted for fear of being isolated from the other's unique experience of group life. The attitude develops that everyone has something to offer. There is much active listening, helpful feedback, openness, trust and warmth. Members bask in the euphoria of a solidaric group.

Task behavior is more results oriented. There is less emphasis on rights and prerogatives for their own sakes. There is greater flexibility in member roles and greater preoccupation with getting the task accomplished. There is also a greater appreciation of the complexity of the task. Realistic pessimism often develops over the group's capacity to reach its goals.

There comes a point in the latter part of my courses, usually about five or six weeks from the end, when people seem to get tired of vigorous presentation and debate, and they start to dwell more and more on how their personal experiences relate to the course. It is at this time when people from different walks of life in the class, e.g., different professional schools, occupations, ethnic backgrounds, begin to talk about their own worlds.

It is also a time when I feel especially comfortable about discussing my personal background, not just my research interests but my career, consulting, and family life. In terms of my own mental energy, the course takes on a different character. I am less concerned with getting others to understand new concepts and more focused on using the concepts we have learned to search collaboratively for new insights into our own lives. All of this indicates to me that the group has reached Stage Four.

Implications

Be especially attentive to the direction the class wants to move.

This is the period when some of the most insightful conversations in the whole course can take place if you let them happen. I try to encourage this by putting the session's agenda on the board and asking the class to comment on what they want to talk about. We will make a contract to get the other work done as expeditiously as possible and then spend extra time on topics of particular interest.

Invite some of the more interesting people in the class to talk about the course material in terms of their experience.

I am occasionally lucky enough to have some people in their 40s and 50s in my introductory courses, and this is when they shine. By this time they have had a chance to assess the curriculum in terms of their own experience, and having lived longer, they typically have more insights to offer. The rest of the class is also ready to listen because they, too, have sized up the course by now, have released their competitive urges, and are beginning to ponder the broader implications of the organizational behavior perspective.

This is also the time when people discover especially interesting things about each other. The fellow who did not like the movie *12 Angry Men* reveals that he is in a joint program with the law school. The woman who was especially involved in the nonverbal exercises during a recent class reveals that she teaches deaf and dumb children. The black radical who has periodically frustrated the class's activities with attacks on American management ideology expresses his ambivalence about succeeding in a white-dominated world.

Let your heart do most of the talking in response to personal comments.

With a PhD in sociology and a preoccupation with theory building, I often have a difficult time preventing myself from spinning theories around people's personal revelations. I have found that, at least in this part of the course, this is not what class members want or need to hear. What they really want is to make an emotional connection with me. Simple direct statements that come from the heart—"I understand, I am with you, I have felt that way, too"—are more important. This does not mean that conceptualization is lost. Instead, when I let myself do this, I find other people making the conceptual connections in the context of their own experience.

Stage Five: Interdependence vs. Withdrawal

Here the issue of intimacy is the underlying theme. There is a major incentive to make everything fit together, to make the most out of everyone's capabilities while accepting and appreciating their human qualities.

The focal question is "Who are we to each other in all of our overlapping relationships?"

The goal of the group is rather idealistic. To achieve it often requires a great deal of back tracking, of reexamining unclear relationships and unfinished issues. The overall thrust is toward a state of complex interdependency.

Structurally, the group is both highly differentiated and tightly integrated around the task issues which are the raison d'etre of the group and its entire resocialization process.

The leader is now a fully functioning member contributing according to his or her expertise.

Intermember relationships are reality oriented, placing top priority on task accomplishment. Conflict is dealt with openly and constructively. Differences in the support and affection particular people give to others is accepted as valid, so long as it does not interfere with task accomplishment. There is mutual trust even in the face of conflict over methods and personal styles. Members can evaluate themselves and task demands realistically and act in behalf of their own and the group's education.

I do not know whether my classes have ever fully gotten into this stage. Perhaps they have in the sense that the sessions of the preceding stage often lead to the cooperative reworking of earlier material. For instance, someone may finally grasp Maslow's concept of "the need to know and the fear of knowing" and for ten minutes the dynamics it points to will be retraced through the history of the class. The urge to make all the pieces fit together is clearly evident.

More often, however, preoccupation with the end of the course will bring an end to the group's development before much interdependence is achieved. In my opinion this is probably a healthy outcome. People naturally want to protect themselves from too great a sense of psychological loss when the end of the group is predetermined. The task of the teacher at this time, I think, should be to manage the withdrawal process.

Implications

Set time aside for review and integration with the students' broader educational objectives.

People need to feel that they are taking something away from a course that their other reference groups approve of. For instance, while integrating concepts with personal experience may be a major outcome of the course, integration of the concepts themselves may seem more important for the official objectives of a school of management. Just as it is useful to start a course by relating it to broader objectives, it is important to end here as well.

Review the experience of the class as a developmental phenomenon.

The intent here is to put the learning process itself into perspective so that people can manage their own participation in the process in the future with greater awareness.

Encourage people to share their satisfactions and dissatisfactions with the course and with their or others' participation in it.

This kind of purely evaluative feedback helps the class to bring psychological closure to its experience. I try to get people to say something negative as well as positive so that those who really have some unfinished business can get it off their chests, and so that those who are feeling euphoric might recognize the uniqueness of their own experiences and the reality that there is always unfinished business.

Caveats to the Theory

Complete group development is never achieved. As in human development, the treatment of later issues reveals inadequacies in the resolution of earlier ones.

Groups regress as well as progress. This is caused not only by the developmental process itself but also by members' experiences outside the group and by the group's interaction with other groups. Often a group can become stuck or fixated around a particular developmental issue. The leader's own behavior is critical in determining how well the group progresses.

In relating this theory to classroom management, I have talked about the general trends I have seen in my classes. The caveats listed above help to explain some of the less typical events, such as especially frustrating sessions or whole segments of courses where groups seem to be stuck in their development.

In particular, there are many exogeneous variables that can influence the developmental process and, therefore, need to be taken into account when attempting to apply the theory, e.g., the presence of other teachers with different content and styles who are teaching their own courses to the same group of students simultaneously, the scheduling of one's course in an integrated curriculum so that one enters a particular group when it has already gone through several stages of development, the occurrence of holidays and vacations and, one's own place in the adult life cycle and its impact on one's teaching concerns and style.

While these qualifications may make the theory more difficult to apply than one might imagine at first blush, its basic outlines are relevant to everyone in the teaching profession. They provide a wealth of hypotheses for directing one's attention to the impact on students and on their classroom experience. The hypotheses have concrete implications that can be tested and modified through individual experience. At the same time, the theory as a whole provides a framework for cumulative research into the teaching process.

REFERENCES

Bion, W. R., *Experiences in Groups and Other Papers*. London: Tavistock Publications; New York: Basic Books, 1961.

Erikson, Erik H., *Childhood and Society*. Second Edition. New York: W. W. Norton and Company, 1963.

McCaskey, M. B., "Collecting Feedback throughout the Course," *The Teaching of Organization Behavior*, 1976, II(3), 34-36.

Schutz, William, *FIRO: A Three Dimensional Theory of Interpersonal Behavior*. New York: Rinehart & Company, 1958.

Srivastva, S., S. L. Obert, and E. H. Neilsen, "Organizational Analysis through Group Processes: A Theoretical Perspective for Group Development," to appear in Cary Cooper (ed.), *New Perspectives in Organization Development and Analysis*. London: MacMillan Press, 1977.

2

Research

Introduction

The few carefully selected research articles in this section provide a sound basis for the articles on application in Part I and also indicate, by the years in which they were produced, something of the history of study and research into groups.

Over many years, occasional articles and books about groups have appeared. Freud devoted a small portion of his writing to groups. John Dewey foretold the later concern with small group feeling and with the effect of atmosphere on group functioning. However, an analysis of the *Psychological Abstracts* from the thirties through the middle forties indicates only an occasional article about groups. Brown's first edition of *Social Psychology*, published in 1934, devotes only four of over six-hundred pages to a discussion of groups and this discussion deals mainly with cultural forces and the influence of the primary group on the individual.

It required the theoretical and action-research interests of Kurt Lewin, combined with his establishment of the first Research Center for Group Dynamics at the Massachusetts Institute of Technology (MIT) in 1945, to focus research and action interest on the small group. The classic study of autocracy-democracy by Lewin, Lippitt, and White (1939); Lewin's (1943) food habit studies; Moreno's (1946) development of psychodrama and sociodrama; the Marrow and French (1945) study of changing a stereotype in industry—all preceded the large number of studies to appear in the forties and fifties. The *Psychological Abstracts* list well over a hundred articles in the fifties that deal with small group behavior. Most of the best known books appeared in the fifties: *Group Dynamics* by Cartwright and Zander (1953); *Small Groups* by Hare, Borgatta, and Bales (1955); *Emotional Dynamics and Group Culture* by Stock and Thelen (1958). In addition, work on group behavior was being conducted during the forties and fifties by the Tavistock Institute in London.

Kurt Lewin's concern for action research created an immediate bridge between basic research and application. The T-group, the progenitor of most of the experientially-based training today, came serendipitously from research conducted at the Workshop on Community Relations (see R. Lippitt, 1951) held in Connecticut during the summer of 1946. This workshop led to the establishment of the National Training Laboratory in Group Development (now the NTL Institute). At its first session in 1947, an interdisciplinary team composed of social and clinical psychologists, sociologists, and an anthropologist conducted a number of exploratory studies, which lead to more thorough studies. For the next decade, research into small group behavior was carried on jointly with the training efforts.

Articles leading to application, two of which appear in Part I of this book, grew out of the action-research and training efforts of the first two sessions of the National Training Laboratory in Group Development. During the early fifties, the new Adult Education Association, with grants from the Fund for Adult Education of the Ford Foundation, published *Adult Leadership* and, for a few years, offered opportunities for applied articles to be published.

During the late forties and fifties, research and application into small group behavior reached its apex. This interest continues to be vital in today's world and this book, containing some of the best application and research articles, can help to keep this interest vibrant.

REFERENCES

Brown, L. G., *Social Psychology* (1st ed.), New York: McGraw-Hill, 1934.

Cartwright, D. & A. Zander, *Group Dynamics: Research and Theory*, Evanston, IL: Harper & Row, 1953.

Hare, P., E. F. Borgatta & R. F. Bales, *Small Groups*, New York: Knopf, 1955.

Lewin, K., *The Relative Effectiveness of a Lecture Method and a Method of Group Decision for Changing Food Habits*, Washington, DC: National Research Council, 1943.

Lewin, K., R. Lippitt & R. K. White, Patterns of aggressive behavior in experimentally created social climates, *Journal of Social Psychology*, 1939, *10*, 271-279.

Lippitt, R., *Training in Community Relations*, New York: Harper & Row, 1949.

Marrow, A. J. & J. R. P. French, Jr., Changing a stereotype in industry, *Journal of Social Issues*, 1945, *1*(3).

Moreno, J. L., *Psychodrama* (3 vols.), New York: Beacon House, 1946.

Stock, D. & H. A. Thelen, (Eds.), *Emotional Dynamics and Group Culture*, New York: New York University Press, 1958.

Informal Communication in Small Groups

by Leon Festinger

Spontaneous, informal social communication is a vital part of the functioning of groups. It appears, when we consider group action from a theoretical point of view, that the sharing of information, the exertion of influence and other such processes whereby one part of a group communicates with another part are very basic. A better understanding of the dynamics of such communication points, in turn, to a better understanding of how groups function and the ways in which they affect their members.

The program of research in social communication which we shall describe has thus attempted to focus on various types of communication and various aspects of the communication process. It is not possible to give here a detailed account of the experiments and findings related to the several problems of communication which we have pursued. We shall, however, list briefly the various problems on which we have worked and examine more fully the work on one of these problems, namely, communication as the exertion of influence.

1. *The transmission of rumor and information in groups:* A number of studies have been conducted which were concerned with discovering the factors which determine when rumors or information will spread, and the direction of the transmission of such rumors. One such study was done by following up the transmission of a rumor which started spontaneously in a community (4). Two other studies were conducted by following up the transmission of rumors which were deliberately planted within a group in a prearranged manner (5,2).

2. *Restraints against communication in hierarchies:* Studies have been performed on the determinants of the direction of communication and

From Harold Guetzkow (Ed.), *Groups, Leadership, and Men*. Pittsburgh, PA, Carnegie Press, Carnegie-Mellon University, 1951. Reprinted by permission.

the kind of information which does or does not get communicated in hierarchical structures. One such experiment was done in a functioning organization (2). Two experiments were performed in artificially created hierarchies in which we studied the communication process which existed between and within the hierarchical layers thus created (7,9).

3. *Communication and influence:* The first study related to this problem investigated the determinants of group formation and the development and maintenance of group standards in a housing project (5). As a result of it, numerous new insights and hypotheses were gained concerning the part that communication plays in small groups. In order to clarify and add to our knowledge, a number of laboratory experiments were performed to test and elaborate some of the specific hypotheses which had emerged (1,6,8). We shall in the ensuing pages describe in detail the development of the research on this problem.

SOCIAL PRESSURES IN INFORMAL GROUPS

There are many beliefs and attitudes that people hold which cannot be checked with objective data. Yet people are in need of support for these beliefs and one method employed to gain it is by agreement with others. The attempt to get such support, that is, the attempt to have others in a group, of which one is a member, agree on a given opinion or belief or behavior pattern, leads to a process of influence among members of the group and consequent mutual adjustment of opinion. An individual may try to influence others to accept his beliefs or he may be willing to be influenced by others. Under appropriate circumstances the result of such a process of influence by communication is that a number of people find support for their opinions by achieving a state of relative uniformity within a group.

It is, of course, not necessary that everybody accept a certain opinion in order that it seem correct and valid for a particular individual. We tend to refer our opinions to certain groups and not to others. In general people tend to hold opinions which are accepted by the people with whom they associate. Such considerations, then, seem to be important for the formation of groups and for the influence processes which act in these groups. An attempt was made to investigate these phenomena in groups that had developed in a housing project (5).

The housing project consisted of one hundred houses arranged in courts. These houses were all occupied by the families of married veteran students at the Massachusetts Institute of Technology. About half of the families had children, in almost all cases, one child per family.

After achieving a working knowledge of the kind of people who lived in the project, the type of social life they led, and their interests and backgrounds, it seemed appropriate to study the conditions for friendship and group formation within this neighborhood community. When our data were assembled, the most striking item was the dependence of friendship formation on the mere physical arrangement of the houses. People who lived close to one another became friendly while people who lived farther apart did not. Mere accidents of geography such as where a path led or whose doorway a staircase passed were major determinants of friendships within this community. The small face-to-face social groups which formed were, to a large extent, limited to the number of people who lived in the same court.

Certainly other factors operated. If two people did not like each other they did not become friends even if they lived right next door to one another. It was impressive, however, to see how large a part mere physical arrangement did play. Since the courts did play such an important role in determining friendship formation and, consequently, the formation of social groups within the community, we were able to study other aspects of the functioning of these groups, considering each court as a potential social group. We could then examine to what extent these potential groups had become actual psychological groups and how membership affected people's attitudes and behavior.

We were fortunate in being able to study these processes in connection with a new issue which arose in the community. A few months after our investigation had begun the tenants spontaneously formed a tenant organization. We were able to study the growth of this organization and to observe, from the beginning, the development of attitudes toward it and the participation in its activities by the residents of the project. The fact that the organization would affect equally all sub-groups in the project made relevant an investigation of the ways in which different group standards had developed in the different courts and the factors which affected their strength and nature.

Both the qualitative and quantitative data which we gathered in this community pointed clearly to a high degree of uniformity within each of the courts in the project concerning attitudes toward and activity in this tenant organization. They also pointed to great differences between courts in this respect. Each group, it seems, had developed more or less strong group standards concerning this issue and exerted strong influences on its members to conform. How effectively this influence was exerted on its members depended to a great extent on how cohesive the small social group was. Those groups to which the members were strongly attracted were able to exert strong forces on their members to conform and those toward which the members were little attracted were not able to maintain uniform group standards. Furthermore, the people who did not conform to the group standards of the court in which they lived were not as integral a part of the group as those who did conform. These nonconformers tended to have fewer friends in their own court and fewer friends in the project as a whole.

In attempting to explain the data which we obtained in this study we were led to the following interpretations. The informal pressures which a group exerts on its members are frequently subtle ones which are difficult to localize. The weight of other's opinions, the gradual change in one's ideas of what is the "normal" thing to do simply because every one else does it, and the mutual influences of people on one another are the kinds of things that serve effectively as pressures toward conformity with the behavior pattern of the group.

Under such circumstances the consequences of nonconformity are also subtle. These consequences may merely be the tendency to prefer those people who are not "different." There was no indication in this project that there was any overt or formalized pressure on court members to conform to their court standards. Many of the residents realized that the people in their court were different from the people in some other court, but the influences which created and maintained these differences among courts were indirect and the residents were not aware of them. Members of the courts were influenced in their opinions and behavior merely by virtue of their association with others without any formalized "group intent" to influence.

The strength of the influence which the group could effectively exert in this manner depended partly upon the attractiveness of the group for the member and partly on the degree to which the member was in communication with others in the group. No matter how attractive a group is to a particular person, it will be impossible for the group to exert any influence on him if he is never in communication with the group. In general there seem to be three conditions under which individuals would be able to resist group influences of this nature.

1. The member may not be strongly attracted to belong to the group. Under these circumstances the relatively weak influence which the group exerts cannot overcome personal considerations which may happen to be contrary to the group standards. This person may, if the influence attempts become overt, simply leave the group.

2. There may not be sufficient communication between the member and others in the group. Under these conditions the pressures from the group are simply not brought to bear on the member, although, if they had been exerted, they might have been effective. In such instances the non-conformer may not even be aware of the fact that he is different from most of the others in his group.

3. The influence of some other group to which the person belongs may be stronger than the influence which the court is able to exert

on him. Under these circumstances the person who appears as a non-conformer is one only because we have chosen to call him a member of the court group. He does deviate from his own court but he conforms to some other group to which he actually belongs.

In order to understand more fully these group processes involving communication, the following three questions must be asked and answered: (1) When do pressures toward uniformity arise in groups and what are the conditions for the effective exertion of influence in response to such pressures? (2) How does perceived group membership, attraction to the group, and strength of pressure toward uniformity affect the direction of communication? That is, upon whom are influences exerted and upon whom are they not exerted? (3) What determines when a non-conformer is or is not rejected by the group?

These three questions were investigated in three separate laboratory experiments specifically designed to answer them.

THE EXERTION OF INFLUENCE THROUGH SOCIAL COMMUNICATION

On the basis of the results of the previous study, the hypothesis may be advanced that pressure towards uniformity in a group, the amount of influence exerted and how effective the exertion of influence will be is a function of how attractive the group is for its members. In order to test this hypothesis specifically, Back (1) conducted an experiment with the following focus:

1. Determination of the exact relationship between attraction to the group and the accomplishment of influence.
2. Determination of whether these same relationships will exist irrespective of the particular source of the attraction to the group.

In the experiment in question three sources of attraction to the group were experimentally varied. In some groups the source of attraction was the personal liking among the members, in some it was the possibility of a reward which could be attained by membership in the group, and in still others the source of attraction was the prestige which the group had in the eyes of the experimenter. For each of these sources of attraction to the group some high cohesive and some low cohesive groups were created. There were then, in all, six different types of groups employed in the experiment.

The procedure which was followed attempted to control other variables which could affect the influence process. In essence the procedure was as follows: Pairs of subjects of the same sex, who did not know each other prior to the experiment, were scheduled to appear in the laboratory at the same time. After the subjects were introduced to each other they were each taken to a different room and were each given a set of three photographs. They were told that the pictures had been taken from a film strip and formed a sequence which they were to reconstruct and then write a story connecting the pictures. They were also informed that after having written the story they would have an opportunity to discuss their ideas and their stories with the other person in the group and afterwards they would be able to write a final story. It was emphasized that their story should be closely tied to the pictures and should make use of the available clues that were present in the set of three pictures.

At this time each subject was also given additional instructions which, depending upon which of the six experimental conditions he was to be in, was calculated to increase or decrease the attraction he felt toward being in this group. While it would not be feasible to go into the details of this manipulation of the attraction to the group, suffice it to say that there is evidence that the strength of the attraction to the group was successfully manipulated for each of these three types of attraction.

When they had completed their stories, the two partners were brought together to discuss what they had written. Before this discussion they were reminded that the object of it was to help them improve their own story. It was emphasized that they were not going to write a common story and that they could stop the discussion at any time when they saw its usefulness at an end. The length and manner of the discussion were therefore left entirely to the subjects.

After they had concluded the discussion the subjects returned to their separate rooms to write their final story. They were instructed to "write what you now think to be the best story." They could not see the pictures again and, therefore, could not check information which they had received from their partners.

The data obtained from this experiment fall into three categories:

1. Data obtained from observing the discussion process which went on between the two members of each group.

2. Data showing how much each member had been influenced by the discussion. This was obtained from coding the initial and final stories and counting the number of changes which could be traced to the partner's influence.

3. Data from an interview with each subject conducted at the end of the session.

Summarized, the major results are the following:

1. *Patterns of discussion.* On the basis of the observations of the discussion in each group, ratings were made in terms of whether or not the discussion seemed to be an active attempt at influence. Of the 30 high cohesive pairs, 16 were rated as actively attempting to influence each

other, while only 7 of the 30 low cohesive pairs were thus rated. Consistent with this is the finding from answers to questions in a post-experimental interview. The subjects were asked whether or not they felt pressure from their partners to change their story. Out of the 60 subjects in the 30 high cohesive groups, 36 reported that they did feel such pressure, while only 21 members of the 60 low cohesive subjects reported that they felt such pressure to change their opinion. We may thus conclude that stronger attraction to the group did make for greater pressure towards uniformity as seen by the amount of influence which was attempted.

2. *Reaction to partner's influence attempts.* After the experiment was finished each subject was asked the question, "If your partner had tried all he could, do you think you would have accepted his story?" For each of the different sources of attraction to the group the members of the high cohesive groups reported feeling less resistance to influence from the partner than did the members of the low cohesive groups. In other words, the members of the high cohesive groups, irrespective of the source of the attraction to that group, tended to report more readiness to change their opinion in response to pressure from their partner.

3. *The effect of cohesiveness on the amount of influence actually accomplished.* We have seen that in the high cohesive groups the subjects tried harder to influence their partners and were also more willing to accept their partners' opinions. We may therefore expect to find more influence accomplished in the high than in the low cohesive groups. This is indeed the case. Irrespective of the source of the attraction to the group, the high cohesive pairs showed more change which could be attributed to the influence of their partners than did the low cohesive groups.

This experiment, performed under controlled laboratory conditions, with experimental manipulation of the variables with which we were concerned, substantiates the hypothesis arrived at in our field study of a neighborhood community. We may now state somewhat more precisely the hypotheses emerging from these studies. The greater the attraction of members to a group, given some discrepancy in opinion concerning a relevant issue, the more pressure towards uniformity will develop within the group and, consequently, there will be greater attempts to influence others in the group and greater readiness on the part of the members to change their opinions in line with the opinions of others. The result of this, of course, is more rapid progress toward a state of uniformity.

INTERPERSONAL COMMUNICATION IN SMALL GROUPS

With the establishment of the theory that groups tend to exert pressures on members to change their opinions when difference of opinion exists, we must look further and examine the determinants of the direction of communication, that is, upon whom in a group will such pressures be exerted. It would seem that if a group has the property of moving toward uniformity, then any discrepancy among the different parts of the group will give rise to pressures which will be exerted differentially on the parts of the group to effect a change in order to re-establish uniformity. The strength of these pressures is a function of the magnitude of the tendencies toward uniformity which the group possesses. In a group where the tendencies toward uniformity concern an opinion about a particular issue, the exertion of pressures on persons to change their opinion must make itself felt through a process of communication among them.

What can we infer about this process of communication?

1. If we assume that the magnitude of pressure applied to any member of a group is a direct function of the discrepancy between that person's opinion and the opinion of the rest of the group, it would follow that within a psychological group we would expect communication to be directed mainly toward those members whose opinions are extreme as compared to the opinions of the others.

2. The less the pressure toward uniformity in a group, the less should be this tendency to communicate mainly to the extremes of the opinion range within the group. We would also expect to find here, in line with the results reported in the preceding pages, that the less the pressure toward uniformity in a group, the less will be the actual exertion of influence and the less will be the actual accomplishment of influence within that group.

The experiment by Festinger and Thibaut (6) which we shall summarize here was specifically designed to test these hypotheses under controlled laboratory conditions. Groups of volunteers ranging in size from six to fourteen members, all of whom were strangers to one another, assembled in the experimental room. Each member was asked to sit down at one of a number of small tables arranged in a circle. Each member was identified to the others by a letter printed on a card placed on a stand in front of him so that all others could see it.

After all the members were present the group was given a problem to consider. The problem was such that opinions concerning it could be placed on a suggested seven point scale. The members were instructed to consider the problem and then each to place on a stand in front of him a card which would indicate to the others in the group what his opinion was on the problem. Thus, at the start of the experiment all members had formed opinions and were aware of what the opinions of everyone else in the group were. The problems which we used in this experiment were chosen so as to produce adequate dispersion of opinion within each group.

When these preliminaries were over the experimenter described to the group the manner in which the problem was to be discussed. Paper pads were distributed to the subjects and they were informed that discussion about the problem was to be restricted to writing notes to one another. They were free to include anything they liked in the notes. They could address a note to only one person at a time, but they could write as many notes as they pleased. As soon as a note was written the experimenter would take it and deliver it to the person to whom it was addressed. It was emphasized that, in order to have the discussion proceed sensibly, if any member of the group at any time changed his opinion he should change the card in front of him so that everyone in the group would be aware at all times of what the opinions of the other members were.

In addition to this general procedure, instructions were given which attempted to manipulate the magnitude of the pressure toward uniformity operating in the group. Some were given instructions calculated to produce rather high pressure toward uniformity, other groups were given instructions calculated to produce moderate pressure toward uniformity, while still others were given no additional instructions. In the last groups any pressures toward uniformity which existed would be spontaneously generated.

The results obtained were as follows:

1. *The direction of communication.* It is possible to examine the direction of communication by examining the number of communications addressed to those individuals whose opinions were at the extreme of the range in the group, to those whose opinions were one step removed from the extreme of the range, two steps removed from the extreme of the range and so on. It is found that uniformly 70 per cent to 90 per cent of the communications are addressed to persons whose opinions are at the extremes of the existing range of opinion in the group. The number of communications received falls off very rapidly for those people whose opinions are closer to the middle of the range. This result is uniform. It is true for all groups irrespective of the particular problem they were discussing. We may conclude unequivocally that the volume of communication directed toward a group member is a function of his proximity to the extreme of the existing range of opinions.

2. *The effect of increasing the pressure toward uniformity.* It was possible to calculate an index for each group which would reflect to what extent the communications were being directed toward the extremes of the opinion range. We can consequently compare these indices for groups in which high pressure toward uniformity had been induced with those in which medium pressure toward uniformity or low pressure toward uniformity had been created. The results show that there is least tendency to communicate to the extreme opinions in the "low pressure" groups and there

is the greatest tendency to communicate to the extremes of the opinion range in the "high pressure" groups. The "medium pressure" groups tend to fall between the other two in their tendency to communicate to the extremes. We may conclude therefore, that the higher the pressure toward uniformity the greater will be the proportion of the communications addressed to the extremes of the psychological group.

3. *The relation between pressure toward uniformity and amount of influence accomplished.* It was possible in this experiment to check once more on the hypothesis with which the Back experiment (1) was concerned. In this experiment cohesiveness was varied and consequently the pressure toward uniformity was indirectly manipulated. In the present experiment pressure toward uniformity was manipulated directly. To be consistent it is clear that one should find the same difference between the high pressure and the low pressure toward uniformity groups as was found between the high cohesive and the low cohesive groups in the Back experiment. We would expect then, to find greater actual change toward uniformity, the greater the experimentally induced pressure toward uniformity.

In order to test this hypothesis a measure of the amount of change toward uniformity was calculated for each experimental group. In all of the comparisons the "high pressure" groups showed most change toward uniformity, the "medium pressure" groups showed the next largest amount of change toward uniformity and "low pressure" groups showed the least amount of such change.

We may conclude that pressure toward uniformity in a group has the following effects:

1. The greater the pressure, the more is influence exerted on extreme opinions.

2. The greater the pressure, the more influence is actually accomplished.

DEVIATION, REJECTION AND COMMUNICATION

In the light of the effects of pressures toward uniformity which we have already examined, we may now try to formulate, more adequately, the various types of reactions to such pressures which a group may show. We have already seen that one response is to attempt to exert influence on other members of the group and another is to be more amenable to influence and more ready to change. Both of these act to move the members of the group closer towards uniformity. There is still a third reaction to pressures toward uniformity which also, in a sense, acts to hasten the achievement of uniformity. This type of behavior is the rejection from the psychological group of those individuals who do not conform or do not agree with the others. In the extreme instance, of course, if one excludes from the group all of the divergent opinions, one then has already achieved uniformity within the psychological group. The existence of three simultaneous tendencies whenever pressures toward uniformity exist may then be postulated:

1. A tendency to attempt to change the opinions of others.
2. A tendency to be ready to change one's own opinion.
3. A tendency to reduce one's dependence on those who disagree.

It is the last tendency which gives rise to the overt symptom of rejection from the group.

An experiment by Schachter (8) was designed to measure the extent to which the existence of pressures towards uniformity makes for the rejection from the group of nonconformers or deviates. It is, of course, of importance in this connection not only to know that once pressures toward uniformity exist those who deviate are rejected, but also to know the conditions under which the rejection of deviates is stronger or weaker. The experiment by Schachter was designed to test the hypothesis that the strength of rejection of deviates responded to the same factors which increased tendencies to influence others and greater readiness to change one's self. Specifically, that the higher the cohesiveness of the group and the greater the degree of relevance of the issue to the group, the greater would be the magnitude of the rejection of members who do not conform on that issue.

The experiment was conducted as follows: students on the campus of the University of Michigan were offered an opportunity to join various clubs that were being organized. Each of the clubs eventually consisted of ten members who were to meet for discussion purposes. Interest in joining these clubs was stimulated by making the discussion topics and the purposes of the discussion attractive to potential members. When each club group actually met, among the ten members were three trained participants who were instructed to behave in certain patterns.

Each group was given a topic to discuss which was in line with the members' reasons for joining. This topic was selected so that almost everyone would have opinions about it which would cluster closely together. One of our confederates was instructed to take an extremely deviant position with respect to the opinion on this issue and to maintain it throughout the course of the discussion. Another of the confederates was instructed to adopt a very deviant opinion but gradually, as others tried to get him to change his opinion, to yield so that by the end of the discussion he would agree with most of the others. The third trained participant was instructed to adopt that opinion which most of the other members of the group supported and to remain at that opinion.

Again a full description of the way these experiments were performed would be inappropriate. We proceeded, however, to create some groups which were highly cohesive (that is, there was a strong attraction for the members to be in the group) while other groups were made into low cohesive groups. Similarly, the variable of relevance of the issue to the functioning of the group was manipulated. For some groups, both in high and low cohesive conditions, the issue was very relevant to the performance and purpose of the group. For other groups the issue which they discussed was made largely irrelevant to the functioning and purpose for which the club had come together. The course of the discussion was observed and records were kept of those who spoke, of whom they spoke to, and what kinds of remarks were addressed to various people. After the discussion, in the guise of electing officers and committees to insure the continued successful existence of the club, measurements were obtained from which could be inferred the degree to which members of the group rejected others. From these data it was then possible to analyze the extent to which the variables of cohesiveness and relevance operated to affect rejection by the group of members who deviated.

1. *Factors determining degree of rejection from the group.* We may first look at the extent to which the confederates who played different roles in the group were rejected by the group. It should be pointed out that, of course, the trained participants were rotated from role to role so that the effect of personality would be cancelled out in the analysis.

It is of course not surprising that the confederate who started out agreeing with the other members of the group, and continued to agree with them, was not at all rejected. He was accepted by the group as were the other members. It is also interesting to note that the paid participant who at the start of the discussion held an extremely divergent opinion, but who gradually was influenced by the others so that he ended up agreeing with the group, was never rejected by the group. He too was accepted as well as the other members and as well as the trained participant who had always conformed.

On the other hand, the consistent deviate, that is the accomplice who had started out voicing extremely divergent opinions and remained divergent throughout the course of the discussion, was consistently rejected by almost all of the groups. The variables of cohesiveness of the group and relevance of the issue to the group did affect the degree to which the deviate was rejected. The highly cohesive groups rejected the deviate considerably more than the less cohesive groups. Those groups where the issue was relevant rejected the deviate more than did those groups where the issue was largely irrelevant to the functioning of the group. These two factors acted together so that in the low cohesive groups where the issue was irrelevant there was virtually no rejection of the deviate.

2. *The pattern of communication.* In order to be sure that the same factors are indeed operating here which acted in the other experiments we have examined, we may look to see if we can corroborate some of the results which we had found previously. It will be recalled that in the Back experiment (1) there was evidence from the observation of the discussion that the high cohesive groups attempted more actively to influence the members than did the low cohesive groups. This was true in the present experiment. There is observational evidence of the same kind that the high cohesive groups tended to exert more influence in the discussion than the low cohesive groups and that the groups where the issues were relevant tended to exert more influence in the discussion than the groups where the issues were irrelevant.

It will also be recalled that in the Festinger and Thibaut experiment (6) it was found that the great majority of the communications tended to be addressed to those whose opinions were extreme with respect to the range of opinion present in the group at the time. We would then expect to find in the present experiment that the great majority of the communications were addressed to the consistent deviate. This is indeed true. In all groups many more communications were addressed to the consistent deviate during the course of the meeting than were addressed to any of the other members of the group.

An additional result was obtained with regard to the communications addressed to the deviate. If we examine changes in the communication pattern as the discussion proceeded in the high cohesive groups where the issue was relevant (the group in which rejection was strongest) we find differences to exist between those members who do and those members who do not reject the deviate at the end of the meeting. Those who do not reject the deviate steadily increase in the frequency of communications addressed to him as the discussion proceeds. This same set of data for those members who do reject the consistent deviate at the end of the meeting shows quite a different pattern. As the discussion progresses the number of communications addressed to the deviate increases to a maximum and then drops steadily off. The maximum was reached when the discussion had gone on for about twenty-five minutes. The number of communications addressed to the deviate by those who reject him at the end of the meeting decreases steadily from then on.

This would seem to indicate that as long as a nonconformer is still included in the group and accepted as a member of the group, the great majority of communications will be addressed to him in an attempt to get him to change and conform to the group opinion. Once he is rejected from the group, however, or when the tendency to reject him becomes strong, there will be a corresponding decrease in the number of communications addressed to him. This reinforces the interpretation that the bulk of communications intended to influence the opinion of others are addressed to the opinions that are extreme within the psychological group. They are not addressed to extreme opinions held by persons who are not considered part of the group.

It seems clear then that the same factors which affect the amount of influence exerted and the readiness of members to change their own opinion, also affect the tendency to lessen one's dependence on those who disagree and to reject the disagreers from the group.

SUMMARY

We have discussed in detail a number of research studies on processes of influence by communication in small groups and the effects of these processes. In brief we have explored the following problems:

1. What are the determinants of the magnitude of pressures to attempt to influence others?
2. What determines just what persons one attempts to influence within a group?
3. What are the determinants of how much change is accomplished by an influence process?
4. What are the determinants of rejection of members because of non-conformity?

It is interesting to note the relationship between this program of theoretically based research and another program which has oriented itself more at the level of finding applications in actual life settings. Many of the findings from the program in informal social communication and much of the theory which has been developed in connection with these researches has had great practical value in studies of industrial productivity, and in leadership training. . . . It is to be hoped that continued development of basic areas of knowledge concerning the communication process in groups and the continued application of such findings will lead to a firm and fruitful body of data which will offer many more possibilities of application to problems of group functioning and group life.

BIBLIOGRAPHY

1. Back, K. The exertion of influence through social communication. *J. abnorm. soc. Psychol.*, 1950.

2. Back, K., Festinger, L., Hymovitch, B., Kelley, H. H., Schachter, S., and Thibaut, J. The methodology of studying rumor transmission. *Human Relations*, 1950, *3*, 307-312.

3. Festinger, L., Informal social communication. *Psychol. Rev.*, 1950, *57*, 271-282.

4. Festinger, L., Cartwright, D., et al. A study of a rumor: its origin and spread. *Human Relations*, 1948, *1*, 464-486.

5. Festinger, L., Schachter, S., and Back, K. *Social Pressures in Informal Groups: a Study of a Housing Project*. New York: Harper & Bros., 1950.

6. Festinger, L., and Thibaut, J. Interpersonal communication in small groups. *J. abnorm. soc. Psychol.*, 1951.

7. Kelley, H. H. Communication in experimentally created hierarchies. *Human Relations*, 1950, *4*.

8. Schachter, S. Deviation, rejection, and communication. *J. abnorm. soc. Psychol.*, 1951.

9. Thibaut, J. An experimental study of the cohesiveness of underprivileged groups. *Human Relations*, 1950, *3*, 251-278.

Task Roles and Social Roles
in Problem-Solving Groups

by Robert F. Bales

During the last ten years, a number of laboratories for the study of social interaction within small groups and organizations have been started in university research centers, hospitals, clinics, and military installations. The studies and experiments I shall describe were conducted in one of these laboratories, which was established in 1947 at Harvard University.

The laboratory consists of a large, well-lighted room for the group under study and an adjoining room for observers who listen and watch from behind windows with one-way vision. The subjects are told at the beginning that the room has been constructed for the special purpose of studying group discussion, that a complete sound recording will be made, and that there are observers behind the one-way mirrors. The purpose of the separation is not to deceive the subjects but to minimize interaction between them and the observing team.

Over a number of years we have evolved a more or less standard type of group and task which has formed the setting for a number of studies. The data I shall report came from several studies, all done under essentially the same conditions, so that a description of the most recent investigation will serve in substance for the others.

PROCEDURES

The sample which provided data for the most recent investigation consisted of 30 five-man experimental groups. Subjects were 150 Harvard freshmen who were recruited by letters sent to a random sample of the entering class which briefly described the experiment as one concerned

From *Readings in Social Psychology* (3rd Ed.) by Eleanor E. Maccoby, Theodore M. Newcomb & Eugene L. Hartley (Eds.). Copyright 1947, 1952 (©1958) by Holt, Rinehart & Winston. Reprinted by permission of Holt, Rinehart & Winston.

with group problem-solving and decision-making. Volunteers were offered a dollar an hour. The groups were randomly composed. Typically the members of a group did not know each other, nor were they introduced to each other. In effect, they were faced with the problem of getting organized as well as with the more obvious problem that was issued to them.

The more obvious problem, which we call the standard task, involved the discussion of a human-relations case, a five-page presentation of facts about a problem facing an administrator in his organization. Members were given separate identical copies of the case to read ahead of time and were told that, although each was given accurate information, we intended to leave them uncertain as to whether they each had exactly the same range of facts. The cases were collected after they had been read by the members individually, to prevent direct comparison of typed copies, although members were allowed to take notes. The task defined for each group was to assemble the information, to discuss why the people involved were behaving as they did, and to decide what should be recommended as action for the solution to the problem presented. The groups were asked to time themselves for 40 minutes and to dictate the group solution for the sound record in the final one or two minutes of the meeting.

While the group members began to organize themselves and to solve the case problem, the observers got to work in the observation room. They systematically recorded every step of the interaction, including such items as nods and frowns. Each observer had a small machine with a moving paper tape on which he wrote in code a description of every act—an act being defined essentially as a single statement, question, or gesture. Acts ordinarily occurred at the rate of 15 to 20 per minute. The recorded information on each act included identification of the person speaking and the person spoken to and classification of the act according to predetermined categories. The categories included attempts to solve either the organizational problems of the group or the task problems by the offering of information, opinions, and suggestions.

Questions and several types of positive and negative reactions completed the set of 12 categories (see Figure 1). This method is called "interaction-process analysis."[1] The categories are meant to have a general-purpose usefulness for group research and their use is not confined in any way to the laboratory conditions described here, although the

---

[1]Robert F. Bales, *Interaction Process Analysis: A Method for the Study of Small Groups* (Cambridge, Mass.: Addison-Wesley Co., Inc., 1950).

best norms exist for the standard task and the group type described here.[2]

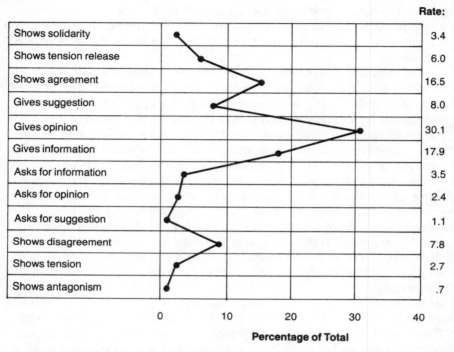

Fig. 1. Types of interaction and their relative frequencies. This profile of rates is the average obtained on the standard task from 24 different groups, four of each size from two to size seven, each group meeting four times, making a total of 96 sessions. The raw number of scores is 71,838.
(From Robert F. Bales. "How People Interact in Conferences," *Scientific American*, Vol. 192 [March, 1955].

As Figure 1 shows, on the average about half (56 percent) of the acts during a group session on the standard task fall into the categories of problem-solving attempts; the remaining 44 percent are distributed among positive reactions, negative reactions, and questions. In other words, the process tends to be two-sided, with the reactions serving as a more or less constant feedback on the acceptability of the problem-solving attempts. The following example will illustrate the pattern of interchange.

Member 1: I wonder if we have the same facts about the problem? [Asks for opinion.] Perhaps we should take some time in the beginning to find out. [Gives suggestion.]

---

[2]For norms, see Robert F. Bales and Edgar F. Borgatta, "Size of Group as a Factor in the Interaction Profile," in A. Paul Hare, Edgar F. Borgatta, and Robert F. Bales, *Small Groups, Studies in Social Interaction* (New York: Alfred A. Knopf, Inc., 1955), pp. 396-413.

Member 2: Yes. [Agrees.] We may be able to fill in some gaps in our information. [Gives opinion.] Let's go around the table and each tell what the report said in his case. [Gives suggestion.]

Member 3: Oh, let's get going. [Shows antagonism.] We've all got the same facts. [Gives opinion.]

Member 2: (Blushes) [Shows tension.]

A number of interesting generalizations can be made about the way in which rates of activity in the various categories tend to differ according to group size, time periods within a meeting, development of a group over a series of meetings, pre-established status characteristics of members, and the like.[3] The present article, however, will be concerned with a particular set of problems in which the interaction data have played an important part—whether there are tendencies for persons to develop different roles during interaction, even though there are no pre-established status differences, and if so, what kind, and why? There are several plausible views about this set of problems. The following account presents four distinguishable views and shows how research led from one view to another in the course of several studies.

THE HYPOTHESIS OF A SINGLE-STATUS ORDER

Perhaps the most ordinary conception of a group is that it consists of a leader and several followers who fall into a kind of status order from highest to lowest. The leader is the best-liked member of the group, participates most actively, and is felt to be the best performer of whatever task activities the group undertakes. No matter which of these criteria the researcher takes, he will come out with the same rank order of members. The expectation that most groups are structured like this and that departures from this simple form of organization may be treated as the result of special circumstances may be called the hypothesis of a "single-status order."

This is a plausible hypothesis. It underlies much research on leadership. It is congruent with the ideological position that for good leadership it is very important that a good leader should be an all-around "great man," and it assumes that there are such men, at least relative to the other members in a given group.[4] This hypothesis assumes role differen-

---

[3]For a short review, see Robert F. Bales "Some Uniformities of Behavior in Small Groups" in the previous edition of this book, Guy E. Swanson, Theodore M. Newcomb, and Eugene L. Hartley (eds.), *Readings in Social Psychology* (New York: Henry Holt & Co., Inc., 1952), rev. ed., pp. 146-159.

[4]For some evidence that there are some such men, in relative terms, see Edgar F. Borgatta, Arthur S. Couch, and Robert F. Bales, "Some Findings Relevant to the Great Man Theory of Leadership," *Am. Sociol. Rev.*, 1954, XIX, 755-759.

tiation but essentially only along a single quantitative dimension, leadership status.

Early in the research we began to ask group members about their likes and dislikes for each other, their opinions of who had the best ideas and who showed the most leadership, and other similar questions. We wanted to know how these questions related to each other and to our observations of interaction. The question as to whether or not there is role differentiation within a group can be reduced in part to whether group members show some consensus that certain members stand higher than others on a given criterion and whether different criteria give different status orders rather than a single-status order.

When I first began to examine data from our experimental groups, I worked under the assumption that there might be some such thing as a "simply organized group," that is, one in which the rank order of members on activity, task ability, and likeability would coincide, and that these groups would in some sense or other be the most successful or best satisfied.[5]

Figure 2 shows the results which raised a most interesting set of questions. The total interaction initiated by one man in the course of a meeting establishes the basis for ranking him relative to the others on activity. If there is a strong tendency toward a single-status order, top men on activity should also rank highest in group-member responses to such questions as "who has the best ideas," and should also receive the highest number of "liking" votes and lowest of "disliking."[6] The second man on activity should, on the average, be second highest on the other criteria of excellence, and so on. The rank order on each criterion should be highly correlated to the rank order on the other criteria.

What does Figure 2 suggest? First, there seems to be a positive correlation between activity rank and idea rank, although the second man seems a little low. But on liking-received rank, there is a marked discrepancy. The top man on activity appears considerably lower than expected on liking received. Both the second and the third men are higher on the average than he. Is the top man doing something to lose likes and provoke dislikes? Here one notes the dislike curve. The differences are small and probably not significant but they suggest that the top man is possibly the highest on dislikes received. Liking seems to be centering on the second

---

[5]Robert F. Bales, "The Equilibrium Problem in Small Groups," Ch. IV in Talcott Parsons, Robert F. Bales, and Edward A. Shils (eds.), *Working Papers in the Theory of Action* (Glencoe, Ill.: Free Press, 1953).

[6]The actual questions used are presented in the source indicated at the foot of Figure 3. They are omitted in the present paper for the sake of brevity.

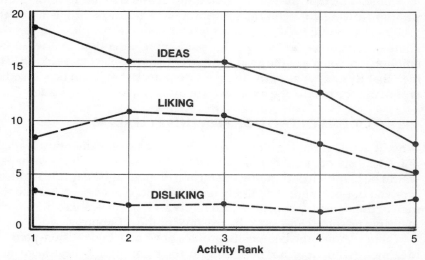

Fig. 2. Average ratings* received on ideas, liking, and disliking by men of each activity rank.

(From Robert F. Bales, "The Equilibrium Problem in Small Groups," Ch. IV in Talcott Parsons, Bales, and Edward A. Shils [eds.], *Working Papers in the Theory of Action* [Glencoe, Ill.; Free Press, 1953], p. 146.)

*Each entry at a given activity rank is a mean over 12 sessions for the persons who occupied that rank as of each meeting. (Four separate five-man groups were involved.) The idea index is not actually a rating but an index obtained by adding rankings received (including self-rankings) and subtracting the total from the highest possible, 25. The like and dislike indexes are average ratings received, with the highest possible, 28.

and third man in activity, and they both seem to be lower than expected on idea ranking. Can it be that these men are tending to avoid too heavy an emphasis on the task area for fear of being disliked?

On further investigation of this problem it turned out that something happened in groups over a series of four sessions that was equally thought-provoking. In the first sessions, if a given man held top position on the idea ranking by his fellow members, the probability was about 50-50 that he would *also* hold a top position on a likeability ranking. But in the second meeting the probability dropped markedly, and by the fourth meeting was only about one in ten. The percentage of cases in which the same man held the top position on liking and idea rankings at the same time, divided by session, may be charted as follows:

Sessions

1	2	3	4
56.5	12.0	20.0	8.5

Could it be that there was something about arriving in a top-status position, owing to technical contribution to the task problems of the group, that tended to "lose friends and alienate people"? If so, was another man likely to arise who paid more attention to the social-emotional problems of the group and so tended to collect more liking? The idea that this happens with sufficient frequency that it can be viewed as typical may be called "the hypothesis of two complementary leaders."

THE HYPOTHESIS OF TWO COMPLEMENTARY LEADERS

Why, if at all, should groups tend to have two complementary leaders, one a task specialist, the other a social-emotional specialist?[7] Perhaps it would be helpful to look at the interaction of men highest on idea ranking received but not highest on liking received, and vice versa. It may be that men of these two types behave differently and the differences in behavior may give us some clues as to the reasons for the differences.

Table 1 shows the composite profiles of 44 matched session-pairs[8] of idea men (who were not best liked in their group) and best-liked men (who were not top in idea ranking). Slater, from whose paper the table is taken, comments: "The most salient general difference in Table 1 is the tendency for the Idea man to initiate interaction more heavily in Area B (Problem-Solving Attempts) and the Best-liked man in Area A (Positive Reactions). The Idea man also seems to disagree somewhat more, and show a little more antagonism, while the Best-liked man asks more questions and shows more tension."[9]

On the receiving end, the situation is largely reversed, with the idea man receiving more agreement, questions, and negative reactions, while the best-liked man receives more problem-solving attempts, and more solidarity and tension release. The general picture is thus one of specialization and complementarity, with the idea man concentrating on the task and playing a more aggressive role, while the best-liked man concentrates more on social-emotional problems, giving rewards and playing a more passive role.

---

[7]A theory is advanced in Robert F. Bales and Philip E. Slater, "Role Differentiation in Small Decision-making Groups," Ch. V in Talcott Parsons *et al.* (eds.), *Family, Socialization, and Interaction Process* (Glencoe, Ill.: Free Press, 1955).

[8]Although the number of *sessions* was 44, the number of separate individuals involved was not 88, since each group ran over four sessions, and some individuals were in the same position more than once.

[9]Slater, *op. cit.* in footnote to Table 1. It is not possible to state that all of the detailed differences indicated are significant, because rates in the various categories are interdependent. However, Slater shows that the two types are in general significantly different from each other.

Table 1*
Composite Profiles in Percentages of 44 Top Men on Idea Ranking and 44 Top Men on Like Ranking for the Same Sessions

	Interaction category	Initiated		Received	
		Idea men	Best-liked men	Idea men	Best-liked men
Area A: Positive reactions	Shows solidarity	3.68	4.41	2.57	3.15
	Shows tension release	5.15	6.98	7.95	9.20
	Shows agreement	14.42	16.83	23.29	18.27
Area B: Problem-solving attempts	Gives suggestion	8.97	6.81	7.01	7.22
	Gives opinion	32.74	28.69	25.52	31.09
	Gives orientation	18.54	17.91	14.06	14.54
Area C: Questions	Asks orientation	3.04	3.71	3.62	2.80
	Asks opinion	1.84	2.94	1.94	1.74
	Asks suggestion	.93	1.33	.85	.84
Area D: Negative reactions	Shows disagreement	8.04	7.60	10.65	9.35
	Shows tension increase	1.92	2.16	1.59	1.35
	Shows antagonism	.73	.63	.95	.45

*From Philip E. Slater, "Role Differentiation in Small Groups," *Am. Sociol. Rev.*, 1955, XX, 305.

The kind of complementarity that shows in the behavior, then, is a kind that occurs in short interchanges in conversations where a problem-solving attempt by one person is followed by an agreement or disagreement from some other, or where a pleasant remark or a joke by one is followed by a smile or a laugh from the other. Such a division of labor by type of act is very common and easily recognized. There may or may not be a specialization so that one person continues to produce more of one form of behavior than the other.

But now consider an important fact. Almost exactly the same sort of difference in interaction profile tends to be found between high participators and low participators,[10] even if one ignores the idea and like ratings. High participators tend to specialize in problem-solving attempts, low participators tend to specialize in positive or negative reactions or questions. Moreover, the proportion of problem-solving attempts increases when a man is placed with lower participators and decreases when he is working with higher participators.[11] What do these facts suggest?

---

[10]See Edgar F. Borgatta and Robert F. Bales, "Interaction of Individuals in Reconstituted Groups," *Sociometry*, 1953, XVI, 302-320.

[11]*Op. cit.*

For one thing, these facts seem to imply that the qualitative differences in the type of act attributed to a given person may be more or less forced by the tendency of others in the group to talk a little or a great deal, thus giving him an opportunity to make the problem-solving attempts or leaving him only in a position to respond to the quicker or more valuable proposals of others.

Insofar as the ratings a man receives are based on the way he behaves, the ratings others give him will surely be dependent on how much he talks. Let us suppose that a man can receive a high rating on ideas only if he makes many problem-solving attempts. He can do this only by talking a good deal. Then, to receive a high rating on ideas he will have to talk a lot. Or, conversely, let us suppose that a man can receive a high rating on liking only if he rewards others by positive reactions. He can do this only if he permits them to make many problem-solving attempts, which in turn requires that he let the other(s) talk a lot. Then, to receive a high rating on liking he will have to talk less.

This line of reasoning seems to fit with the facts so far presented and, moreover, has a certain plausibility in terms of common organizational arrangements. The husband and wife in many families seem to play complementary roles of the sort described. Many administrators find cases from their experience where organizations in fact have two leaders, one who specializes on the task side, one on the social-emotional side. It is a kind of political maxim that it is almost impossible to elect the person who is technically best suited for an office—he is generally not popular enough. Surely there must be many persons in leadership positions who welcome any theory that explains to them that their lack of popularity is no fault of their own but a result of a specialization that is in the nature of things.

The problem now is that it might be inferred from this ideological version of the theory that there is no essential distinction between sheer activity and ratings received on goodness of ideas and, moreover, that there is a negative correlation between these two and liking received. Is it true that leaders must choose between task effectiveness and popularity?

THE HYPOTHESIS OF THREE ORTHOGONAL FACTORS

Fortunately, a number of studies in the literature bear on this question and the results of a number of researchers tend to converge on an answer. When members of small groups are asked to rate and choose each other on a wide variety of descriptive criteria or are assessed by observers, three factors or distinct dimensions generally tend to appear.

Carter[12] indicates the frequency with which these factors are found in reviewing a series of factor analytic studies, such as those of Couch and himself, Sakoda, Wherry, and Clark.[13] A recent study by Wispe[14] may be added to the list.

Carter describes the factors as follows:

Factor I. *Individual prominence and achievement:* behaviors of the individual related to his efforts to stand out from others and individually achieve various personal goals.

Factor II. *Aiding attainment by the group:* behaviors of the individual related to his efforts to assist the group in achieving goals toward which the group is oriented.

Factor III. *Sociability:* behaviors of the individual related to his efforts to establish and maintain cordial and socially satisfying relations with other group members.

These factors seem to represent underlying dimensions in the evaluations persons make of each other, whether as observers or as fellow group members. It may be that the best way of looking at these factors is not as personality traits but as frameworks in which the perceiver responds to personality traits of others.

But the important thing to note is that in these studies the three factors, which I shall call "activity," "task ability," and "likeability," are not, in general, mutually exclusive: a high standing on one does not preclude or interfere with a high standing on the other. Nor are they mutually supportive in general but, rather, they tend to be uncorrelated.

The fact that they are uncorrelated in general does not necessarily mean, of course, that there are no dynamic relationships between the phenomena represented by the factors. It means that there is no simple linear relationship that tends to be found over all populations, so that knowing where a man stands on one does not allow for a prediction of his

---

[12]Launor F. Carter, "Recording and Evaluating the Performance of Individuals as Members of Small Groups," *Personn. Psychol.*, 1954, VII, 477-484.

[13]Arthur S. Couch and Launor F. Carter, "A Factorial Study of the Rated Behavior of Group Members," Paper read at Eastern Psychological Association, March 1952; J. M. Sakoda, "Factor Analysis of OSS Situational Tests," *J. Abnorm. & Soc. Psychol.*, 1952, XLVII, 843-852; R. J. Wherry, *Factor Analysis of Officer Qualification Form QCL-2B* (Columbus: Ohio State University Research Foundation, 1950); R. A. Clark, "Analyzing the Group Structure of Combat Rifle Squads," *Am. Psychologist*, 1953, VIII, 333.

[14]Lauren G. Wispe, "A Sociometric Analysis of Conflicting Role-Expectations," *Am. J. Sociol.*, LXI (1955), 134-137.

standing on either or both of the others. If there are dynamic relationships between the factors they must be more complicated, nonlinear, or circumstantial. What suggestions of relationship are there left?

THE HYPOTHESIS OF INDIVIDUAL DIFFERENCES IN OVERTALKING

Although it is not true that simply by talking a great deal does one guarantee a high rating on the quality of his ideas, it is still probably true that in groups of the sort we were studying it is very difficult to make a substantial contribution to the task without talking a great deal, especially in the first meeting, and overtalking may be resented by other members as a threat to their own status and a frustration of their own desire to talk. Results of other experimenters provided some findings that are congruent with this line of thought. Let us look for a moment at some of these results.

Leavitt and Mueller[15] explored the effect of one-way communication in a restricted communication situation where the receiver of the information is given no opportunity to "feed back" acknowledgements, questions, or negative reactions to the sender. They find that an initial reaction of hostility toward the sender tends to appear.

Thibaut and Coules[16] find that receivers who are not permitted to communicate to a person who has sent them an act of hostility show less post experimental friendliness to the sender than those permitted to reply.

A peripheral position in a restricted network approximates in some ways the position of a receiver with no opportunity for feedback. In an experiment where members were allowed to communicate only in written form through set channels on a task of assembling information, Leavitt[17] finds that members in peripheral positions are less well satisfied with their jobs than those in central positions.

These results suggested to us that the relatively low average of likeability preferences received by top participators might be due to the presence of some men in the total population of top men who overtalk, in the sense that they do not allow an appropriate amount of feedback of objections, qualifications, questions, and countersuggestions to occur. Our method of observation allowed us to examine the amount of interaction a given

---

[15]H. J. Leavitt and R. A. H. Mueller, "Some Effects of Feedback on Communication," *Hum. Relat.*, 1951, IV, 401-410.

[16]J. W. Thibaut and J. Coules, "The Role of Communication in the Reduction of Interpersonal Hostility," *J. Abnorm. & Soc. Psychol.*, 1952, XLVII, 770-777.

[17]H. J. Leavitt, "Some Effects of Certain Communication Patterns on Group Performance," see pp. 546-563 in this volume.

man received in relation to the amount he initiated. We thus arrived at the hypothesis that the ratio of interaction received to that initiated might help distinguish between those top interactors who were proportionately well liked and those who were not.

In general, as has been indicated, activity, task-ability ratings, and liking ratings appear in many studies as orthogonal factors, uncorrelated with each other over the total population assessed. It is important to recognize, however, that subparts of a population, or a different population, may show the variables related in a different way. It is the possibility that subparts of our population may show different relationships of these variables that we now explore.

We first make a basic division of the population according to the rank of each person within his own group on the gross amount of participation he initiated and call this his activity. Five ranks are thus recognized, since the groups were five-man groups.

The second division of the population is made within each rank. All the men of each rank are divided into three subpopulations according to their own ratio of amount of participation received from others to the amount of participation they initiate. This ratio is known as the R/I, or the feedback ratio. Within each rank, then, there are three subpopulations of ten men each, low, medium, and high on the feedback ratio.

Figure 3 shows the average values of ratings or ranking received for each of the subpopulations of ten men on liking, disliking, and ideas. The ratings or rankings were given to each man by his four fellow group members and have been converted for plotting in such a way that high numbers mean high average rankings received.

The point of greatest interest is the difference in the relations of liking to activity when the feedback ratio is taken into account. Figure 3 indicates that among the third of the population with a low feedback ratio, the top two men seem definitely lower than would be expected if liking received increased linearly in proportion to activity. The correlation between activity and liking received is near zero.

However, both the medium R/I and the high R/I thirds show a positive correlation. From these data it is still plausible to suppose that the top man even in the high R/I third shows a little less liking received than one would expect. But the effect is slight.

The data obtained by asking about dislikes present essentially the same picture. The highest participators among the third of the population with the lowest feedback ratio not only are less well liked but are more disliked than their less active colleagues in the same subpopulation. In this third of the population, the more the person talks, the more he is disliked. But in the opposite third of the population, those who have a

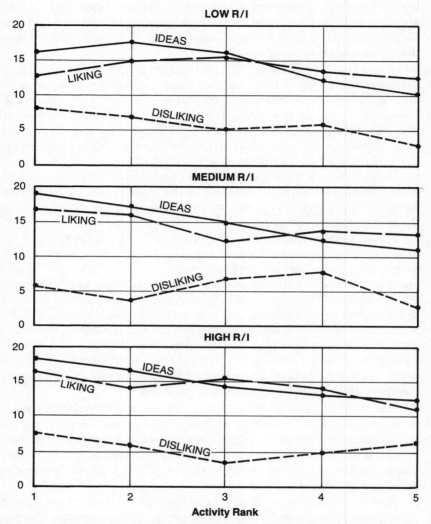

Fig. 3. Average ratings* received on ideas, liking, and disliking by men of each activity rank, according to their feedback ratio (R /I).

(Condensed from Robert F. Bales, "Task Status and Likeability as a Function of Talking and Listening in Decision-making Groups," in Leonard D. White [ed.], *The State of the Social Sciences* [Chicago: University of Chicago Press, 1956], pp. 148-161.)

*Each entry at a given activity rank is the mean for ten persons. The idea index is not actually a rating, but an index obtained by adding rankings received (including self-rankings) and subtracting the total from the highest possible, 25. The like and dislike indexes are average ratings, with the highest possible, 28.

high feedback ratio, there is no relation between how much a man talks and how much he is disliked.

With regard to idea rankings received, there is a definite indication that the highest participators in the third of the population with the low feedback ratio tend to suffer on idea rankings received, as they do on liking received, although the effect is not so marked. This effect seems to disappear completely in the medium R/I and high R/I groups.

It is plain, however, that there is an appreciable linear correlation between activity and idea rankings received over the total of the three subpopulations. This finding thus differs from other studies which find these two variables to be generally orthogonal. We attribute the correlation in our groups at least partly to the fact that we are dealing in this study with data from first meetings entirely. Data on groups running over four sessions indicate that this correlation tends to fall over time, especially in groups where the initial consensus as to who has the best ideas is low.[18] The correlation between ideas and liking also tends to fall as indicated above in Table 1. In short, the three factors tend to separate out as independent more clearly in later meetings than in the first.

To summarize briefly: In the groups in this total sample there is only a weak correlation between liking received and activity, providing one makes no breakdown into subpopulations. But for about one third of the population there is a positive and linear correlation between how much a man talks and how well he is liked. This is the third, who receive more interaction in proportion to the amount they initiate, that is, who have a high feedback ratio. The falling-off of liking received among the individuals who talk the most in total population is attributable especially to the other extreme third of the population, who talk proportionately most above the amount they receive. The same may be said for their rankings.

CONCLUSION

It appears that activity, task-ability ratings, and likeability ratings should be treated as three distinct factors, since over a large population of members, meetings, and groups they tend to be uncorrelated with each other. If one accepts this assumption a simple and very useful classification of role types in small groups suggests itself.

1. A member who is high on all three of the factors corresponds to the traditional conception of the good leader, or the "great man." Such men are found, but, if the factors are uncorrelated, are rare.

---

[18]Philip E. Slater, "Role Differentiation in Small Groups," *Am. Sociol. Rev.*, 1955, XX, 300-310.

2. A member who is high on activity and task-ability ratings but less high on likeability is a familiar type who may be called the "task specialist." This type is not so rare as the first type and may operate effectively in cooperation with the third.

3. A member who is high on likeability but less high on activity and task ability may be called the "social specialist." This type is much less rare than the first type and groups which operate under the dual leadership of a man of this type and of the second type are common.

4. A member who is high on activity but relatively low on task ability and likeability ratings may be called an "overactive deviant." This type is not rare. This is the person who, in the leadership literature, is said to show "domination" rather than "leadership."

5. A member who is low on all three may be called an "underactive deviant" and may indeed be a kind of scapegoat. On the assumption that the factors are uncorrelated this type should be as rare as the first type, but since the lack of correlation traces mainly to discrepancies at the upper end of the scales, this type is not actually so rare as the first type and is, in fact, probably very common.

Logically, of course, one can distinguish many additional types. Those mentioned, however, have a certain intuitive distinctness and for present purposes serve to summarize and harmonize the various views on role differentiation that have been examined in this paper.

level of performance below which they should not drop if they wish to have a respectable record. Following each vote, each member is told what the others expect him to produce and by implication is told what his share of the total work should be. Suppose, finally, that each person knows that the rest of the group cannot identify either his votes or his contributions to the total production. In this situation once each member learns what the group expects of him, he may set his own private and personal goal to match the group's expectations of him or he may set his own goal elsewhere, and he may produce as much as is asked of him, or more, or less. An illustration of such a group in a natural setting is a committee of financial canvassers who set quotas for each member, or a group of workmen on a group piece-rate payment plan who establish goals for themselves each day anew.

Although we have described a fairly specific type of group, it is useful to note that it allows distinctions to be made within it among four closely related concepts concerning group goals and individual goals. (a) The *member's goal for the group* is a region toward which a member exerts pressures on his group. In the above example it describes the level of production each member believes the group should try to achieve. (b) The *group goal* is a region of positive valence toward which a group tends to locomote and is usually some synthesis of the members' goals for the group. In our example the group goal is the result of the votes of the individual members concerning the group's objectives. (c) The *group's goal for a member* is a region toward which a group (excluding the member's vote in the matter) exerts pressures on a member. Usually, but not always, this region is similar to or on the path to the region the group holds as its goal. The pressures to achieve this goal may vary in strength from weak to strong. In the example the group's goal for a member is the quota the member is assigned during the next time-interval. (d) The *personal goal* is a region of positive valence toward which a person tends to locomote. In the example this is the personal and private goal each person sets for himself, while knowing what others are expecting of him. There is a circular causal relationship among these four goals in the direction (a), (b), (c), (d), and back again to (a). A change in any one of the four then will have effects to some degree on the other three, in the indicated sequence.

The first interest of this study is in the determinants of congruency between the location of (c), the *group's goal for a member* and the location of (d), the *member's personal goal*. *Congruency* is defined as the inverse of the distance between the locations of the personal goal and the group's goal for the member. The second purpose is to compare the attitudes and behaviors of persons whose personal goals are more congruent and the attitudes and behaviors of persons whose personal goals are less congruent. Are highly congruent persons more concerned with the group than the less congruent? Do highly congruent persons internalize the goal set for them by the group more than the less congruent do? Do the more congruent produce more than the less congruent?

Both the group's goal for the member and the member's goal for himself will be described in the present instance in terms of a specified number of units of production. A group's goal for a member may, in principle, be set at any level from very difficult to extremely easy. We shall, accordingly, describe goals set for a member in terms of their degree of *difficulty*, where difficulty is determined by the amount of energy or skill required to attain that level. A personal goal may likewise be set at various levels. We shall designate the level of the personal goal hereafter as the member's *level of aspiration*, where a high level means that he has chosen a difficult goal and a low level means that he has chosen an easier goal.

Will a member set his level of aspiration more congruent with the level of the group's goals for him when that goal is more difficult or when it is easier? Drawing upon theories of aspiration-setting (Lewin *et al.*, 1944) and theories of social influence (Raven & French, 1958), we can advance plausible arguments supporting the prediction that he will more readily set his level of aspiration closer to the difficult goal; and equally plausible assertions can be made supporting the prediction that he will set his level of aspiration closer to the easier goal. Because there is at hand no reliable means of choosing the most appropriate assumptions and predictions, we propose to postpone speculation on this issue until we see what the results provide in response to the question.

When a group determines a goal for a member, it is common for some indication to be given to the member concerning how important achievement of that goal is to the group. This indication of importance is conceived as the *strength of the group's pressures* on a member toward achievement of the suggested goal. Here it seems quite reasonable that the stronger the pressures to attain a given goal placed on a member by the group, the closer is he likely to set his level of aspiration to the given goal, all other matters being equal.

We cannot assume, however, that all other matters are always equal for persons who have a particular goal set for them and who have a particular degree of pressure upon them to achieve that goal. Schachter *et al.* (1951) and Berkowitz (1954), for example, have demonstrated that members who are attracted to their groups are more disposed to accept (and to act in accordance with) inductions from other members concerning how hard they should work, than are members who are less attracted to their groups. We predict, then, that members who are highly attracted to their groups will set their levels of aspiration more congruent with the group's goal for them than will those who are less attracted to their groups.

In a group where the members are facilitatively interdependent (Thomas, 1957), as is the case in the present study, we anticipate that those who set their levels of aspiration to be highly congruent with the goal put before them will be more concerned to ensure that the group has a high quality of effort than those who set their levels of aspiration to be less congruent with that goal. This hypothesis is based on the assumption that persons whose levels of aspiration are highly congruent with the group's goal value the achievement of that goal and can ensure their attainment of it by exercising forces on others to work toward that goal. Specifically, we predict that members who place their levels of aspiration closer to the group's goal for them will set higher goals for the group when asked to vote on this matter and will give their goals for the group greater strength; that is, they will more strongly desire the group to achieve the goals they set for it.

If the assumption is correct that members who place their levels of aspiration highly congruent with the goals set for them by the group strongly value the achievement of that goal, it follows that such persons will likewise be concerned with their own achievement. The pressures persons place on themselves to achieve an established level of aspiration is the *personal strength* of that aspiration. We predict that highly congruent persons will have greater personal strength of aspiration than less congruent persons.

Members who place their levels of aspiration congruent with the goals set for them are, we assume, more likely to internalize these goals. Internalization is defined as the degree to which a person takes the expectations of others as expectations he holds for himself. In the present instance a person who has *strongly* internalized the group's goal for him not only sets his level of aspiration close to the location of that goal, but also evaluates the success or failure of his behavior in the light of the proximity of his performance to his internalized goal. A person who has *weakly* internalized the group's goal for him tends to set his level of aspiration less congruent to that goal and not to evaluate the success or failure of his performance in terms of attainment of that goal. We predict, then, that persons whose levels of aspiration are more congruent with the group's goal for them will more often evaluate their performances in terms of how close these performances are to the level of the group's goals than will persons whose levels of aspiration are less congruent with these goals.

How much will members individually produce under the various conditions thus far considered? One may readily anticipate from the earlier assumptions that persons whose levels of aspiration are more highly congruent with the goal set for them by the group will more often produce as asked by the group, that is, if the group's goal is high they will produce more than if the group's goal is low.

DESCRIPTION OF THE EXPERIMENT

The participants in this experiment were 160 undergraduate men at the University of Michigan. They were recruited from college classes by inviting them to take part in research on the productivity of groups. Eight subjects were asked to appear at each experimental session. Care was taken to ensure that they were strangers to one another.

At the outset of the session they were informed that this study was being done for the United States Air Force to 'survey the general ability of college students to get things done, according to rules and in good time'. The importance of an individual's 'aptitude' for this type of achievement was emphasized by stating in some detail that the results on this test have been found to be good indicators of how well a person conducted himself in a variety of jobs. Each group was told that the members' individual tasks were to find marked beans in a box containing a large quantity of marked and unmarked beans, to place them in a bottle, and to work at this for an indefinite number of three-minute trials. It was said that the task was made simple so that motor skill would not be a primary factor in determining their scores. They were also told that the group would have the freedom to determine the pace of its members by means of a voting procedure, to be described later on.

'Your score', they were told, 'will be determined by the number of marked beans credited to you. One-half of your score is the number of beans you select, the other half is the number of beans found by your group as a whole.' This was stated so that the participants would see themselves as interdependent, and so that it would appear reasonable for the remaining members of the group to make demands on each member and for each member to make demands on the others. It was stated that their scores would be privately reported to them at the end of the session.

Following these instructions, the subjects were seated at eight cubicles. No subject could see or talk to another. On the table within each cubicle was a cardboard box containing five pounds of ordinary navy beans, half a pound of which were marked with a black India-ink spot. Attached to the left side of each partition was an opaque bottle. During the task participants wore work gloves which made it difficult to pick up more than one bean at a time.

At the end of each three-minute period box and bottle were removed and a fresh box and bottle were substituted. During each intermission between trials each subject filled out a brief form asking for two types of information. One question concerned the *member's goal for the group*. He was asked to complete the statement: 'The group should increase its speed by _____% during the next work-interval.' The percentage was to describe the increase in number of marked beans to be picked in the next trial over those found in the present trial. Note that the subjects had no way of knowing exactly how many marked beans one another had found in the previous trial. The second query concerned the *strength* members placed upon their goal for the group. Here the subject was asked to check a preferred point on a five-item scale (very strongly to very slightly) in response to the question: 'How strongly do you want them to do this?'

The experimenter collected these forms and visibly computed average percentages for the group, excluding the vote of each subject in turn. The appropriate percentage was then reported to each member as the *group's goal for the member*. The report read: 'Your group wants you to increase by _____% during the next work interval.' This report, however, did not depend upon what the subjects had written but instead followed a pre-determined series of percentages and each group member in a given condition received the same percentage on any one trial. The varied degree of difficulty inherent in the group's goal for the member was created by the size of the percentage put before the subjects at the beginning of each trial, starting with trial No. 2. Percentages reported to the subjects in order to generate *difficult* and *easy* goals for each trial are shown in the following tabulation.

Number of trial	2	3	4	5	6	7	8	Mn.
Difficult group goal for member, percentages	14	12	12	11	10	10	9	11·4
Easy group goal for member, percentages	14	7	7	6	5	5	4	6·85

The easy goals were known, from pretests, to be achieved by most persons with some effort, while the difficult goals were known to be achievable only with great effort. The first amount (14 per cent) was made the same for both difficult and easy conditions in order to establish a common baseline against which subsequent percentages could be evaluated as high or low. The decreasing size in the percentages in each series was adopted since it was consistent with the inclinations of subjects in pretests gradually to ease their goals for the members. The participants were told that a good score required that a group performance must improve by at least 4 per cent on each trial, a statement intended to give them a point of reference in evaluating the adequacy of their own aspirations and of the group's goal for the member on each trial.

The slip given to the subject by the experimenter also described the *strength* of the particular goal for the member. It read, referring to the level of the group's goal for the member: 'They want you to do this [very strongly or very slightly, as the case may have been].' In any one experimental condition all members received the same reports.

The two conditions of difficulty and the two degrees of strength were created in a 2-by-2 factorial design.

Each subject now completed a second brief form. First, he was asked to state his *level of aspiration* with the question: 'I should increase my speed by _____ % during the next interval.' In the analysis of the data, levels of aspiration were examined in respect to their congruence with the goal for the members that had been reported to them before the immediately preceding trial. Second, he was asked about his *strength of aspiration* with the query: 'How strongly do you want yourself to do this?' (a five-item scale, very strongly to very slightly, was to be marked). These were collected by the experimenter and not revealed to the rest of the subjects.

The *production* of the subjects was measured, by the use of a graduated tube, in terms of cubic millimeters of marked beans found during each trial.

After the eighth trial subjects were asked to complete a questionnaire with the understanding that they would return to work when it was completed. The instrument contained queries concerning their reactions to the group in which they had worked and to other conditions created in the experiment. When this form had been completed, the purposes of the experimental conditions were explained and all questions were answered.

RESULTS

Levels of Aspiration

We consider first how much the difficulty of the group's goal for the member and the strength of this goal serves to determine the members' stated levels of aspiration. A summary of these results, averaged across all trials, is shown in *Table 1*.

In general, variations in the difficulty of the group's goal for them bore little relationship to the members' levels of aspiration. Persons who had the more difficult goals placed their levels of aspiration somewhat higher than those who had easier goals, holding strength of the pressures constant, but this difference was not statistically significant. Further, curves showing the mean levels of aspiration trial by trial, for those with a difficult goal and for those with an easy goal, are almost identical after the second trial. The average discrepancy between the members' levels of aspiration and the goals set for them is greater when the goal is difficult (discrepancy = 3·54) than when the goal is easy (discrepancy = · 51), but the difference between these discrepancies is unimportant, given the facts that the difficult goals set for the member were much higher (Mn. = 11·14) than the easy goals (Mn. = 6·85), and that the levels of aspiration do not differ significantly under separate degrees of difficulty.

Table 1. Group's Goal for Member and Members' Levels of Aspiration

	Mean level of group's goals for members	Mean members' levels of aspiration	*t*
1. Difficult goals for members	11·14	7·60 [a]	a vs. b= ·98
2. Easy goals for members	6·85	6·34 [b]	
3. Strong social pressures	9·00	8·41 [c]	c vs. d=3·94***
4. Weak social pressures	9·00	5·99 [d]	
5. Difficult goals, strong press.	11·14	8·87 [e]	e vs. f=3·16***
6. Difficult goals, weak press.	11·14	6·33 [f]	
7. Easy goals, strong press.	6·85	7·93 [g]	g vs. h=2·58**
8. Easy goals, weak press.	6·85	5·62 [h]	

$**p < ·01$, $***p < ·001$, by *t* test.
Note. e vs. g, and f vs. h, not significant.

For each particular goal, it will be recalled, the member was told how strongly the rest of the group desired him to reach that goal. The results reveal that the stronger the pressure on the member to achieve any given goal, the higher the member placed his level of aspiration. This result held true regardless of the difficulty of the goal, as may be seen in the lower four rows of *Table 1*. In the context of this experiment, apparently, stronger pressures were interpreted by members and accepted by them as inductions to set higher levels of aspiration.

When the goal was a difficult one, stronger pressures generated greater congruence than weaker pressures, as may be seen in rows 5 and 6 of *Table 1*. Where the goal was an easy one (rows 7 and 8), it is evident that stronger pressures caused members to place their aspirations above the easy goal (mean members' aspiration of 7·93 exceeded the mean group goal of 6·85 by 1·08 units), and that weaker pressures caused members to place their aspirations below the goal for the member (mean members' aspirations of 5·62 below groups's goal of 6·85 by −1·23 units). The 1·08 and the −1·23 are not significantly different. We conclude that stronger pressures generated greater congruence than weaker pressures, but only when goals were difficult.[1]

It is useful, for the examination of subsequent results, to consider two separate categories of subjects: those whose levels of aspiration were highly congruent with the goal set before them and those whose levels of aspiration were less congruent with that goal. *Highly congruent* members are those who set their levels of aspiration at least as high as the group's goal for them on four or more of the seven trials (excluding the first trial). *Less congruent* members are those who set their levels of aspiration lower than the group's goal for them on four or more of the seven trials. A larger proportion of highly congruent persons ($N=45$) appeared under easier goals and stronger pressures ($p < \cdot 001$) and a larger proportion of less congruent persons ($N=115$) occurred under more difficult goals and weaker pressures ($p < \cdot 001$).

Concern with Group

Are those members whose levels of aspiration were highly congruent with the goals set for them by their group more attracted to their group than those whose aspirations were less congruent? It was predicted that they would be. In the questionnaire given at the end of the session the subjects were provided the following statement: 'There is another group of students who are taking this Achievement Aptitude Test at this very moment in another part of the building . . . You have an opportunity to complete this test either with this group or with your own group. Do you want to remain a member of your group?' Response alternatives were yes, no, or undecided. It can be seen in *Table 2* that highly congruent persons were more attracted to their group than less congruent persons.

The highly congruent members in addition set higher goals for the group than did the less congruent (see *Table 2*), and they more often

---

[1]To see if the level of aspiration remains high when difficulty is further increased while pressure is held constant and strong, a number of subjects, now included in the above results, were given during the fifth and sixth trial bottles with narrower openings, which allowed only one bean to be put in the bottle at a time, and that with care. (The special bottles were used rather than a further numberical increase in difficulty on the assumption that extremely high levels of difficulty would not be credible as typical of a group's vote.) All other conditions were the same. It was assumed that the special bottles made a given group goal more difficult to achieve than the same level goal with the regular bottles. That this assumption is probably correct was shown by a significantly slower production among those who had the special bottles. Persons who had the more difficult bottles set significantly lower ($p < \cdot 01$) levels of aspiration (Mn. $= 6 \cdot 72$) during the fifth and sixth trials than those who had the regular bottles (Mn. $= 8 \cdot 15$). The effect of strong pressures in generating higher levels of aspiration, then, apparently no longer holds at some greater level of difficulty.

placed high strength on their goals for the group than did the less congruent persons. These results indicate that highly congruent persons, as expected, were more concerned about the quality of effort by the group as a whole.

Table 2. Concern with Group by Highly Congruent and Less Congruent Members

	Highly congruent (N=45) %	Less congruent (N=115) %	χ^2
Want to remain in group?			
Yes	80	63	3·19*
No, undecided	20	37	
Difficulty of members' goals for group			
High	88	39	31·25***
Low	12	61	
Strength of members' goals for group			
Strong	81	47	14·61***
Weak	19	53	

*$p < ·05$, ***$p < ·001$.

Personal Strength of Aspirations

The personal strength of aspiration is an indication of how much an individual desires to attain his established level of aspiration. We anticipated that the strength of aspiration would be greater for persons with high congruity than for those with less congruity. Among the highly congruent, 75 per cent rated their strength of aspiration high (above median of all trials) and 25 per cent rated it low, while among the less congruent 40 per cent rated their strength of aspiration high and 60 per cent low. This distribution provides a chi-square of 14·96, significant at better than the ·001 level of confidence. Clearly, members with high congruity had stronger desires to achieve their levels of aspiration than did members with low congruity.

Internalization of Goals for Members

We expected that highly congruent members would more often internalize the goal set for them than would less congruent members and that highly congruent members, therefore, would more often evaluate their performances in terms of how close these performances came to the attainment of that goal. To test this hypothesis, the subjects were presented with this statement in the post-questionnaire: 'If during a ten-minute work period my actual percentage of increase in speed were *less* than the percentage my group said I should increase by, I would probably feel . . .' They then checked a preferred point on a seven-item scale, from 'very dissatisfied with myself' to 'very satisfied with myself'. In response to this hypothetical issue, highly congruent persons rated themselves as likely to be more dissatisfied than did less congruent ($t=3 \cdot 52$, $p < \cdot 01$). It appears that a larger number of strong internalizers were among the highly congruent members than among the less congruent ones.

In theories of aspiration-setting (Lewin *et al.*, 1944; Stotland, 1957) it is assumed that persons who fail to attain their aspired level will have stronger dissatisfactions (feelings of failure): (a) the easier the goal, and (b) the greater the valence of the goal. We inquire, then, whether highly congruent and less congruent individuals differ in their fulfillment of this assumption. In respect to the difficulty of the goal for the member, it may be seen, in *Table 3*, that when the goal is easy less congruent persons, compared to highly congruent ones, are likely to feel less dissatisfaction from failing to attain the easy goal. When the goal is difficult, however, highly congruent and less congruent persons do not differ significantly in the amount of dissatisfaction they state they would feel.

Table 3. Dissatisfaction from Performing Below Group's Goal for Member

	Highly congruent (N=45)		Less congruent (N=115)		
	High dissat.	Low dissat.	High dissat.	Low dissat.	χ^2
Difficult goals for members	3	9	16	51	$\cdot 25$
Easy goals for members	18	14	4	44	$15 \cdot 90$***
χ^2	2$\cdot$27		3$\cdot$69		
Strong social pressures	17	15	7	40	$13 \cdot 23$***
Weak social pressures	4	8	13	55	$\cdot 53$
χ^2	1$\cdot$16		$\cdot 11$		

***$p < \cdot 001$.

We may assume, in the light of previous results, that the stronger the pressures on a member the more he tends to place value on the goal set for him. When the pressures were strong a greater proportion of persons with less congruity than of those with high congruity were little dissatisfied with their performances, but where the pressures were weak there was no significant difference in the dissatisfactions between persons with high and low congruity.

All in all, persons with high congruity, more than those with low congruity, reacted to the hypothetical failure as level of aspiration theory would lead us to expect. Thus, we conclude that the levels of aspiration stated by persons with high congruity were more likely to have been the result of internalizing the goal set for them than were the levels of aspiration among persons with low congruity.

Speed of Work

The number of marked beans selected by each person indicates the amount of his movement toward the goal. The average group goals for the member for all conditions required a 9 per cent increase in speed of production, whereas the average *actual* percentage of increase by subjects was just under 6 per cent. Thus, on the whole, members did not perform as well as asked to by their groups.

Highly congruent persons did not produce significantly more than less congruent persons, nor did they conform more closely in their actual increases of production, from trial to trial, to the increases requested of them by their groups. We conclude that highly congruent persons who, as we have already noted, apparently accepted the goal set for them came no closer to reaching that goal than less congruent persons who apparently rejected the goal set for them.

In so far as difficulty of the goal for the member is concerned, it was found that those who were given more difficult goals tended to produce slightly better than those with easy goals, but the relationship was not statistically significant. In respect to the strength of the pressures there was an inverse relationship: the weaker the pressures the more members produced ($t=1 \cdot 90$, $p < \cdot 05$). This inverse relationship between the strength of the pressures and the rate of production was statistically significant, regardless of the difficulty of the goal, on all but two of the seven trials. It seems evident that members worked in opposition to the social pressures acting upon them: when the pressures were strong members worked slowly, and when they were weak members worked rapidly. Apparently the stronger pressures developed resistance in the participants in respect to the speed of production.

We may develop some understanding of this resistance by determining under what conditions the inverse relationship is stronger. It seems reasonable, for example, that persons with high congruity would be less likely to develop actions opposing the pressures than those with low congruity, because, as we have seen earlier, persons with high congruity appeared to internalize the goals set for them more than did those with low congruity. This anticipation, however, was not supported. In both highly congruent and less congruent persons the inverse relationship between strength of pressures and amount of production occurred. Furthermore, the inverse relationship between strength of pressures and rate of production was present regardless of the amount of internalization among persons with either high congruity or low congruity. Thus, the inverse relationship was apparently not affected by the degree that members' levels of aspiration were congruent with the goals held for them by their groups.

We consider, next, the strength of the members' personal levels of aspiration, defined earlier as the strength of the desire to achieve an established level of aspiration. We assume that those with a greater strength of aspiration have a clearer and more distinct own goal, toward which they intend to direct their efforts, than do those with weaker strengths of aspiration. The inverse relationship (between strength of pressures and rate of production) is reasonably strong among persons with greater strengths of aspiration (see *Table 4*) but is almost exactly what would be obtained by chance among persons with weaker aspirations. Plainly, it is members with greater strengths of aspiration who acted opposite to the intended pressures of their groups. This held true, incidentally, regardless of the absolute height of the members' levels of aspiration.

Table 4. Number of Persons with a Given Personal Strength of Aspiration and Their Rates of Production

	Greater strength of aspiration		Weaker strength of aspiration		
	High prod.	Low prod.	High prod.	Low prod.	χ^2
Strong social pressures ($N=79$)	23	32	12	12	n.s.
Weak social pressures ($N=80$)	19	6	27	28	$4 \cdot 05^*$
χ^2	$6 \cdot 74^{**}$		n.s.		

$^*p < \cdot 025$, $^{**}p < \cdot 01$.

It appears likely that persons with stronger aspirations desired to achieve their aspirations on their own, independently of the group. This desire for independence, then, manifested itself in actions opposing the pressures from the group. Persons with weaker strength of aspiration, in contrast, were not differentially influenced by variations in the strength of the pressures on them in so far as their rates of production were concerned, seemingly, because they were not greatly concerned to obtain a respectable score.

In summary, variations in the difficulty of the goal for the member had no clear consequence for members' rates of production. Weaker pressures appeared to generate greater production than stronger pressures primarily among persons who had a strong desire to achieve their established aspirations. The congruity among personal aspirations and the group's goal for the member had no effect upon rate of production.

SUMMARY

This experiment was concerned with the sources of congruity between a member's level of aspiration and the group's goal for the member. The goal put before him, which each member viewed as the choice of others in his group excluding his own vote, was predetermined by the experimenter for each of seven trials. It was either an easy goal or a difficult one and was reported to each member by the experimenter as being either a region the group strongly desired the member to reach or as one the group weakly desired the member to reach. A second purpose of the study was to examine the relationship between degree of congruity and the attitudes and behaviors of members.

The major findings were the following.

1. Variations in difficulty of the group's goal for the member had no appreciable effect upon where members set their levels of aspiration or upon congruence between levels of aspiration and the group's goal for the member.

2. Members set higher levels of aspiration the stronger the pressures on them to attain a given goal. When the goal was difficult, stronger pressures generated greater congruence than did weaker pressures. When the goal was easy, however, the strength of pressures bore no relationship to congruence.

3. Members who set their levels of aspiration more congruent with the goal that the group had voted for them showed greater involvement in their group than the members who set their levels of aspiration less congruent with that goal: they were more attracted to membership in the group, they set higher goals for the group, and they attached higher strength to the goals they set for the group.

4. Persons who set their levels of aspiration more congruent with the goal set for them had greater strengths of aspiration (i.e. more desire to achieve their established levels of aspiration) than persons who set their levels of aspiration less congruent with the goal.

5. Members who placed their levels of aspiration more congruent with the group's goal more often internalized that goal than did persons who placed their levels of aspiration less congruent with the goal; as

shown by their tendency to evaluate their performances in terms of proximity of achievement of the internalized group goal.

6. Persons exposed to weak pressures tended to produce more than those exposed to strong pressures. This inverse relationship between strength of pressures and rate of production was limited to those persons who had greater strengths of personal aspiration. Apparently they desired independence from the group and thus worked in opposition to the pressures placed upon them. Members given easy goals by their groups produced no more nor less than those given difficult goals.

The conclusion is obvious that members, who apparently accept as individual aspirations the goals that are put before them by their group, do not thereafter always perform so as to fulfill these personal aims. The distinctions among (a) the member's goal for the group, (b) the group's goal, (c) the group's goal for the member, and (d) the member's personal goal were found to be an heuristic aid, but further study is needed before the relations among these concepts (or substitutes for them) can be fully understood and before the effects of social pressures within this system of goals can be explained.

REFERENCES

Berkowitz, L. (1954). Group standards, cohesiveness, and productivity. *Hum. Relat.*, *7*, 509-19.

French, J. R. P., Jr., & Raven, B. (1959). The bases of social power. In D. Cartwright (Ed.), *Studies in social power*. Ann Arbor, Mich.: Inst. for Soc. Research.

Horwitz, M. (1954). The recall of interrupted group tasks. *Hum. Relat. 7*, 3-38.

Lewin, K., Dembo, Tamara, Festinger, L., & Sears, Pauline (1944). Level of aspiration. In J. McV. Hunt (Ed.), *Personality and the behavior disorders*. New York: Ronald.

Raven, B., & French, J. R. P., Jr. (1958). Group support, legitimate power and social influence. *J. Personality 26*, 400-9.

Schachter, S., Ellerton, Nancy, McBride, Dorothy, & Gregory, Doris (1951). An experimental study of cohesiveness and productivity. *Hum. Relat. 4*, 229-38.

Stotland, E., Thorley, S., Thomas, E., Cohen, A., & Zander, A. (1957). The effects of group expectations and self-esteem upon self evaluation. *J. abnor. soc. Psychol. 54*, 55-63.

Thomas, E. J. (1957). Effects of facilitative role interdependence on group functioning. *Hum. Relat.*, *10*, 347-66.

Trust and Managerial Problem Solving

by Dale E. Zand

This paper presents a model of trust and its interaction with information flow, influence, and control, and reports on an experiment based on the model to test several hypotheses about problem-solving effectiveness. The subjects were managers and the independent variable was the individual manager's initial level of trust. Groups of business executives were given identical factual information about a difficult manufacturing-marketing policy problem; half the groups were briefed to expect trusting behavior, the other half to expect untrusting behavior. There were highly significant differences in effectiveness between the high-trust groups and the low-trust groups in the clarification of goals, the reality of information exchanged, the scope of search for solutions, and the commitment of managers to implement solutions. The findings indicate that shared trust or lack of trust apparently are a significant determinant of managerial problem-solving effectiveness. [1]

There is increasing research evidence that trust is a salient factor in determining the effectiveness of many relationships, such as those between parent and child (Baldwin *et al.*, 1945), psychotherapist and client (Fiedler, 1953; Seeman, 1954), and members of problem-solving groups (Parloff and Handlon, 1966). Trust facilitates interpersonal acceptance and openness of expression, whereas mistrust evokes interpersonal rejection and arouses defensive behavior (Gibb, 1961).

During the past fifteen years many managers have been introduced to programs, variously called sensitivity training (Bradford *et al.*, 1964), grid laboratories (Blake and Mouton, 1964), or group workshops (Schein and

---

[1]This article is based on a paper presented to the 17th International Congress of Applied Psychology, Liege, Belgium, July 1971.

From *Administrative Science Quarterly*, 1972, 17(2). Reprinted by permission.

Bennis, 1965), to improve their skills in developing trust and thus, presumably, their managerial effectiveness. It has been difficult, however, to show a direct correlation between trust and managerial effectiveness in a working organization (Dunnette and Campbell, 1968; House, 1967), so that there is a need to clarify the theoretical basis for assertions about trust and managerial effectiveness and to devise experiments to test them.

INTRODUCTION

Rogers (1961) found that in an effective helping relationship, one participant (counselor, therapist, helper) behaved in ways that developed trust and the other experienced an increase in trust, and concluded that the development of trust is a crucial initial factor and a necessary continuing element in such a relationship. He summarized extensive research in which an increase in trust appeared to be causally related to more rapid intellectual development, increased originality, increased emotional stability, increased self-control and decreased physiological arousal to defend against threat.

The level of trust in a relationship affects the degree of defensiveness. Gibb (1961) found that members of small groups that developed a "defensive climate," had difficulty concentrating on messages, perceived the motives, values, and emotions of others less accurately, and increased the distortion of messages. Other studies suggest that some interpersonal trust is required for effective problem solving in a group. Parloff and Handlon (1966) found that intensive, persistent criticism increased defensiveness and mistrust among members of a group and decreased their ability to recognize and accept good ideas. Meadow *et al.* (1959) reported that defensiveness induced a lasting decrease in problem-solving effectiveness. They found that groups penalized for poor ideas and admonished to produce only good ideas while working on early problems produced poorer solutions to later problems when these restrictions were removed than groups that were not penalized and admonished during their early problem assignments.

This paper: (1) analyzes the concept of trust, (2) presents a model of the interaction of trust and problem-solving behavior, and (3) reports the results of an experiment that attempted to test several hypotheses derived from the model.

ANALYSIS OF CONCEPT

Trusting behavior, following Deutsch (1962), is defined here as consisting of actions that (a) increase one's vulnerability, (b), to another whose behavior is not under one's control, (c) in a situation in which the penalty (disutility) one suffers if the other abuses that vulnerability is greater than the benefit (utility) one gains if the other does not abuse that vulnerability. For example, a parent is exhibiting trusting behavior in hiring a baby sitter so he can see a movie. The action significantly increases his vulnerability, since he cannot control the baby sitter's behavior after leaving the house. If the baby sitter abuses that vulnerability, the penalty may be a tragedy that may adversely affect the rest of his life; if the baby sitter does not abuse that vulnerability, the benefit will be the pleasure of seeing a movie. Thus trust, as the term will be used in this paper, is not a global feeling of warmth or affection, but the conscious regulation of one's dependence on another that will vary with the task, the situation, and the other person.

MODEL

The following model, based on Gibb, (1964), conceptualizes the transforming of one's inner state of trust (or mistrust) into behavior that is trusting (or mistrusting) through (1) information, (2) influence, and (3) control.

One who does not trust others will conceal or distort relevant information, and avoid stating or will disguise facts, ideas, conclusions and feelings that he believes will increase his exposure to others, so that the information he provides will be low in accuracy, comprehensiveness, and timeliness; and therefore have low congruence with reality. He will also resist or deflect the attempts of others to exert influence. He will be suspicious of their views, and not receptive to their proposals of goals, their suggestions for reaching goals, and their definition of criteria and methods for evaluating progress. Although he rejects the influence of others, he will expect them to accept his views. Finally, one who does not trust will try to minimize his dependence on others. He will feel he cannot rely on them to abide by agreements and will try to impose controls on their behavior when coordination is necessary to attain common goals, but will resist and be alarmed at their attempts to control his behavior.

When others encounter low-trust behavior, initially they will hesitate to reveal information, reject influence, and evade control. This short cycle feedback will reinforce the originator's low trust, and unless there are changes in behavior, the relationship will stabilize at a low level of trust.

All of this behavior, following from a lack of trust, will be deleterious to information exchange, to reciprocity of influence, and to the exercise of self-control, and will diminish the effectiveness of joint problem-solving efforts.

To the objective uncertainty inherent in a problem, for example, unavailable facts and unknown causal relationships between actions and results, low trust will add social uncertainty; that is, uncertainty introduced by individuals withholding or distorting relevant information and concepts.

Persons lacking trust attempting to solve a problem jointly will attempt to minimize their vulnerability. There will be an increase in the likelihood of misunderstanding or misinterpretation. The social uncertainty induced by their low trust will increase the probability that underlying problems may go undetected or be avoided, and that inappropriate solutions may be more difficult to identity. If the group is incapable of breaking out of this ineffective pattern of problem solving, it may seize an expedient solution as a device to end its work and dissolve itself.

Persons who trust one another will provide relevant, comprehensive, accurate, and timely information, and thereby contribute realistic data for problem-solving efforts. They will have less fear that their exposure will be abused, and will therefore be receptive to influence from others. They will also accept interdependence because of confidence that others will control their behavior in accordance with agreements, and therefore will have less need to impose controls on others, (see Figure 1). Consequently they will contribute to a decrease in social uncertainty, and be less likely to misinterpret the intentions and the behavior of others. As a result, underlying problems are more likely to be identified and examined, and solutions more likely to be appropriate, creative, and long-range.

Hypotheses

It is not assumed here that trust alone will solve a technical problem; it is assumed that group members collectively have adequate knowledge, experience, and creativity to define and solve a complex problem. It is also assumed that it is possible to increase or decrease trust in members of a problem-solving group.

On the basis of the model described, the following differences can be predicted in the problem-solving behavior of groups with high and low trust.

An increase in trust will increase the exchange of accurate, comprehensive, and timely information. Problem-solving groups and high trust will:

Hypothesis 1. Exchange relevant ideas and feelings more openly,

Hypothesis 2. Develop greater clarification of goals and problems.

Hypothesis 3. Search more extensively for alternative courses of action,

Hypothesis 4. Have greater influence on solutions.

Finally, an increase in trust will increase willingness to control one's own behavior, will increase confidence in the reliability of others, and will decrease efforts to control the behavior of others, all of which will contribute to increased satisfaction and motivation. Hence, problem-solving groups with high trust will:

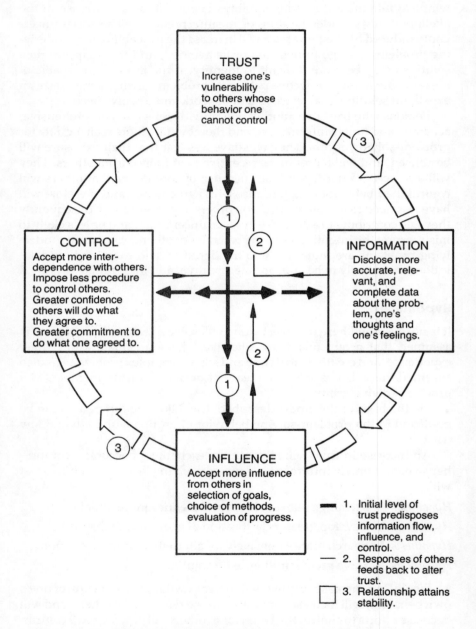

Figure 1. A model of the relationship of trust to information, influence, and control.

Hypothesis 5. Be more satisfied with their problem-solving efforts,

Hypothesis 6. Have greater motivation to implement conclusions,

Hypothesis 7. See themselves as closer and more of a team,

Hypothesis 8. Have less desire to leave their group to join another.

Dynamics of Trust

Trust takes form in the interaction of two (or more) people, and the dynamics of this interaction is illustrated in Figure 2.

An increase in trust will increase the willingness to influence others and the receptivity to the influence of others. Hence, problem-solving groups with high trust will:

Let P denote one person and O the other. If (1) P lacks trust, (2) he will disclose little relevant or accurate information, be unwilling to share influence, and will attempt to control O. (3) Assume O also lacks trust, (4) perceives P's initial behavior as actually untrusting, and (5) concludes he was right to expect P to be untrustworthy; then (6) he will feel justified in his mistrust of P. Since (7) P sees O's behavior as untrusting, he (8) will be confirmed in his initial expectation that O would not be trustworthy and (2) P will behave with less trust than when he entered.

The interaction will continue around the loop inducing O and P to behave with less and less trust until they arrive at an equilibrium level of low trust, each attempting to minimize his vulnerability and to maximize his control of the other. In the process the effectiveness of problem solving will decrease. After interaction has continued, each will tend to hold more firmly to his entering beliefs. They will not have a reliable basis for accepting or sharing influence, and the mutual resistance to influence will arouse feelings of frustration in both. If they have a deadline, each will attempt to impose controls on the other. If P is O's organizational superior, he may command O's compliance, which will reinforce O's mistrust. Usually, by the middle of the meeting the level of trust will be lower than the initial level.

Gibb (1964) offers support for the dynamics of this interaction. In observing small group behavior he noted that the defensive behavior of a listener generated cues which subsequently increased the defensiveness of the communicator, resulting, if unchecked, in a circular pattern of escalating defensiveness.

The pattern of spiral reinforcement illustrated in Figure 2 would operate constructively if it is assumed that both P and O entered the relationship with trust in the other. Gibb (1964) observed that when defensiveness was reduced, members were better able to concentrate on the content and meaning of a message, became more problem oriented, and were less concerned about imposing controls on each other's behavior.

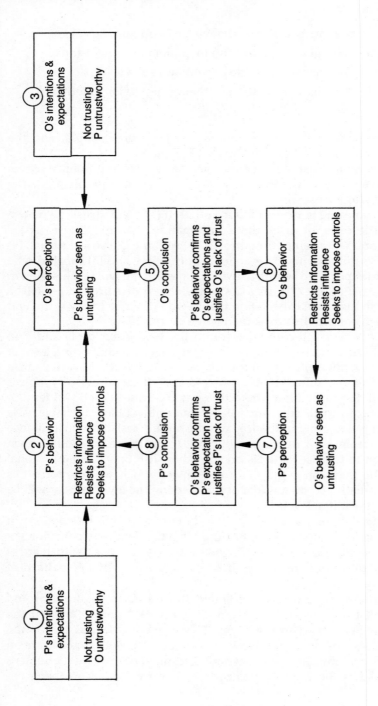

Figure 2. A model of the interaction of two persons with similar intentions and expectations regarding trust.

METHOD

The spiral reinforcement model of the dynamics of trust (Figure 2) has been presented to establish a theoretical rationale for the methods used to induce different levels of trust, but this study did not focus on a test of the spiral reinforcement model. The aim of this study was to examine the relation between trust and problem-solving effectiveness as formulated in the eight hypotheses.

To test the hypotheses derived from the model, the research was designed so that half of the experimental groups started work on a business-management problem with a mental set toward low trust and half with a mental set toward high trust. Mental set, as used here, includes intentions as to one's behavior, expectations as to the behavior of others, feelings such as anxiety or discomfort, and cognitive frame used to interpret events and form perceptions. In this research trust was not examined as a personality variable; that is, an element of individual character, but as an induced attitude, one that the individual could alter in a situation in which he was led to intend and to expect trust (or mistrust) from others as he attempted to solve a problem. Because trust as a personality trait was not relevant, and to avoid alerting the subjects to the issue of trust, no prior measures were taken of the subject's attitude toward trust.

Subjects. Because of their high potential for top management, upper-middle managers from all functions and product divisions of a large, international electronics company were periodically selected by their superiors, after discussion with the corporate personnel staff, to attend an off-site, four-week, in-residence program in management development given several times a year that accepted sixteen managers at a time. Eight managers in each program, were randomly chosen to be subjects and distributed into two problem-solving groups, each with four members. The remaining eight managers were observers; each was randomly assigned to a group with four members and each group observed one problem-solving group. Data were gathered in eight programs providing a total of sixty-four subjects in sixteen problem-solving groups and fifty-nine observers (five programs were short one manager) in sixteen observing groups. There were no subordinates, superiors, or peers from the same department or division in any program. Interviews confirmed that the subjects and the observers did not know about the experiment, which was designed as a learning event embedded in the program.

Problem. The central problems involved (1) developing a strategy to increase short-term profits without undermining long-term growth of a medium-sized electronics company with very low return on investment, outdated manufacturing facilities, whose labor force had been cut 25 percent and whose top management personnel had been changed and reorganized two years before, and (2) obtaining commitment to implement such a program despite strong managerial disappointment because expectations of immediate investment for expansion and modernization would not be met. The situation, a variation of one described by Maier *et al.* (1959), involved four executive roles: president and vice presidents for marketing, manufacturing, and personnel. Subjects were randomly assigned to the roles.

Procedure. All subjects and observers were given a written description of the production, marketing, financial, and personnel difficulties of the company.

In the presence of the observers, subjects were told they were to conduct a meeting lasting thirty minutes in the president's office to make appropriate management decisions. Ostensibly, they were to demonstrate their decision-making competence to their fellow managers, the observers.

Each subject was then given an additional written statement with factual and attitudinal information relevant to his function. He had no knowledge of the role information given to other subjects. The subjects privately read and absorbed this problem information for twenty-five minutes so there would be minimal need to refer to it during the meeting.

Treatments. Subjects were randomly assigned to one of two group conditions: an entering mental set toward high or low trust.

The factual data about production, marketing, finance, and so on was identical in both conditions, and all vice presidents were led to expect that the president would announce approval of a long-studied plant expansion.

In both conditions the president's statement told him that on the preceding day, he had received an ultimatum from the board of directors demanding an increase in profits within one year or else he would be forced to resign. Furthermore, he was told that expansion was not feasible because it would reduce short-term profits, take more than a year to build and start up a new plant, and the board was not likely to approve the financing, so as a first step toward increasing profits, he would have to announce his decision against expansion. The vice presidents had no knowledge of the president's dilemma when they started their thirty-minute problem-solving meeting.

Induction of conditions of trust. The induction of the two levels of trust was accomplished by operating on the following entering beliefs of subjects: (1) the task competence of others, (2) norms on introducing information and new ideas, (3) norms on attempts to influence managers outside of one's primary responsibility, (4) likelihood that others would abuse trusting behavior, and (5) competitiveness or collaborativeness for rewards.

In a high-trust group, a manager's entering mental set toward trust was shaped by the following paragraph, which followed the factual information in the role statement:

> You have learned from your experiences during the past two years that you can trust the other members of top management. You and the other top managers openly express your differences and your feelings of encouragement or of disappointment. You and the others share all relevant information and freely explore ideas and feelings that may be in or out of your defined responsibility. The result has been a high level of give and take and mutual confidence in each other's support and ability.

Subjects in low-trust groups had a similar paragraph in their role information, but worded to induce a decrease in trust.

The reward system was operated on by information placed only in the president's statement. In the high-trust condition, the president was led to see his relation to his vice presidents as collaborative. His role statement said that "although the Board's decision considered you specifically, since you appointed the current top management team it is likely that the Board will go outside for a successor and possibly other vice presidents."

In the low-trust condition the president was led to see his relation to his vice presidents as potentially competitive. His role statement said that since the board's ultimatum pertained to him, it was possible that they might appoint one of the vice presidents as his successor. The vice presidents in both conditions were given no information about whether their relation to the president was potentially competitive or collaborative.

All subjects were told that "whenever information is incomplete, introduce whatever facts and experiences seem reasonable under the circumstances."

Observers. In addition to reading the written general description of the company's problems, before observing the problem-solving meeting, the observers were told of the vice presidents' factual basis for seeking and expecting to get final approval for plant expansion and that the president had received a one-year ultimatum from the board the preceding day, but they were given no information about the attitudinal parts of the statements.

Measures. After thirty minutes, group discussion was stopped and each subject and observer completed a questionnaire with eight or nine items. The respondent was to indicate whether in his group, or the group he observed, there was "much" or "little" of the property described in each item.

The items were: (1) trust, (2) openness about feelings, (3) clarification of the group's basic problems and goals, (4) search for alternative courses of action, (5) mutual influence on outcomes, (6) satisfaction with the meeting, (7) motivation to implement decisions, (8) closeness as a management team as a result of the meeting. The subjects' questionnaire had a ninth item: "As a result of this meeting would you give little or much serious consideration to a position with another company?" The written statement could only suggest to each subject an entering mental set toward high or low trust. By the end of the meeting each subject's level of trust would depend on the extent to which his entering beliefs were confirmed by the behavior of the other managers.

RESULTS

Measures of Trust. The responses of subjects and of observers are reported separately in Table 1, with the chi-square value for each item.

The subjects' rating of level of trust confirms that the induction of high and low trust was successful ($p < .001$) after one-half hour of problem discussion. This result, although not a direct test of the spiral reinforcement model, does offer support for it.

Since the observers used only their personal standards for their ratings, it is noteworthy that they had little difficulty recognizing the behavior indicative of low or high trust ($p < .001$).

The hypotheses about differences between groups with high or low trust were confirmed by the responses of the subjects (items 2-9, $p < .001$) and observers (items 3-9, $p < .001$; item 2, $p < .05$).

Qualitative Differences. There were also observable qualitative differences in the comprehensiveness and creativity of the problem solving of the two groups.

High-Trust Groups. In the high-trust groups the president consistently disclosed voluntarily the board's demand for better short-term performance. These teams, after initial frustration with the disapproval of immediate expansion, dealt with the short-range plans to increase profitability and then began to design long-range plans for modernization and expansion that they would present to the board.

Short-range plans emerging from the discussion among the vice presidents included straightforward proposals to review the product line, to identify and promote sales of high-profit items, and to cut back output of low-profit items. Their more creative proposals, flowing from substantial changes in their perceptions, included, for example, leasing space in a nearby vacant plant, rearranging work flow, selectively modernizing equipment that would provide greatest cost benefits and require minimal capital, subcontracting standard components, and rapidly converting

Table 1. Frequency of Response to Each Item by Subjects and Observers Under High Trust and Low Trust with Chi-Square Values for Differences

Item	Response	Subjects			Observers		
		Condition			Condition		
		High trust	Low trust	χ^{2*}	High trust	Low trust	χ^{2***}
1. Trust	Much	30	9	28.1	19	7	16.7
	Little	2	23		6	26	
2. Openness about feelings	Much	31	15	26.4	15	12	4.2
	Little	1	17		7	21	
3. Clarification of problems and goals	Much	24	10	10.8	18	7	12.9
	Little	8	22		8	26	
4. Search	Much	21	6	13.8	11	5	14.7
	Little	11	26		11	28	
5. Influence	Much	29	6	30.8	19	2	32.0
	Little	3	26		6	31	
6. Satisfaction	Much	28	7	25.6	20	2	32.7
	Little	4	25		6	31	
7. Motivation to implement conclusions	Much	30	10	26.6	19	4	22.2
	Little	2	22		7	29	
8. Closeness as a team	Much	27	9	19.1	17	5	16.6
	Little	5	23		9	28	
9. Desire to take a job in another company	Much	8	22	10.8			
	Little	24	10				

*$p < .001$ for all χ^2 values in this column.
**$p < .001$ for all χ^2 values in this column except item 2 for which $p < .05$.

two new products from research to production. In one group the managers agreed to invest their personal savings to help finance modernization, to show the board their strong commitment to the company's future.

Low-Trust Groups. In low-trust groups, the vice presidents had difficulty understanding the basis for the president's decision against expansion and his desire for short-range profits. In several groups they asked him if there were reasons behind his decision other than those he had disclosed, but he steadfastly refused to reveal information about the board's demands. As a result the vice presidents in low-trust groups could not sense how close the company might be to reorganization and possibly dissolution. They spent most of the meeting disagreeing with the president by repeating their basic arguments for immediate expansion. Finally, after prolonged frustration, the president would impose directives on the group. Usually he would demand review of the product line to eliminate low-profit items. If there was any creativity it came from the president, who was desperately seeking a solution in spite of the resistance of his vice presidents. Occasionally, the president would propose that it might be possible to lease space in a nearby vacant plant, but his idea would be discarded as unworkable by the belligerent vice presidents. In several groups the president threatened to dismiss a vice president.

Conversation among subjects of the low-trust groups after they had answered the questionnaire, showed the high defensiveness and antagonism they had induced in each other. For example, half the vice presidents said that they were so discouraged they had started to think of looking for another job in the middle of the meeting, and several said they hoped the president's plane would be hijacked or crash. The president usually retorted that he had decided to dismiss them before the next meeting.

Discussion. One might contend that the managers were attempting to follow rigidly the attitude toward trust suggested in their briefing, but in the debriefing interviews, the managers said that after their meeting had started, their level of trust varied in response to the behavior of the other managers. In low-trust groups, for example, about half of the vice presidents said that by the end of the meeting they found themselves trusting one or another vice president more than they expected to and trusting the president much less than when they had started.

That the pattern of spiral reinforcement requires all members of a group to hold similar intentions to trust (or not trust) may be too stringent a condition. The following anecdotal evidence suggests that several members with similar intentions may be sufficient. An unanticipated incident illustrates how difficult it may be for one person acting alone to break the reinforcement pattern even though he has formal power. In one low-trust group, in an effort to behave with trust toward his vice presidents, the president early in the meeting disclosed that the board wanted better profit performance in one year or else might ask for his resignation, but this attempt to show trust did not alter the emergence of low-trust behavior among the vice presidents. Indeed, in interviews after the meeting, the vice presidents said they interpreted the president's statement as a means of shifting blame to the board for his decision not to approve expansion, so that instead of increasing their trust, his behavior confirmed their mistrust. Also, they interpreted the president's comment that he might be forced to resign as evidence that the board did not trust him, so they should not either. Two vice presidents in this group said that by the middle of the meeting they were thinking about how they might hasten the president's resignation. It seems that behaving with high trust towards others who are not trusting will not necessarily induce trust, and if one does so it is wise to limit one's increase in vulnerability.

Another illustration of the difficulty of interrupting the spiral reinforcement pattern occurred in a high-trust group, in which the president did not reveal the board's demand for short-term profits. The vice presidents said that the president seemed troubled, and asked him if he was explaining all the reasons behind his decision not to expand. In the debriefing interviews, after they learned about the president's predicament, one vice president turned to the president and said, "Why didn't you tell us? We could have done so much more to help you and ourselves." The group's level of trust had remained high, but the creativity and comprehensiveness of its solutions had suffered in comparison with other high trust groups.

Because of the many limitations of the experiment—that is, the small number of subjects, data gathered over several years, the study conducted within the context of a management development program—the study was restricted to conditions in which all managers in a group had the same initial level of trust. The condition of mixed trust, in which some members would tend to trust and others would tend to mistrust, was not included; but one could predict that the effects on creativity and comprehensiveness of solutions, and on motivations to implement solutions might be intermediate between those of the high-trust and low-trust groups. The two incidents described above are consistent with such a prediction.

Furthermore the problem used in this study was quite complex, required that the participants generate the alternatives, and had no unique, optimal solution. There might be less of a difference in the output of high-trust and low-trust groups working on highly structured problems; that is, problems with clear, tangible goals, with well-defined information, with alternatives provided, and with a unique solution. Theoretically, the structure inherent in the problem might reduce a group's susceptibility to the social uncertainty generated by low-trust behavior. On the basis of the data in Table 1, however, it would seem that, given similar member competence, groups that develop high trust would solve problems more effectively than low trust groups, that is, they would do better in locating relevant information, in using their members' skills to generate alternatives, and in eliciting commitment.

The data also indicate that patterns of low-trust and high-trust group behavior are recognizable by untrained observers. Possibly the consistency between the responses of subjects and observers was increased by the fact that they were all managers in one company, presumably exposed to a common organizational culture, but any such effect was probably offset by the fact that they came from widely separated divisions, and some were foreign nationals who had worked in overseas subsidiaries.

Finally, this study revealed that theory and research on group forces have had only a minor impact on the thinking of managers. The managers in this study were among the best educated and the most sophisticated to be found in corporate organizations. After completing the questionnaires, but without any information about the trust model, they were brought together and asked for their explanation of what had happened in the two groups. They consistently responded that the outcomes were the result of the personalities of the men (who had been randomly assigned to the different roles) or the president's style (which they interpreted as autocratic or democratic) or the time he stated his decision not to expand (early or late in the meeting). The possibility that a shared level of trust, that is, a group force or a belief held by several or all members of a group, could constitute a social reality which could significantly affect problem-solving effectiveness was not mentioned.

CONCLUSIONS

The findings of this study confirm the hypotheses derived from the model. The results indicate that it is useful to conceptualize trust as behavior that conveys appropriate information, permits mutuality of influence, encourages self-control, and avoids abuse of the vulnerability of others.

It appears that when a group works on a problem, there are two concerns: one is the problem itself, the second is how the members relate to each other to work on the problem. Apparently in low-trust groups, interpersonal relationships interfere with and distort perceptions of the problem. Energy and creativity are diverted from finding comprehensive, realistic solutions, and members use the problem as an instrument to minimize their vulnerability. In contrast, in high-trust groups there is less socially generated uncertainty and problems are solved more effectively.

This study also offers qualitative support for the spiral-reinforcement model. It suggests that mutual trust or mistrust, among members of a group, are likely to be reinforced, unless there is marked or prolonged disconfirming behavior. Exactly what disconfirmation is needed and how much requires further investigation.

Finally, this research offers evidence that a social phenomenon, trust, can significantly alter managerial problem-solving effectiveness.

REFERENCES

Baldwin, Alfred L., Joan Kalhorn, and Fay Hoffman Breese, 1945. "Patterns of parent behavior." *Psychological Monograph*, 58, 268, pp. 1-75.

Blake, Robert R., and Jane S. Mouton, 1964. *The Managerial Grid*. Houston: Gulf Publishing.

Bradford, Leland P., Jack R. Gibb, and Kenneth D. Benne, 1964. *T-Group Theory and Laboratory Method*. New York: John Wiley.

Deutsch, Morton, 1962. "Cooperation and trust: some theoretical notes." In Marshall R. Jones (ed.), *Nebraska Symposium on Motivation*. Lincoln, Nebraska: University of Nebraska Press, pp. 275-319.

Dunnette, Marvin D., and John P. Campbell, 1968. "Laboratory education: impact on people and organizations." *Industrial Relations*, 8, 1, pp- 1-27.

Fiedler, Fred E., 1953. "Quantitative studies on the role of therapists' feelings toward their patients," in Orval H. Mowrer (ed.), *Psychotherapy: Theory and Research*. New York: Ronald Press, Ch. 12.

Gibb, Jack R., 1961. "Defense level and influence potential in small groups." In Luigi Petrillo and Bernard M. Bass (eds.), *Leadership and Interpersonal Behavior*. New York: Holt, Rinehart Winston, pp. 66-81.

Gibb, Jack R., 1964. "Climate for trust formation." In Leland P. Bradford, Jack R. Gibb and Kenneth D. Benne (eds.), *T-Group Theory and Laboratory Method*. New York: John Wiley, pp. 279-301.

House, R. J., 1967. "T-group education and leadership effectiveness: a review of the empiric literature and a critical evaluation." *Personnel Psychology*, 20, 1, pp. 1-32.

Maier, Norman R. F., Allen R. Solem, and Ayesha A. Maier, 1959. Supervisory and Executive Development. New York: John Wiley, pp. 308-315.

Meadow, Arnold S., Sidney J. Parnes, and Hayne Reese, 1959. "Influence of brainstorming instructions and problem sequence on creative problem-solving tests." Journal of Applied Psychology, 43, pp. 413-416.

Parloff, Morris B., and Joseph H. Handlon, 1966. "The influence of criticalness on creative problem solving dyads." Psychiatry, 29, pp. 17-27.

Rogers, Carl R., 1961. On Becoming A Person. Boston: Houghton Mifflin, 39-58.

Seeman, Julius, 1954. "Counselor judgments of therapeutic process and outcome." In Carl R. Rogers and Rosalind F. Dymond (eds.), Psychotherapy and Personality Change. Chicago: University of Chicago Press, Ch. 7.

Schein, Edgar H., and Warren G. Bennis, 1965. Personal and Organizational Change Through Group Methods. New York: John Wiley.

Assets and Liabilities in Group Problem Solving: The Need for an Integrative Function

by Norman R. F. Maier

Research on group problem solving reveals that the group has both advantages and disadvantages over individual problem solving. If the potentials for group problem solving can be exploited and if its deficiencies can be avoided, it follows that group problem solving can attain a level of proficiency not ordinarily achieved. The requirement for achieving this level of group performance seems to hinge on developing a style of discussion leadership which maximizes the group's assets and minimizes its liabilities. Since members possess the essential ingredients for the solutions, the deficiencies that appear in group solutions reside in the processes by which group solutions develop. These processes can determine whether the group functions effectively or ineffectively. The critical factor in a group's potential is organization and integration. With training, a leader can supply these functions and serve as the group's central nervous system, thus permitting the group to emerge as a highly efficient entity.[1]

A number of investigations have raised the question of whether group problem solving is superior, inferior, or equal to individual problem solving. Evidence can be cited in support of each position so that the answer to this question remains ambiguous. Rather than pursue this generalized approach to the question, it seems more fruitful to explore the forces that influence problem solving under the two conditions (see reviews by Hoffman, 1965; Kelley & Thibaut, 1954). It is hoped that a better recognition of these forces will permit clarification of the varied dimensions of the problem solving process, especially in groups.

[1]The research reported in the following reading was supported by Grant No. MH-02704 from the United States Public Health Service. Grateful acknowledgment is made for the constructive criticism of Melba Colgrove, Junie Janzen, Mara Julius, and James Thurber.

The forces operating in such groups include some that are assets, some that are liabilities, and some that can be either assets or liabilities, depending upon the skills of the members, especially those of the discussion leader. Let us examine these three sets of forces.

GROUP ASSETS

Greater Sum Total of Knowledge and Information

There is more information in a group than in any of its members. Thus problems that require the utilization of knowledge should give groups an advantage over individuals. Even if one member of the group (e.g., the leader) knows much more than anyone else, the limited unique knowledge of lesser-informed individuals could serve to fill in some gaps in knowledge. For example, a skilled machinist might contribute to an engineer's problem solving and an ordinary workman might supply information on how a new machine might be received by workers.

Greater Number of Approaches to a Problem

It has been shown that individuals get into ruts in their thinking (Duncker, 1945; Maier, 1930; Wertheimer, 1959). Many obstacles stand in the way of achieving a goal, and a solution must circumvent these. The individual is handicapped in that he tends to persist in his approach and thus fails to find another approach that might solve the problem in a simpler manner. Individuals in a group have the same failing, but the approaches in which they are persisting may be different. For example, one researcher may try to prevent the spread of a disease by making man immune to the germ, another by finding and destroying the carrier of the germ, and still another by altering the environment so as to kill the germ before it reaches man. There is no way of determining which approach will best achieve the desired goal, but undue persistence in any one will stifle new discoveries. Since group members do not have identical approaches, each can contribute by knocking others out of ruts in thinking.

Participation in Problem Solving Increases Acceptance

Many problems require solutions that depend upon the support of others to be effective. Insofar as group problem solving permits participation and influence, it follows that more individuals accept solutions when a group solves the problem than when one person solves it. When one individual solves a problem he still has the task of persuading others. It follows, therefore, that when groups solve such problems, a greater number of persons accept and feel responsible for making the solution work. A low-quality solution that has good acceptance can be more effective than a higher-quality solution that lacks acceptance.

Better Comprehension of the Decision

Decisions made by an individual, which are to be carried out by others, must be communicated from the decision-maker to the decision-executors. Thus individual problem solving often requires an additional stage—that of relaying the decision reached. Failures in this communication process detract from the merits of the decision and can even cause its failure or create a problem of greater magnitude than the initial problem that was solved. Many organizational problems can be traced to inadequate communication of decisions made by superiors and transmitted to subordinates, who have the task of implementing the decision.

The chances for communication failures are greatly reduced when the individuals who must work together in executing the decision have participated in making it. They not only understand the solution because they saw it develop, but they are also aware of the several other alternatives that were considered and the reasons why they were discarded. The common assumption that decisions supplied by superiors are arbitrarily reached therefore disappears. A full knowledge of goals, obstacles, alternatives, and factual information is essential to communication, and this communication is maximized when the total problem-solving process is shared.

GROUP LIABILITIES

Social Pressure

Social pressure is a major force making for conformity. The desire to be a good group member and to be accepted tends to silence disagreement and favors consensus. Majority opinions tend to be accepted regardless of whether or not their objective quality is logically and scientifically sound. Problems requiring solutions based upon facts, regardless of feelings and wishes, can suffer in group problem-solving situations.

It has been shown (Maier & Solem, 1952) that minority opinions in leaderless groups have little influence on the solution reached, even when these opinions are the correct ones. Reaching agreement in a group often is confused with finding the right answer, and it is for this reason that the dimensions of a decision's acceptance and its objective quality must be distinguished (Maier, 1963).

Valence of Solutions

When leaderless groups (made up of three or four persons) engage in problem solving, they propose a variety of solutions. Each solution may receive both critical and supportive comments, as well as descriptive and explorative comments from other participants. If the number of negative and positive comments for each solution are algebraically summed, each may be given a valence index (Hoffman & Maier, 1964). The first solution that receives a positive valence value of 15 tends to be adopted to the satisfaction of all participants about 85 percent of the time, regardless of its quality. Higher quality solutions introduced after the critical value for one of the solutions has been reached have little chance of achieving real consideration. Once some degree of consensus is reached, the jelling process seems to proceed rather rapidly.

The critical valence value of 15 appears not to be greatly altered by the nature of the problem or the exact size of the group. Rather, it seems to designate a turning point between the idea-getting process and the decision-making process (idea evaluation). A solution's valence index is not a measure of the number of persons supporting the solution, since a vocal minority can build up a solution's valence by actively pushing it. In this sense, valence becomes an influence in addition to social pressure in determining an outcome.

Since a solution's valence is independent of its subjective quality, this group factor becomes an important liability in group problem solving, even when the value of a decision depends upon objective criteria (facts and logic). It becomes a means whereby skilled manipulators can have more influence over the group than their proportion of membership deserves.

Individual Domination

In most leaderless groups a dominant individual emerges and captures more than his share of influence on the outcome. He can achieve this end through a greater degree of participation (valence), persuasive ability, or stubborn persistence (fatiguing the opposition). None of these factors is related to problem-solving ability, so that the best problem solver in the group may not have the influence to upgrade the quality of the group's solution (which he would have had if left to solve the problem by himself).

Hoffman and Maier (1967) found that the mere fact of appointing a leader causes this person to dominate a discussion. Thus, regardless of his problem-solving ability a leader tends to exert a major influence on the outcome of a discussion.

Conflicting Secondary Goal: Winning the Argument

When groups are confronted with a problem, the initial goal is to obtain a solution. However, the appearance of several alternatives causes individuals to have preferences and once these emerge the desire to support a position is created. Converting those with neutral viewpoints now enters into the problem-solving process. More and more the goal becomes that of winning the decision rather than finding the best solution. This new goal is unrelated to the quality of the problem's solution and therefore can result in lowering the quality of the decision (Hoffman & Maier, 1966).

FACTORS THAT SERVE AS ASSETS OR LIABILITIES, DEPENDING LARGELY UPON THE SKILL OF THE DISCUSSION LEADER

Disagreement

The fact that discussion may lead to disagreement can serve either to create hard feelings among members or lead to a resolution of conflict and hence to an innovative solution (Hoffman, 1961; Hoffman, Harburg, & Maier, 1962; Hoffman & Maier, 1961; Maier, 1958, 1963; Maier & Hoffman, 1965). The first of these outcomes of disagreement is a liability, especially with regard to the acceptance of solutions; while the second is an asset, particularly where innovation is desired. A leader can treat disagreement as undesirable and thereby reduce the probability of both hard feelings and innovation, or he can maximize disagreement and risk hard feelings in his attempts to achieve innovation. The skill of a leader requires his ability to create a climate for disagreement which will permit innovation without risking hard feelings. The leader's perception of disagreement is one of the critical factors in this skill area (Maier & Hoffman, 1965). Others involve permissiveness (Maier, 1953), delaying the reaching of a solution (Maier & Hoffman, 1960b; Maier & Solem, 1962), techniques for processing information and opinions (Maier, 1963; Maier & Hoffman, 1960a; Maier & Maier, 1957), and techniques for separating idea-getting from idea-evaluation (Maier, 1960, 1963; Osborn, 1953).

Conflicting Interests versus Mutual Interests

Disagreement in discussion may take many forms. Often participants disagree with one another with regard to solutions, but when issues are explored one finds that conflicting solutions are designed to solve different problems. Before one can rightly expect agreement on a solution, there should be agreement on the nature of the problem. Even before this, there should be agreement on the goal, as well as on the various obstacles that prevent the goal from being reached. Once distinctions are made between goals, obstacles, and solutions (which represent ways of overcoming obstacles), one finds increased opportunities for cooperative problem solving and less conflict (Hoffman & Maier, 1959; Maier, 1960, 1963; Maier & Solem, 1962; Solem, 1965).

Often there is also disagreement regarding whether the objective of a solution is to achieve quality or acceptance (Maier & Hoffman, 1964b), and frequently a stated problem reveals a complex of separate problems, each having separate solutions so that a search for a single solution is impossible (Maier, 1963). Communications often are inadequate because the discussion is not synchronized and each person is engaged in discussing a different aspect. Organizing discussion to synchronize the exploration of different aspects of the problem and to follow a systematic procedure increases solution quality (Maier & Hoffman, 1960a; Maier & Maier, 1957). The leadership function of influencing discussion procedure is quite distinct from the function of evaluating or contributing ideas (Maier, 1950, 1953).

When the discussion leader aids in the separation of the several aspects of the problem-solving process and delays the solution-mindedness of the group (Maier, 1958, 1963; Maier & Solem, 1962), both solution quality and acceptance improve; when he hinders or fails to facilitate the isolation of these varied processes, he risks a deterioration in the group process (Solem, 1965). His skill thus determines whether a discussion drifts toward conflicting interests or whether mutual interests are located. Cooperative problem solving can only occur after the mutual interests have been established and it is surprising how often they can be found when the discussion leader makes this his task (Maier, 1952, 1963; Maier & Hayes, 1962).

Risk Taking

Groups are more willing than individuals to reach decisions involving risks (Wallach & Kogan, 1965; Wallach, Kogan, & Bem, 1962). Taking risks is a factor in acceptance of change, but change may either represent a gain or a loss. The best guard against the latter outcome seems to be primarily a matter of a decision's quality. In a group situation this depends upon the leader's skill in utilizing the factors that represent group assets and avoiding those that make for liabilities.

Time Requirements

In general, more time is required for a group to reach a decision than for a single individual to reach one. Insofar as some problems require quick decisions, individual decisions are favored. In other situations acceptance and quality are requirements, but excessive time without sufficient returns also represents a loss. On the other hand, discussion can resolve conflicts, whereas reaching consensus has limited value (Wallach & Kogan, 1965). The practice of hastening a meeting can prevent full discussion, but failure to move a discussion forward can lead to boredom and fatigue-type solutions, in which members agree merely to get out of the meeting. The effective utilization of discussion time (a delicate balance between permissiveness and control on the part of the leader), therefore, is needed to make the time factor an asset rather than a liability. Unskilled leaders tend to be too concerned with reaching a solution and therefore terminate a discussion before the group potential is achieved (Maier & Hoffman, 1960b).

Who Changes

In reaching consensus or agreement, some members of a group must change. Persuasive forces do not operate in individual problem solving in the same way they operate in a group situation; hence, the changing of someone's mind is not an issue. In group situations, however, who changes can be an asset or a liability. If persons with the most constructive views are induced to change the end-product suffers; whereas if persons with the least constructive points of view change the end-product is upgraded. The leader can upgrade the quality of a decision because his position permits him to protect the person with a minority view and increase his opportunity to influence the majority position. This protection is a constructive factor because a minority viewpoint influences only when facts favor it (Maier, 1950, 1952; Maier & Solem, 1952).

The leader also plays a constructive role insofar as he can facilitate communications and thereby reduce misunderstandings (Maier, 1952; Solem, 1965). The leader has an adverse effect on the end-product when he suppresses minority views by holding a contrary position and when he uses his office to promote his own views (Maier & Hoffman, 1960b, 1962; Maier & Solem, 1952). In many problem-solving discussions the untrained leader plays a dominant role in influencing the outcome, and when he is more resistant to changing his views than are the other participants, the quality of the outcome tends to be lowered. This negative leader-influence was demonstrated by experiments in which untrained leaders were asked to obtain a second solution to a problem after they had obtained their first one (Maier & Hoffman, 1960a). It was found that the second solution tended to be superior to the first. Since the dominant individual had influenced the first solution, he had won his point and therefore ceased to dominate the subsequent discussion which led to the second solution. Acceptance of a solution also increases as the leader sees disagreement as idea-producing rather than as a source of difficulty or trouble (Maier & Hoffman, 1965). Leaders who see some of their participants as troublemakers obtain fewer innovative solutions and gain less acceptance of decisions made than leaders who see disagreeing members as persons with ideas.

THE LEADER'S ROLE FOR INTEGRATED GROUPS

Two Differing Types of Group Process

In observing group problem solving under various conditions it is rather easy to distinguish between cooperative problem-solving activity and persuasion or selling approaches. Problem-solving activity includes searching, trying out ideas on one another, listening to understand rather than to refute, making relatively short speeches, and reacting to differences in opinion as stimulating. The general pattern is one of rather complete participation, involvement, and interest. Persuasion activity includes the selling of opinions already formed, defending a position held, either not listening at all or listening in order to be able to refute, talking dominated by a few members, unfavorable reactions to disagreement, and a lack of involvement of some members. During problem solving the behavior observed seems to be that of members interacting as segments of a group. The interaction pattern is not between certain individual members, but with the group as a whole. Sometimes it is difficult to determine who should be credited with an idea. "It just developed," is a response often used to describe the solution reached. In contrast, discussions involving selling or persuasive behavior seem to consist of a series of interpersonal interactions with each individual retaining his identity. Such groups do not function as integrated units but as separate individuals, each with an agenda. In one situation the solution is unknown and is sought; in the other, several solutions exist and conflict occurs because commitments have been made.

The Starfish Analogy

The analysis of these two group processes suggests an analogy with the behavior of the rays of a starfish under two conditions: one with the nerve ring intact, the other with the nerve ring sectioned (Hamilton, 1922; Moore, 1924; Moore & Doudoroff, 1939; Schneirla & Maier, 1940). In the intact condition, locomotion and righting behavior reveal that the behavior of each ray is not merely a function of local stimulation. Locomotion and righting behavior reveal a degree of coordination and interdependence that is centrally controlled. However, when the nerve ring is sectioned, the behavior of one ray still can influence others, but internal coordination is lacking. For example, if one ray is stimulated, it may step forward, thereby exerting pressure on the sides of the other four rays. In response to these external pressures (tactile stimulation), these rays show stepping responses on the stimulated side so that locomotion successfully occurs without the aid of neural coordination. Thus integrated behavior can occur on the basis of external control. If, however, stimulation is applied to opposite rays, the specimen may be "locked" for a time, and in some species the conflicting locomotions may divide the animal, thus destroying it (Crozier, 1920; Moore & Doudoroff, 1939).

Each of the rays of the starfish can show stepping responses even when sectioned and removed from the animal. Thus each may be regarded as an individual. In a starfish with a sectioned nerve ring the five rays become members of a group. They can successfully work together for locomotion purposes by being controlled by the dominant ray. Thus if uniformity of action is desired, the group of five rays can sometimes be more effective than the individual ray in moving the group toward a source of stimulation. However, if "locking" or the division of the organism occurs, the group action becomes less effective than individual action. External control, through the influence of a dominant ray, therefore can lead to adaptive behavior for the starfish as a whole, but it can also result in a conflict that destroys the organism. Something more than external influence is needed.

In the animal with an intact nerve ring, the function of the rays is coordinated by the nerve ring. With this type of internal organization the group is always superior to that of the individual actions. When the rays function as a part of an organized unit, rather than as a group that is physically together, they become a higher type of organization—a single intact organism. This is accomplished by the nerve ring, which in itself does not do the behaving. Rather, it receives and processes the data which the rays relay to it. Through this central organization, the responses of the rays become part of a larger pattern so that together they constitute a single coordinated total response rather than a group of individual responses.

The Leader as the Group's Central Nervous System

If we now examine what goes on in a discussion group we find that members can problem-solve as individuals, they can influence others by external pushes and pulls, or they can function as a group with varying degrees of unity. In order for the latter function to be maximized, however, something must be introduced to serve the function of the nerve ring. In our conceptualization of group problem solving and group decision (Maier, 1963), we see this as the function of the leader. Thus the leader does not serve as a dominant ray and produce the solution. Rather, his function is to receive information, facilitate communications between the individuals, relay messages, and integrate the incoming responses so that a single unified response occurs.

Solutions that are the product of good group discussions often come as surprises to discussion leaders. One of these is unexpected generosity. If there is a weak member, this member is given less to do, in much the same way as an organism adapts to an injured limb and alters the function of other limbs to keep locomotion on course. Experimental evidence supports the point that group decisions award special consideration to needy members of groups (Hoffman & Maier, 1959). Group decisions in industrial groups often give smaller assignments to the less gifted (Maier, 1952). A leader could not effectually impose such differential treatment on group members without being charged with discriminatory practices.

Another unique aspect of group discussion is the way fairness is resolved. In a simulated problem situation involving the problem of how to introduce a new truck into a group of drivers, the typical group solution involves a trading of trucks so that several or all members stand to profit. If the leader makes the decision the number of persons who profit is often confined to one (Maier & Hoffman, 1962; Maier & Zerfoss, 1952). In industrial practice, supervisors assign a new truck to an individual member of a crew after careful evaluation of needs. This practice results in dissatisfaction, with the charge of *unfair* being leveled at him. Despite these repeated attempts to do justice, supervisors in the telephone industry never hit upon the notion of a general reallocation of trucks, a solution that crews invariably reach when the decision is theirs to make.

In experiments involving the introduction of change, the use of group discussion tends to lead to decisions that resolve differences (Maier, 1952, 1953; Maier & Hoffman, 1961, 1964a, 1964b). Such decisions tend to be different from decisions reached by individuals because of the very fact that disagreement is common in group problem solving and rare in individual problem solving. The process of resolving difference in a constructive setting causes the exploration of additional areas and leads to solutions that are integrative rather than compromises.

Finally, group solutions tend to be tailored to fit the interests and personalities of the participants; thus group solutions to problems involving fairness, fears, facesaving, etc., tend to vary from one group to another. An outsider cannot process these variables because they are not subject to logical treatment.

If we think of the leader as serving a function in the group different from that of its membership, we might be able to create a group that can function as an intact organism. For a leader, such functions as rejecting or promoting ideas according to his personal needs are out of bounds. He must be receptive to information contributed, accept contributions without evaluating them (posting contributions on a chalk board to keep them alive), summarize information to facilitate integration, stimulate exploratory behavior, create awareness of problems of one member by others, and detect when the group is ready to resolve differences and agree to a unified solution.

Since higher organisms have more than a nerve ring and can store information, a leader might appropriately supply information, but according to our model of a leader's role, he must clearly distinguish between supplying information and promoting a solution. If his knowledge indicates the desirability of a particular solution, sharing this knowledge might lead the group to find this solution, but the solution should be the group's discovery. A leader's contributions do not receive the same treatment as those of a member of the group. Whether he likes it or not, his position is different. According to our conception of the leader's contribution to discussion, his role not only differs in influence, but gives him an entirely different function. He is to serve much as the nerve ring in the starfish and to further refine this function so as to make it a higher type of nerve ring.

This model of a leader's role in group process has served as a guide for many of our studies in group problem solving. It is not our claim that this will lead to the best possible group function under all conditions. In sharing it we hope to indicate the nature of our guidelines in exploring group leadership as a function quite different and apart from group membership. Thus the model serves as a stimulant for research problems and as a guide for our analyses of leadership skills and principles.

CONCLUSIONS

On the basis of our analysis, it follows that the comparison of the merits of group versus individual problem solving depends on the nature of the problem, the goal to be achieved (high quality solution, highly accepted solution, effective communication and understanding of the solution, innovation, a quickly reached solution, or satisfaction), and the skill of the discussion leader. If liabilities inherent in groups are avoided, assets capitalized upon, and conditions that can serve either favorable or unfavorable outcomes are effectively used, it follows that groups have a potential which in many instances can exceed that of a superior individual functioning alone, even with respect to creativity.

This goal was nicely stated by Thibaut and Kelley (1961) when they

> wonder whether it may not be possible for a rather small, intimate group to establish a problem solving process that capitalizes upon the total pool of information and provides for great interstimulation of ideas without any loss of innovative creativity due to social restraints [p. 268].

In order to accomplish this high level of achievement, however, a leader is needed who plays a role quite different from that of the members. His role is analogous to that of the nerve ring in the starfish which permits the rays to execute a unified response. If the leader can contribute the integrative requirement, group problem solving may emerge as a unique type of group function. This type of approach to group processes places the leader in a particular role in which he must cease to contribute, avoid evaluation, and refrain from thinking about solutions or group *products*. Instead he must concentrate on the group *process*, listen in order to understand rather than to appraise or refute, assume responsibility for accurate communication between members, be sensitive to unexpressed feelings, protect minority points of view, to unexpressed feelings, protect minority points of view, keep the discussion moving, and develop skills in summarizing.

REFERENCES

Crozier, W. J. Notes on some problems of adaptation. *Biological Bulletin*, 1920, *39*, 116-29.

Duncker, K. On problem solving, *Psychological Monographs*, 1945, *58* (5, Whole No. 270).

Hamilton, W. F. Coordination in the starfish. III. The righting reaction as a phase of locomotion (righting and locomotion). *Journal of Comparative Psychology*, 1922, *2*, 81-94.

Hoffman, L. R. Conditions for creative problem solving. *Journal of Psychology*, 1961, *52*, 429-44.

Hoffman, L. R. Group problem solving. In L. Berkowitz (ed.), *Advances in experimental social psychology*, Vol. 2. New York: Academic Press, 1965, pp. 99-132.

Hoffman, L. R., Harburg, E., and Maier, N. R. F. Differences and disagreement as factors in creative group problem solving. *Journal of Abnormal and Social Psychology*, 1962, *64*, 206-14.

Hoffman, L. R. and Maier, N. R. F. The use of group decision to resolve a problem of fairness. *Personnal Psychology*, 1959, *12*, 545-59.

Hoffman, L. R. and Maier, N. R. F. Quality and acceptance of problem solutions by members of homogeneous and heterogeneous groups. *Journal of Abnormal and Social Psychology*, 1961, *62*, 401-07.

Hoffman, L. R. and Maier, N. R. F. Valence in the adoption of solutions by problem-solving groups: Concept, method, and results. *Journal of Abnormal and Social Psychology*, 1964, *69*, 264-71.

Hoffman, L. R. and Maier, N. R. F. Valence in the adoption of solutions by problem-solving groups: II. Quality and acceptance as goals of leaders and members. Unpublished manuscript, 1967 (Mimeo).

Kelley, H. H. and Thibaut, J. W. Experimental studies of group problem solving and process. In G. Lindzey (ed.), *Handbook of social psychology*. Cambridge, Mass.: Addison Wesley, 1954, pp. 735-85.

Maier, N. R. F. Reasoning in humans. I. On direction. *Journal of Comparative Psychology*, 1930, *10*, 115-43.

Maier, N. R. F. The quality of group decisions as influenced by the discussion leader. *Human Relations*, 1950, *3*, 155-74.

Maier, N. R. F. *Principles of human relations*. New York: Wiley, 1952.

Maier, N. R. F. An experimental test of the effect of training on discussion leadership. *Human Relations*, 1953, *6*, 161-73.

Maier, N. R. F. *The appraisal interview*. New York: Wiley, 1958.

Maier, N. R. F. Screening solutions to upgrade quality: A new approach to problem solving under conditions of uncertainty. *Journal of Psychology*, 1960, *49*, 217-31.

Maier, N. R. F. *Problem solving discussions and conferences: Leadership methods and skills*. New York: McGraw-Hill, 1963.

Maier, N. R. F. and Hayes, J. J. *Creative management*. New York: Wiley, 1962.

Maier, N. R. F. and Hoffman, L. R. Using trained "developmental" discussion leaders to improve further the quality of group decisions. *Journal of Applied Psychology*, 1960, *44*, 247-51. (a)

Maier, N. R. F. and Hoffman, L. R. Quality of first and second solutions in group problem solving. *Journal of Applied Psychology*, 1960, *44*, 278-83. (b)

Maier, N. R. F. and Hoffman, L. R. Organization and creative problem solving. *Journal of Applied Psychology*, 1961, *45*, 277-80.

Maier, N. R. F. and Hoffman, L. R. Group decision in England and the United States. *Personnel Psychology*, 1962, *15*, 75-87.

Maier, N. R. F. and Hoffman, L. R. Financial incentives and group decision in motivating change. *Journal of Social Psychology*, 1964, *64*, 369-78. (a)

Maier, N. R. F. and Hoffman, L. R. Types of problems confronting managers. *Personnel Psychology*, 1964, *17*, 261-69. (b)

Maier, N. R. F. and Hoffman, L. R. Acceptance and quality of solutions as related to leaders' attitudes toward disagreement in group problem solving. *Journal of Applied Behavioral Science*, 1965, *1*, 373-86.

Maier, N. R. F. and Maier, R. A. An experimental test of the effects of "developmental" vs. "free" discussions on the quality of group decisions. *Journal of Applied Psychology*, 1957, *41*, 320-23.

Maier, N. R. F. and Solem, A. R. The contribution of a discussion leader to the quality of group thinking: The effective use of minority opinions. *Human Relations*, 1952, *5*, 277-88.

Maier, N. R. F. and Solem, A. R. Improving solutions by turning choice situations into problems. *Personnel Psychology*, 1962, *15*, 151-57.

Maier, N. R. F. and Zerfoss, L. R. MRP: A technique for training large groups of supervisors and its potential use in social research. *Human Relations*, 1952, *5*, 177-86.

Moore, A. R. The nervous mechanism of coordination in the crinoid *Antedon rosaceus*. *Journal of Genetic Psychology*, 1924, *6*, 281-88.

Moore, A. R. and Doudoroff, M. Injury, recovery and function in an aganglionic central nervous system. *Journal of Comparative Psychology*, 1939, *28*, 313-28.

Osborn, A. F. *Applied imagination*. New York: Scribner's, 1953.

Schneirla, T. C. and Maier, N. R. F. Concerning the status of the starfish. *Journal of Comparative Psychology*, 1940, *30*, 103-10.

Solem, A. R. 1965: Almost anything I can do, we can do better. *Personnel Administration*, 1965, *28*, 6-16.

Thibaut, J. W. and Kelley, H. H. *The social psychology of groups*. New York: Wiley, 1961.

Wallach, M. A. and Kogan, N. The roles of information, discussion and consensus in group risk taking. *Journal of Experimental Social Psychology*, 1965, *1*, 1-19.

Wallach, M. A., Kogan, N., and Bem, D. J. Group influence on individual risk taking. *Journal of Abnormal and Social Psychology*, 1962, *65*, 75-86.

Wertheimer, M. *Productive thinking*. New York: Harper, 1959.

Small Group Behavior and Development: A Selective Bibliography

by Gordon Hearn

Group behavior and group development are so complex that any adequate understanding must require observation and study of a considerable number of important factors and the process of their interaction. Hence, any bibliography about group behavior, however extensive, would present difficulties to the user unless carefully annotated.

This selective review of the literature attempts, through its arrangement, to separate out most of the important factors that interactively determine the behavior and development of most small groups. Thirteen of these factors are briefly described and each is followed by a highly selected bibliography directly relating to that factor. It is hoped that such an arrangement not only will make further study easier, but also will, by virtue of this arrangement, provide clearer understanding of the many factors that affect group behavior and their interrelationships.

In addition, the thirteen factors have been arranged under the following five general headings to clarify their importance and the complexity of their interactions:

Group Syntality. The four sections under this heading deal with how a group acquires its own unique characteristics—those qualities that make groups different from one another. Just as individuals have unique personalities, so groups seem to have their own syntality. Organized under this heading are bibliographical references dealing with: The Concept "Group," What the Individual Brings to the Group, The Group Situation, and The Emergence of Group Syntality.

Directed Group Energy. Under this heading are the two subsystems of a group accounting for the group's energy and its direction and focus: the Group Motivation System and the Group Value System.

Group Structure. Postulating the existence of a motivation system and a group value system is an effort to account for the fact that groups move and their movement is directed and purposive. Group movement, however, requires structural systems in the group; without structure the group cannot function. Under this heading, therefore, are such sections as: The Position System, The Role System, and the Relationship System.

Group Functioning. Three subsystems account for the functioning of the group—communication, control, and locomotion. A bibliographical section is presented for each of those subsystems.

Group Survival. Various maintenance systems that are necessary for survival are included under this heading with bibliographies.

GROUP SYNTALITY

1. The Concept "Group"

The first consideration in any theory of small group behavior is the delineation of what is meant by *group*. What is a group? How do we distinguish a group from a non-group? What characteristics define a group?

Definition turns out to be a difficult task. It can be approached in either of two ways: one that seems to work and another that does not. One way to approach the task is to list a number of aggregations that collectively form a comprehensive definition. If aggregations that were found to be in groups could be distinguished from those that were not, a definition could be composed from the elements the group possessed and the non-group lacked. While logical, this approach has proved impossible. Try it and see.

What has proved possible has been the characterization of the various aggregations on the list as *more or less of a group*. When this is done two ingredients seem to appear: (1) interdependency among members, and (2) a *common identification*. These in combination create some degree of *interpersonal bond*.

Another question relates to defining the boundary of a group: who is inside and who is outside. This also becomes a difficult question. Practically any aggregation of persons are in interaction with many others and together their interactions constitute an almost endless network. Where in this network does one draw the boundary defining the group? A variety of ways are used to set boundaries. Usually, some specific arbitrary criterion is used: intensity of interaction, number of interactions, propinquity, color of skin, age, sex, etc.

After considering and rejecting many qualitative definitions as somehow inadequate, I have settled on one formulated by Thelen (1959).

Perhaps we can conclude only that a group is a number of people who think they are a group and act like one. (p. 554)

SELECTED BIBLIOGRAPHY

Asch, S. E., *Social Psychology*, Englewood Cliffs, NJ: Prentice-Hall, 1952.

Bates, F. L., "A conceptual analysis of group structure," *Social Forces*, 1957, *36*, 103-110.

Blumer, J., "Psychological import of the human group," in M. Sherif & W. O. Wilson (Eds.), *Group Relations at the Crossroads*, New York: Harper & Row, 1953.

Borgatta, M. L. "The concept of the group: a brief consideration," *Sociol. Soc. Res.*, 1958, *43*, 83-89.

Deutsch, M., "A theory of cooperation and competition," *Hum. Relat.*, 1949, *2*, 129-152.

Dumphy, D. C., *The Primary Group: A Handbook for Analysis and Field Research*, New York: Appleton-Century-Crofts, 1972.

Eubank, E., *The Concepts of Sociology*, Boston: Heath, 1932.

French, J. R. P., Jr., "Groups under fear and frustration," in R. R. Sears (Ed.), *Authority and Frustration, Studies in Topological and Vector Psychology III*, University of Iowa Studies: Studies in Child Welfare, Vol. 20, Iowa City: University of Iowa Press, 1944, 274-275.

Golembiewski, R. T., *The Small Group*, Chicago: University of Chicago Press, 1969.

Hemphill, J. K. & C. M. Westie, "The measurement of group dimensions," *J. Psychol.*, 1950, *29*, 325-342.

Krech, D. & R. S. Crutchfield, *Theory and Problems of Social Psychology*, New York: McGraw-Hill, 1948.

Lewin, K., "Field theory and experiment in psychology," *American Journal of Psychology*, 1939, *44*, 868-896.

Merton, R. K., *Social Theory and Social Structure*, New York: Free Press, 1957.

Newcomb, T. M., *Social Psychology*, New York: Dryden Press, 1950.

Shepherd, C. R., *Small Groups: Some Sociological Perspectives*, San Francisco: Chandler, 1964, Chapter 3.

Smith, M., "Social situation, social behavior, social group," *Psychol. Rev.*, 1945, *52*, 224-229.

Steiner, I. D., *Group Process and Productivity*, New York: Academic Press, 1972, Chapter 7.

Thelen, H. A., "Work—emotionality theory of the group as organism," in S. Koch (Ed.), *Psychology: A Study of A Science*, New York: McGraw-Hill, 1959, 544-611.

Wilson, G. & G. Ryland, *Social Group Work Practice*, Boston: Houghton Mifflin, 1949.

2. What an Individual Brings to a Group

What the individual members bring to a group is clearly one of the most important factors determining the group syntality that eventually emerges among an aggregation of people. But how does one select and how does one organize all the relevant information about the individual members? What is pertinent and what is not?

One way of thinking about what individual members contribute to the group syntality is to assume that they each bring their several selves. Although a person brings only a single "real" self, there seem to be several manifestations of that central self. First, there is the self as the individual experiences it—the *private self*. Second, there are *public selves*—the images of the self projected toward others; the way one wants to be seen. There can be many of these images because individuals often want to be seen differently by different others. Third, there are several *affective selves* brought to a group situation. These are the projections of the self that are perceived by others; there can be as many of these perceptions as there are others to respond.

Everything that individual members bring to a group can be understood within this conceptual scheme of the several selves: private, public, and affective.

SELECTED BIBLIOGRAPHY

Adorno, T. W., E. Frenkel-Brunswick, D. J. Levinson, & R. N. Sanford, *The Authoritarian Personality*, New York: Harper & Row, 1950.

Asch, S. E., "Forming impressions of personality," *J. Abnorm. Soc. Psychol.*, 1946, *41*, 258-290.

Bion, W. R., *Experiences in Groups*, New York: Basic Books, 1961, 146-153.

Cooley, C. H., *Human Nature and the Social Order*, New York: Scribner's, 1902.

Eisenstadt, S. N., "Reference group behavior and social integration: an explorative study," *Amer. Sociol. Rev.*, 1954, *19*, 175-185.

Hare, A. P., *Handbook of Small Group Research*, New York: Free Press, 1962, Part 2.

Horney, K., *Our Inner Conflicts*, New York: Norton, 1945.

Kelley, H. H., "The warm-cold variable in first impressions of persons," *J. Personality*, 1950, *18*, 431-439.

Luft, J., *Group Processes: An Introduction to Group Dynamics*, Palo Alto, CA: Mayfield, 1970.

McGregor, D., "The Staff Function in Human Relations," *J. Soc. Issues*, 1948, *4*, 6-23.

Mead, G. H., *Mind, Self and Society*, in C. W. Morris (Ed.), Chicago: University of Chicago Press, 1934.

Murray, H. A., *Explorations in Personality*, New York: Oxford University Press, 1948.

Postman, L., J. S. Bruner, & E. McGinnis, "Personal values as selective factors in perception," in G. E. Swanson, T. M. Newcomb, & E. L. Hartley (Eds.), *Readings in Social Psychology*, Revised Edition, New York: Henry Holt, 1952, 375-383.

Redl, F., "Groups, emotion and leadership," *Psychiatry*, 1942, *5*, 573-596.

Stock, D., "Components of valency (affective approach, cultural preference, and areas of concern): a case study," in D. Stock & H. A. Thelen, (Eds.), *Emotional Dynamics and Group Culture*, New York: New York University Press, 1958, Chapter 6.

Wilcox, J., & J. Mitchell, "Effects of group acceptance—reflections of self-esteem levels of individual group members in a task-oriented problem-solving group interaction," *Small Group Behavior*, 1977, *8* (2), 169-178.

3. The Group Situation

In a group situation, there are a great many "givens" determining the group syntality that emerges. These are various pre-existing or contrived conditions that exist independently of group interaction.

One pre-existing condition is the surrounding *culture*, which serves as a context within which interaction occurs. Culture exerts certain constraints on the developing pattern of group syntality; it sets certain limits on interaction. The culture of a society prescribes the ways in which people usually interact in that society. It is important to recognize that group members are influenced not by a single culture, but by a variety of different subcultures within the major culture.

Another of the given conditions is group *size*. The literature on group size is extensive, concerning itself with groups of different sizes, such as the dyad and the triad. The literature also considers the differences among groups of increased size, and it suggests some general rules-of-thumb about the optimum size of groups for different purposes. Examples of the latter suggest that a work group should be as small as possible and still include among its members all the talents required to accomplish the group's purpose. A T-group of twelve to fifteen members works well because it is large enough to allow individual members to "hide" temporarily if they do not want to be part of the present interaction, but it is small enough to allow those members to enter when they desire. From five to seven members seems to be the number preferred for therapy groups.

Another factor that can make a difference is *time*. Some groups, such as families, act as though they will go on forever. On the other hand, encounter groups meet for a limited time and then terminate. All of which makes a difference in what is attended to and how groups function.

The *setting* in which a group meets and works is another important determinant of group syntality. Decor and facilities are important aspects of a setting. A particular room may be good for listening to a didactic lecture but not for interacting in pairs, nor for small group interaction.

Noise, color, movement, and temperature might round out the list of factors that noticeably can affect the form of group syntality emerging in a given instance of group association.

SELECTED BIBLIOGRAPHY

Bales, R. F., & E. F. Borgatta, "Size of a group as a factor in the interaction profile," in A. P. Hare, E. F. Borgatta & R. F. Bales (Eds.), *Small Groups*, New York: Knopf, 1955.

Borgatta, E. F. & R. F. Bales, "Task and accumulation of experience as factors in the interaction of small groups," *Sociometry*, 1953, *16*, 239-252.

Caplow, T., *Two Against One: Coalitions in Triads*, Englewood Cliffs, NJ: Prentice-Hall, 1968.

Deutsch, M., "An experimental study of the effects of cooperation and competition upon group process," *Hum. Relat.*, 1949, *2*, 199-231.

Festinger, L., "Architecture and group membership," *J. Soc. Issues*, 1951, *7*, 152-163.

French, J. R. P., Jr., "Groups under fear and frustration," *University of Iowa Studies: Studies in Child Welfare*, Vol. 20, Iowa City: University of Iowa Press, 1944, 231-308.

Hearn, G., "Leadership and the spatial factor in small groups," *J. Abnorm. Soc. Psychol.*, 1957, *54*, 269-272.

Kecuyer, R., "Social organization and spatial organization," *Hum. Relat.*, 1976, *29*, (1), 1045-1060.

Leavitt, H. J., "Some effects of certain communication patterns on group performance," *J. Abnorm. Soc. Psychol.*, 1951, *46*, 38-50.

Lindsay, J. S. B., "On the number in a group," *Hum. Relat.*, 25 (1), 47-64.

Lippitt, R. & R. White, "The 'social climate' of childrens' groups," in R. G. Barber, J. Kounin & H. Wright (Eds.), *Child Behavior and Development*, New York: McGraw-Hill, 1943, 485-508.

McGrath, J. E., & I. Altman, *Small Group Research*, New York: Holt, Rinehart & Winston, 1966, Chapter 6.

Redl, F. & D. Wineman, *Controls from Within*, New York: Free Press, 1952.

Seta, J. J., P. B. Paulus & J. K. Schkade, "Effects of group size and proximity under cooperative and competitive conditions," *J. Pers. Soc.*, 1976, *34* (1), 47-53.

Stang, D. J., "Group size effects on conformity," *J. Soc. Psychol.*, 1976, *98*, (2), 175-181.

Sommer, R., "Leadership and group geography," *Sociometry*, 1961, *24*, 99-110.

Steiner, I. D., *Group Process and Productivity*, New York: Academic Press, 1972, Chapter 4.

Steinzor, B., "The spatial factor in face-to-face discussion groups," *J. Abnorm. Soc. Psychol.*, 1950, *45*, 552-555.

4. The Emergence of Group Syntality

The manner in which the culture, the endowments of the group members, and the given conditions combine in a group situation determines the group syntality that results and how it occurs. A good deal is known about what occurs but somewhat less is known about how.

When a number of individuals within a certain cultural context come together and interact in a particular group situation, something that may be called group syntality begins to emerge, endowing the group with its unique character. Closely related to the emergence of group syntality is the group's process of development—its movement through a series of identifiable modes of activity toward maturity.

Each member of the group, through participation in the interaction process, contributes something of himself and determines, in part, the pattern of group syntality that develops. To each new group experience, the individual brings certain needs to be satisfied, a capacity to satisfy some of the needs of others, and certain hopes and expectations concerning the prospects of the new experience.

The individual who has given any prior thought to the new experience will already have formulated a number of rather specific hopes, expectations, and ideas about what the group is likely or not likely to do. The member may bring an idealized picture of the group—an image of how a group of this type ought to function, including ideas about the proper role of the leader in contrast to that of a member, the group's goals, and the proper procedures for their pursuance.

However, the needs, capacities, and expectations of group members will be different. One person's needs may be unlike those of any other; each will have somewhat different capacities for satisfying the needs of others; each will have somewhat different expectations.

Out of this diversity arises the interaction that subsequently develops in the group. Members will interact in order to establish need-satisfying relations. They will interact because of the incompatibility of their individual goals, their various perceptions of the group's goal, and in an attempt to reconcile the differences in their expectations. They even may react against the group out of a need to destroy it.

This interaction, born of diversity, generates issues or problems that the group must cope with if it is to survive. The group will continue to exist only if it has sufficient will and ability to resolve its internal problems, as well as those that arise from the group's relation to its environment.

In time, the particular means devised by a group to meet its problems become institutionalized and are woven into the fabric or culture of the group—a process called the emergence of group syntality.

SELECTED BIBLIOGRAPHY

Anderson, R. E. & I. E. Carter, *Human Behavior in the Social Environment*, Chicago: Aldine, 1944, Chapter 4.

Bion, W. R., "Experiences in groups," seven articles in *Hum. Relat.*, beginning in 1948, *I* (3).

Coffey, H. S., "Socio and psyche group process: integrative concepts," *J. Soc. Issues*, 1952, *8*, 65-74.

Eubank, E., *The Concepts of Sociology*, Boston: Heath, 1932, 222-248; 308-324; 391.

Hare, A. P., "Theories of group development and categories for interaction analysis," *Small Group Behavior*, 1973, *4* (3), 259-304.

Hearn, G., "The process of group development," *Autonomous Groups*, 1957, *13* (1 and 2), 1-7.

Jennings, H. H., *Leadership and Isolation*, Second Edition, New York: Longmans Green, 1950, Chapter 13.

Napier, R. W. & M. K. Gershenfeld, *Groups: Theory and Experience*, Boston: Houghton Mifflin, 1973.

Powell, J. W., "The dynamics of group formation," *Psychiatry*, 1948, *11*, 117-124.

Redl, F., "Group emotion and leadership," *Psychiatry*, 1942, *5*, 573-596.

Stock, D. & M. A. Lieberman, "Methodological issues in the assessment of total-group phenomena in group therapy," *Int. J. Group Psychotherapy*, 1962, *12*, 312-325.

Thelen, H. A., *Dynamics of Groups at Work*, Chicago: University of Chicago Press, 1954.

Znaniecki, F., "Social groups as the products of participating individuals," *Amer. J. Sociol.*, 1939, *44*, 799-811.

DIRECTED GROUP ENERGY

5. Group Motivation System

Since movement in all its forms implies the existence of energy, it is necessary to postulate the existence of a motivational subsystem to account for a group's movement. What is the source of the energy that moves a group? The answer to that question identifies the *motivational system* of the group.

A first observation is that the energy of a group is a function of the energy brought to it collectively by the members. It has already been noted that each member brings to the group certain needs to be met in the group. These would seem to combine in some way to constitute the energy source that motivates the group.

Figure 1 suggests a useful way of differentiating the several levels of individual need that combine to move the group:

- Group-related member needs

    Private needs

    Shared social needs

    Universally shared needs

- Group Needs

    Activity-instigated member and group needs

Kurt Lewin made the useful observation that in order to account for a psychological force there must be a perceived goal as well as a need.

When a person (P) has a need in a state of tension and perceives a means of satisfying that need, then that means becomes a goal "region" for *P*; a psychological force operates on *P* to move toward that region. The strength of the force to move depends on the strength of the need and the attractiveness of the goal. Attention must be paid to goals as well as needs in accounting for movement.

There are additional factors in individual members and in a group situation that can affect the strength of group motivation:

1. The origin of the motivating forces, whether they are the members' *own* forces, arising from within, or are *induced* from without the group;
2. The character of the goal itself;
3. How the social field is organized, whether it is autocratic, democratic, or laissez faire;
4. The group's standards and its history of success and failure; and
5. The group situation itself—factors such as size and time perspective.

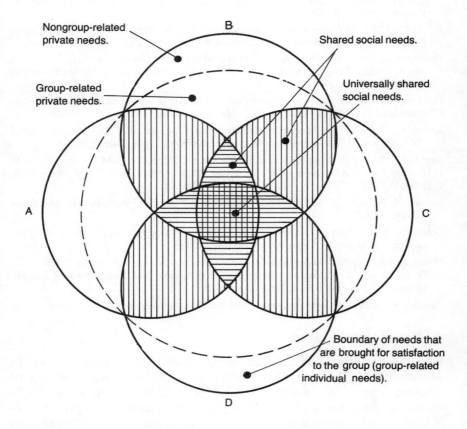

Figure 1. Types of group-related individual needs

SELECTED BIBLIOGRAPHY

Bennett, E. B., "Discussion, decision, commitment and consensus in 'group decision'," *Hum. Relat.*, 1955, *8*, 251-273.

Cartwright, D. & A. Zander, (Eds.), *Group Dynamics: Research and Theory*, Evanston, IL: Harper & Row, 1953, Chapter 22. Also New York: Harper & Row, 1968, Part 6, Chapter 31.

Cattell, R. B., "New concepts for measuring leadership in terms of group syntality," *Hum. Relat.*, 1951, *4*, 161-184.

Cattell, R. B., D. R. Saunders & G. F. Stice, "The dimensions of syntality in small groups," *Hum. Relat.*, 1953, *6*, 331-356.

Coch, L. & J. R. P. French, Jr., "Overcoming resistance to change," *Hum. Relat.*, 1948, *1*, 512-532.

Deutsch, M., "The effects of cooperation and competition upon process," in D. Cartwright & A. Zander, (Eds.), *Group Dynamics: Research and Theory*, Second Edition, Evanston, IL: Harper & Row, 1960, Chapter 22.

Deutsch, M., "Field theory in social psychology," in G. Lindzey (Ed.), *Handbook of Social Psychology*, Vol. I, Cambridge, MA: Addison-Wesley, 1954, Chapter 5.

Festinger, L., S. Schacher, & K. Back, "The operation of group standards," in D. Cartwright and A. Zander (Eds.), *Group Dynamics: Research and Theory*, Second Edition, Evanston, IL: Harper & Row, 1960, Chapter 14.

Horwitz, M., "The recall of interrupted group tasks: An experimental study of individual motivation in relation to group goals," *Hum. Relat.*, 1954, *7*, 3-38.

Lewin, K., "Behavior and development as a function of the total situation," in L. Carmichael (Ed.), *Manual of Child Psychology*, New York: John Wiley, 1946, Chapter 16.

Lewin, K., "Group decision and social change," in E. E. Maccaby, T. M. Newcomb & E. L. Hartley (Eds.), *Readings in Social Psychology*, Third Edition, New York: Henry Holt, 1958, 197-211.

Napier, R. W. & M. K. Gershenfeld, *Groups: Theory and Experience*, Boston: Houghton Mifflin, 1973.

Schachter, S., N. Ellerton, D. McBride & D. Gregory, "An experimental study of cohesiveness and productivity," *Hum. Relat.*, 1951, *4*, 222-238.

White, R. & R. Lippitt, "Leader behavior and member reactions in three 'social climates'," in D. Cartwright & A. Zander, *Group Dynamics: Research and Theory*, Second Edition, Evanston, IL: Harper & Row, 1960, Chapter 28.

Zander, A., *Motives and Goals in Groups*, New York: Academic Press, 1971.

6. Group Value System

Group action usually is directed and purposive, rather than random. In accounting for this fact, it is necessary to postulate the existence of another subsystem, namely, the *value system* of the group. Most simply stated, a group value is any value that is attributed to the group-as-a-whole. Usually, there is no single group value, but a group generally has as many values as there are members. Collectively, these values constitute the group's value orientation.

A group value orientation, like the group itself, is merely an abstraction. It only exists in the minds of the members. But because the members act as if these group values have substance and reality, the values are real and important in their consequences. To understand fully the behavior of any group, one must know the values that the members attribute to it.

The value orientation of the group can be expressed in many forms; it may:

- Define the attributes or behavior pattern of a good group member;

- Be expressed in terms of the characteristics that distinguish the group from other groups;

- Serve to indicate what is good for the group to do or not to do;

- Provide a frame of reference to guide the group in making decisions and choices; it helps to develop consistency in its ways of functioning;

- Be used to justify the ends and means that the group selects to meet its needs;

- Help the group construct a stable, meaningful world for itself;

- Provide a tangible reality with which the members can identify; and

- Enhance the group's prospects of continuity and persistence as it is transmitted to successive generations.

SELECTED BIBLIOGRAPHY

Bavelas, A., "A method of investigating individual and group ideology," *Sociometry*, 1942, 5, 371-377.

Dunphy, D. C., *The Primary Group: A Handbook for Analysis and Field Research*, New York: Appleton-Century-Crofts, 1972.

Havighurst, R. J. and H. Taba, *Adolescent Character and Personality*, New York: John Wiley, 1949.

Kalhorn, J., "Values and sources of authority," *University of Iowa Studies: Studies in Child Welfare*, Vol. 20, Iowa City: University of Iowa Press, 1944, 99-151.

Kluckhohn, C. & H. A. Murray (Eds.), *Personality in Nature, Society and Culture*, New York: Knopf, 1953, 53-67.

Lee, D., "Are basic needs ultimate?" in Kluckhohn, C. & H. A. Murray (Eds.), *Personality in Nature, Society and Culture*, New York: Knopf, 1953, 335-341.

Newcomb, T. M., "Autistic hostility and social reality," *Hum. Relat.*, 1947, I, 69-86.

Olmsted, M. S., "Orientation and role in the small group," *Amer. Sociol. Rev.*, 1954, 19, 741-751.

Parsons, T. & E. A. Shils, *Toward a General Theory of Action*. Cambridge, MA: Harvard University Press, 1951.

Polansky, N., R. Lippitt & F. Redl, "An investigation of behavioral contagion in groups," *Hum. Relat.*, 1950, 3, 319-348.

Seidler, M. B. & M. J. Ravitz, "A Jewish peer group," *Amer. J. Sociol.*, 1955, 61, 11-15.

Sherif, M. & C. W. Sherif, *Groups in Harmony and Tension*, New York: Harper and Row, 1953.

Steiner, I. D., *Group Process and Productivity*, New York: Academic Press, 1972, Chapter 6.

Vickers, Sir Geoffrey, *Value Systems and Social Process*, New York: Basic Books, 1968.

White, R. & R. Lippitt, "Leader behavior and member reaction in three 'social climates'," in D. Cartwright & A. Zander (Eds.), *Group Dynamics: Theory and Research*, New York: Harper & Row, 1968, 318-335.

GROUP STRUCTURE

7. The Position System

One of the ways members manifest their group structure is by the system of positions they occupy in relation to one another. According to Benoit-Smullyon (1944), there are three aspects of social position: *status*, *situs*, and *locus*. It was possible to see these three aspects of the positional system at work in a series of group process seminars:

1. *Status.* The group members enjoyed varied degrees of prestige and exercised diverse amounts of influence on what happened in the seminar. By virtue of these variances, they occupied different relative positions on a prestige hierarchy. This was the status aspect of their social position.

2. *Situs.* Social position was distinguished in terms of a person's membership in various social groupings—an aggregate of persons socially distinguishable by some common characteristic other than status or locus. The common characteristic might be based on sexual, vocational, racial, physiological, and other differences. Distinguishing individuals as men, women, teachers, doctors, black, white, tall, short, fat, or lean would be referring to the situs aspect of social position.

3. *Locus.* Members could be differentiated in terms of the functions they performed in the group. At times, someone would be designated as chairman, recorder, or observer. Occasionally, the members would characterize themselves and others in terms of their typical behavior in the group, such as being a critic, initiator, information-giver, encourager, blocker, and so on. These functional distinctions delineate the locus aspect of social position. (An article by Benne and Sheats, pages 52-61 in this volume, refers to locus.)

The positional system of the group, therefore, refers to all the positions that members may occupy in relation to one another in terms of status, situs, and locus. Although the position of each member may be thus described individually, ultimately, the positional system refers to the status, situs, and locus configurations of the group-as-a-whole.

SELECTED BIBLIOGRAPHY

Adams, S., "Status congruency as a variable in small group performance," *Soc. Forces*, 1953, *32*, 16-22.

Benoit-Smullyon, E., "Status types and status interrelations," *Amer. Sociol. Rev.*, 1944, *9*, 151-161.

Bradney, P., "The joking relationship in industry," *Hum. Relat.*, 1957, *10*, 175-187.

Cartwright, D. & A. Zander, *Group Dynamics: Research and Theory*, Evanston, IL: Harper & Row, 1953, Chapter 11. Also New York: Harper & Row, 1968, Chapter 36.

Chapin, P. S., "Sociometric stars as isolates," *Amer. J. Sociol.*, 1950, *54*, 263-267.

Dunphy, D. C., *The Primary Group: A Handbook for Analysis and Field Research*, New York: Appleton-Century-Crofts, 1972.

Festinger, L., "A theory of social comparison processes," *Hum. Relat.*, 1954, *7*, 117-140.

Festinger, L., S. Schachtor & K. Back, *Social Pressures in Informal Groups*, New York: Harper & Row, 1950.

Heinicke, C. & R. F. Bales, "Developmental trends in the structure of small groups," *Sociometry*, 1953, *16*, 7-38.

Hurwitz, J. I., A. Zander & B. Hymovitch, "Some effects of power on relations among group members," in D. Cartwright & A. Zander, *Group Dynamics: Research and Theory*, Evanston, IL: Harper & Row, 1953, 483-492.

Hyman, H. H., "The psychology of status," *Arch. Psychol.*, 1942, No. 269.

Lewin, K., "Field theory and experiment in social psychology: concepts and methods," *Amer. J. Sociol.*, 1939, *44*, 868-896.

Pellegrin, R. J., "The achievement of high statuses and leadership in the small group," *Social Forces*, 1953, *32*, 10-16.

Schutz, W. C., *FIRO: A Three-Dimensional Theory of Interpersonal Behavior*, New York: Holt, Rinehart & Winston, 1958.

Thibaut, J. W., "An experimental study of the cohesiveness of underprivileged groups," *Hum. Relat.*, 1950, *3*, 251-278.

Whyte, W. F., "The social structure of a restaurant," *Amer. J. Sociol.*, 1948, *54*, 302-310.

Zajonc, R. & D. Wolfe, "Cognitive consequences of a person's position in a formal organization," *Hum. Relat.*, 1960, *19*, 139-150.

8. The Role System

Associated with each position in a group is a role—a prescription for the behavior of anyone who occupies that position. And like positions, the numerous roles in any group constitute a system. The role system is closely related, if not synonymous, with the locus aspect of the positional system.

Position-coordinated roles are the stuff of which groups are made—they are the structural essence of group syntality. Therefore, to whatever extent a human aggregation has evolved an articulated role system, it is a group.

A role is what the person who occupies a particular position in a given situation is expected to feel, think, or do toward members in other related positions as well as how he or she is expected to respond to nonhuman objects. A convenient way to describe a role is to specify the behaviors that are demanded—what one *must* do; that are permitted—what one *may* do; and that are forbidden—what one *may not* do.

Social roles are the meeting ground of the individual and society. And the undertaking of roles is the process by which the reciprocal objectives of socialization and social change are accomplished. The development and survival of both the society and the individual require the assurance of some degree of regularity in human interaction—regularity that is accomplished through the enactment of social roles. Society cannot survive nor perpetuate itself without the assurance that individuals in particular positions will relate to one another in certain prescribed ways. Likewise, the individual, if he is to survive, must have some knowledge of whom to approach, and how, for the satisfaction of his various biological, psychological, and social needs.

Slater (1955) said that:

".... role performance in the small group situation will have both consequences which are important to the functioning of the group in which the role is performed, and personal consequences of importance to the individual who performs it. Similarly, an individual may be motivated to perform a role both by specific inducements offered by the group, and by more general needs operating within the individual himself. (p. 498)

In the final analysis, the enactment of a role in any particular instance is probably determined by a combination of three factors: (1) the demands of the group or society, (2) the needs of the individual role-taker, and (3) the requirements of the particular situation.

SELECTED BIBLIOGRAPHY

Bales, R. F. & F. L. Strodtbeck, "Phases in group problem-solving," *J. Abnorm. Soc. Psychol.,* 1951, *44*, 485-495.

Biddle, B. J. & E. J. Thomas, (Eds.), *Role Theory: Concepts and Research*, New York: John Wiley, 1966.

Benne, K. D. & P. Sheats, "Functional roles of group members," *J. Soc. Issues*, 1948, *4*, 41-49 (also in this volume).

Cottrell, L. S., Jr., "The adjustment of the individual to his age and sex roles," *Amer. Sociol. Rev.*, 1942, *7*, 617-620.

Dunphy, D. C., *The Primary Group: A Handbook for Analysis and Field Research*, New York: Appleton-Century-Crofts, 1972.

Hartley, E. L. & R. E. Hartley, *Fundamentals of Social Psychology*, New York: Knopf, 1952, Chapter 16, "Social role," 483-517; and Chapter 17, "Adjustment of the individual to social rule," 518-554.

Krech, D. & R. S. Crutchfield, *Theory and Problems of Social Psychology*, New York: McGraw-Hill, 1948, 372-374.

Linton, R., *The Cultural Background of Personality*, New York: Appleton-Century-Crofts, 1945.

Neiman, L. J. & J. W. Hughes, "The problem of the concept of role—A resurvey of the literature," *Social Forces*, 1951, *30*, 141-149.

Newcomb, T. M., *Social Psychology*, New York: Dryden Press, 1950, Chapter 9, "Role behavior and the self," 298-334.

Newcomb, T. M., "Role behaviors in the study of individual personality and of groups," *J. Pers.*, 1950, *18*, 273-289.

Sarbin, T. R., "Role theory," in G. Lindzey (Ed.), *Handbook of Social Psychology*, Cambridge, MA: Addison-Wesley, 1954, 223-258.

Slater, P., "Role differentiation in small groups," in A. D. Hare, E. F. Borgatta & R. F. Bales (Eds.), *Small Groups*, New York: Knopf, 1955, 498-515.

Sutherland, E. H., "The professional thief," in G. E. Swanson, T. M. Newcomb & E. L. Hartley (Eds.), *Readings in Social Psychology*, New York: Henry Holt, 1952, 271-279.

Zander, A., A. E. Cohen & E. Statland, *Role Relations in the Mental Health Professions*, Ann Arbor, MI: University of Michigan, Research Center for Group Dynamics, Series No. 5, 1957.

Znaniecki, F., "Social groups as products of participating individuals," *Amer. J. Sociol.*, 1939, *44*, 799-811.

9. The Relationship System

The relationship system is a bridge from structure to function. Viewed as a network connecting those individuals who are occupying the several positions in a group with those who are performing the various roles, it constitutes the third aspect of group structure. Viewed as a dynamic process of interaction, it provides a functional image of the group and a framework within which to describe such functional processes as the communication, control, and locomotion systems of the group.

The relationship system is based on the prescriptions for performances of roles and on the specified kind and amount of behavior expected from member-to-member or member-to-group. Collectively, these prescriptions for interpersonal behavior constitute the relationship system of the group.

To fully understand the relationship system, one must understand the nature of interaction because interaction is the essence of relationship. Newcomb (1950) has defined interaction as a "process in which an individual notices and responds to others who are noticing and responding to him." This is elaborated by Asch (1952), who notes that human interactions are

> happening which are psychologically represented in each of the participants. . . . Interaction of this kind requires a new unique organization in each of the participants, which can no more be further subdivided than we can

separate a question from an answer. The paramount fact about social interaction is that the participants stand on common ground, that they turn toward one another, and that their acts interpenetrate and therefore regulate each other. (p. 161)

The determinants of the relationship system that emerges in a group derive from factors in the individual members, in the society at large, and in the group situation.

Sociometrics, one way in which the relationship system can be analyzed, was developed by J. L. Moreno (1934) in the early thirties. It was further developed by H. S. Dimock (1937) in the late thirties and by Helen H. Jennings (1950) in the following decade. In its simplest form, sociometrics asks informants to indicate who they would choose and who they would not choose as an associate in a given situation. The data gathered in this manner may be shown graphically in the form of sociograms in which choices are usually indicated by a line of solid arrows from the chooser to the chosen and a line of broken arrows from the rejector to the rejected. Sociograms must be examined to determine dyadic and triadic relations, to identify subgroups, leaders, and isolates.

SELECTED BIBLIOGRAPHY

Asch, S. E., *Social Psychology*, New York: Dryden Press, 1950.

Bales, R. F., *Interaction Process Analysis*, Cambridge, MA: Addison-Wesley, 1950.

Deutsch, M., "The effects of motivational orientation upon trust and suspicion," *Hum. Relat.*, 1960, *13*, 123-139.

Dimock, H. S., *Rediscovering the Adolescent*, New York: Association Press, 1937.

Hearn, G., "Leadership and the spatial factor in small groups," *J. Abnorm. Soc. Psychol.*, 1957, *54*, 269-272.

Hill, W. F., "The Hill interaction matrix, progress and prospects," *Small Group Behavior*, 1977, *8*, (3), Whole Issue.

Homans, G. C., *The Human Group*, New York: Harcourt Brace Jovanovich, 1950.

Jennings, H. H., "Sociometric structure in personality and group formulation," in M. Sherif & M. O. Wilson (Eds.), *Group Relations at the Crossroads*, New York: Harper and Row, 1953.

Lewin, K., R. Lippitt & R. K. White, "Patterns of aggressive behavior in experimentally created 'social climates,'" *J. Soc. Psychol.*, 1939, *10*, 271-299.

McGregor, D., "The staff function in human relations," *J. Soc. Issues*, 1948, *4*, 6-23.

Riecken, H. W., "The effect of talkativeness on ability to influence group solutions to problems," *Sociometry*, 1958, *21* (4), 309-321.

Rosenfeld, L. B., *Human Interaction in the Small Group Setting*, Columbus, OH: Charles E. Merrill, 1973, Chapter 8.

Steinzor, B., "The spatial factor in face-to-face discussion groups," *J. Abnorm. Soc. Psychol.*, 1950, *45*, 552-555.

Stock, D. & H. A. Thelen (Eds.), *Emotional Dynamics and Group Culture*, New York: New York University Press, 1958.

Stock, D. & S. Ben-Zeev, "Changes in work and emotionality during group growth," in D. Stock & H. A. Thelen (Eds.), *Emotional Dynamics and Group Culture*, New York: New York University Press, 1958, 192-206.

Thibaut, J. W. & H. H. Kelley, *The Social Psychology of Groups*, New York: John Wiley, 1959.

Weschler, I. R., R. Tannenbaum & E. Talbot, "A new management tool: the multi-relational sociometric survey," *Personnel*, 1952, *29*, 85-94.

GROUP FUNCTIONING

10. The Communication System

Communication is the principal means by which individuals interrelate their behavior and in so doing are able to function as a group. Communication is essential to the emergence of group syntality; it is the means by which a group maintains its wholeness. Not only does communication enable a group to maintain a state of internal equilibrium, it also enables the group to achieve a correspondence between itself and external environment.

Morris (1946) has defined communication in a way that suggests six helpful factors in understanding the total phenomenon:

- The communication situation
- The communicator
- The transmission of a message
- The interpreter
- The reception of a message
- The message

A. The Communication Situation. The conditions that exist in the situation in which the communication takes place determine, in part, what occurs. Some examples include: the structure of the group in terms of its positions, roles, relationships; the spatial relationship of the communicators; the arrangement and the state of the channels for communication—whether they are one-way or two-way; the signal to noise ratio; the loading of the channels.

B. The Communicator or Transmission. Certain other factors affect the communicator and the transmission of a message. How willing is the communicator to transmit? How much encouragement is there to communicate? How much does the communicator know about the interpreter? How available are the signs and the channels required? What is the style, the reputation, and the psychophysiological state of the communicator?

228   *Group Development*

C. *The Interpreter and Reception.* There also are a variety of factors present in receiving and interpreting a message. What is the internal state in terms of the individual's desire and ability to hear and see, both physically and emotionally?

D. *The Message.* Finally, there are a number of semantic characteristics that relate to the form and substance of the message transmitted.

While all this is true and important information about communication, it appears sterile because it is at the cognitive level. It leaves unsaid the kind of things Carl Rogers might say about communication. For him, communication involves hearing and being heard at several levels; being authentic and experiencing another person who is authentic; loving or caring, and being loved. It involves the transmission of meaning in the form of *feelings*, as well as ideas.

SELECTED BIBLIOGRAPHY

Appley, D. G., & A. E. Winder, *T-Groups and Therapy Groups in a Changing Society*, San Francisco: Jossey-Bass, 1973, Chapter 4.

Burgoon, M., J. K. Heston & J. McCroskey, *Small Group Communication: A Functional Approach*, New York: Holt, Rinehart and Winston, 1974.

Cathcart, R. S. & L. A. Samovar, *Small Group Communication: A Reader*, Second Edition, Dubuque, IA: W. C. Brown, 1974.

Festinger, L., "Informal social communication," *Psychol. Rev.*, 1950, *57*, 271-282.

Gibb, C. A., "Leadership" in G. Lindzey (Ed.), *Handbook of Social Psychology*, Cambridge, MA: Addison-Wesley, 1954, 877-920.

Hare, A. P., *Handbook of Small Group Research*, Glencoe, IL: Free Press, 1962, Part 2.

Hearn, G., "Leadership and the spatial factor in small groups," *J. Abnorm. Soc. Psychol.*, 1957, *54*, 269-272.

Johnson, W., "The fateful process of Mr. A. talking to Mr. B., *Harvard Business Review*, 1953, *31* (1), 50.

Leavitt, H. J., "Some effects of certain communication patterns on group performance," *J. Abnorm. Soc. Psychol.*, 1951, *46*, 38-50.

Lewis, G. H., "Organization in communication networks," *Comparative Group Studies*, 1971, *2* (2), 149-160.

March, J. G. & H. A. Simon, *Organizations*, New York: Wiley, 1958.

Morris, C., *Signs, Language and Behavior*, Englewood Cliffs, NJ: Prentice-Hall, 1946.

Parsons, T. & A. E. Shils, *Toward a General Theory of Action*, Cambridge, MA: Harvard University Press, 1952.

Philip, G. M. & E. C. Erickson, *Interpersonal Dynamics in the Small Group*, New York: Random House, 1970.

Polansky, N., R. Lippitt & F. Redl, "An investigation of behavioral contagion in groups," *Hum. Relat.*, 1950, *3*, 319-348.

Ruesch, J. & G. Bateson, *Communication: The Social Matrix of Psychiatry*, New York: Norton, 1951.

Shaw, M. E. "A comparison of two types of leadership in various communication nets," *J. Abnorm. Soc. Psychol.*, 1955, *50*, 127-134.

Simon, H. A., "A formal theory of interaction in small groups," *Amer. Soc. Rev.*, 1952, *17*, 202-211.

11. The Control System

The second functional subsystem of a group is the control system. Some form of control is essential to the existence and the persistence of any group. The control system is analogous to the central nervous system of a human or to the bridge of a ship. Its primary function is accomplished by (1) direction setting and decision making and (2) establishing and maintaining structure through the channeling and circumscription of individual behavior.

By means of its control system, a collection of individuals is able to take collaborative action on corporate tasks; they are able to move together toward the fulfillment of their collective purposes. Control, in its essence, is a process in which individual activity is redirected to serve the collective interests of the whole group.

The Ingredients of Control

Control is accomplished, in a group, through the operation of a number of forces and these forces arise from six sources:

- *Self-Control.* Many of the limitations and constraints operating on an individual member's behavior are self-imposed.
- *Social Control.* Control also derives from the norms of society. Customs, expectations, usages, norms, values, and all behavior prescriptions that emanate from the larger society are forms of social control.
- *System Control.* Some measures of total control derive from the system itself, and therefore, may be regarded as system control.
- *Member Control.* An individual member can be the source of control, if he or she has sufficient power and authority.
- *Task Control.* Sometimes the task exerts control and directs the actions of group members. It is not uncommon for a group to work on a task in a highly coordinated and efficient manner with little apparent control from the kinds of sources already mentioned.
- *Situation Control.* Finally, factors in the group situation may serve as a principal source of control. Time or setting or group size may be such factors.

These are the elements that are combined in the control system of a group. But, how do they combine? Perhaps control results from the competitive interactive process among these six potential sources—from their struggle for dominance. It is likely that each group and each phase in the life of a given group will be a different mix.

SELECTED BIBLIOGRAPHY

Cartwright, D., *Studies in Social Power*, Ann Arbor, MI: University of Michigan Press, 1959.

Cooley, C. H., *Human Nature and the Social Order*, Chicago: Scribner's, 1922.

Gerson, L. W., "Punishment and position: The sanctioning of deviants in small groups," in Paul V. Crosbie, *Interaction in Small Groups*, New York: Macmillan, 1975, 546-553.

Halal, W. E., "Toward a general theory of leadership," *Hum. Relat.*, 1974, *27* (4), 401-416.

Hartley, E. L. & R. E. Hartley, *The Fundamentals of Social Psychology*, New York: Knopf, 1952, Chapter 19, "Leadership—followership."

Hearn, G., *Theory Building in Social Work*, Toronto: University of Toronto Press, 1958.

Hollingshead, A. B., "The concept of social control," *Amer. Soc. Rev.*, 1941, *6*, 217-224.

Lippitt, R., J. Watson & B. Westley, *The Dynamics of Planned Change*, New York: Harcourt, Brace Jovanovich, 1958.

Mills, T. M., *The Sociology of Small Groups*, Englewood Cliffs, NJ: Prentice-Hall, 1967, Chapter 5.

Pigors, P., *Leadership or Domination*, Boston: Houghton Mifflin, 1935.

Roucek, J. S. (Ed.), *Social Control*, Princeton: Van Nostrand, 1956.

Stogdill, R. M., "Leadership, membership and organization," *Psychol. Bull.*, 1950, *47*, 1-14.

Tannenbaum, R. & W. H. Schmidt, "How to choose a leadership pattern," *Harvard Business Review*, 1958, *36* (2), 95-101.

Vickers, Sir Geoffrey, "Control, stability and choice," Ninth Wallberg Memorial Lecture, University of Toronto, 1956. In *Yearbook* of Society for General Systems Research, Vol. II, L. von Bertalanffy & A. Rapaport (Eds.), Ann Arbor, MI: Mental Health Research Institute, University of Michigan, 1957.

12. The Locomotion System

The third functional subsystem is the locomotion system, the means by which a group may change its location in space. In combination with communication and control, it enables the group to take concerted action in pursuit of corporate goals.

Cartwright and Zander (1953) have defined locomotion as follows:

> Whenever it is possible to assert that some location is relatively the most preferred for a group and that a sequence of efforts to change the position of the group will terminate when the location is reached, we shall designate that location as the group's goal. Whenever the group changes its location, we shall speak of group locomotion. (p. 306)

There can be locomotion in three kinds of space: physical, cognitive, and social. A football team physically moving down the field might be thought of as locomotion in physical space. A seminar mentally moving toward the solution of a theoretical problem might be regarded as locomotion in cognitive space. The members of a sensitivity group emotionally moving away from, against, or toward one another might be thought of as locomotion in social space.

SELECTED BIBLIOGRAPHY

Bossard, J. H. S. & E. S. Boll, *Ritual in Family Living*, Philadelphia: University of Pennsylvania Press, 1950.

Cartwright, D. & A. Zander, *Group Dynamics*, Evanston, IL: Harper & Row, 1953, Chapter 22, "Group goals and group locomotion: introduction," 305-318.

Deutsch, M., in G. Lindzey (Ed.), *Handbook of Social Psychology, Vol. I,* Cambridge, MA: Addison-Wesley, 1954, Chapter 5, "Field theory in social psychology," 181-222.

Festinger, L., "Informal social communication," *Psychol. Rev.*, 1950, *57*, 271-282.

King, E. E., "Group locomotion and goal achievement," in *The Sociology of Small Groups*, New York: Pageant Press, 1962, 85-94.

Leeper, R. W., *Lewin's Topological and Vector Psychology: A Digest and a Critique*, University of Oregon Monographs: Studies in Psychology, No. 1, Eugene, OR: University of Oregon, 1943.

Lewin, K., *Principles of Topological Psychology*, New York: McGraw-Hill, 1936.

Merei, F., "Group leadership and institutionalization," *Hum. Relat.*, 1948, *2*, 23-39.

Schutz, W. C., "On group composition," *J. Abnorm. and Soc. Psychol.*, 1961, *62*, 275-281.

Tolman, E. C., in T. Parsons & E. A. Shils (Eds.), *Toward a General Theory of Action*, Cambridge: Harvard University Press, 1951, Part 3, "A psychological model," Chapter 2, "The model," 285-302.

13. Group Survival

Groups require maintenance if they are to survive. Group survival is never a certainty, and it must be actively promoted. The maintenance system of the group is the means by which the survival of the group is assured.

There are several ways of thinking about group survival. One way is to assume that it depends on the group holding its members. Another assumption is that the group must remain distinct from its environment while it maintains some kind of continuity in the qualities by which it is recognized as separate. Finally, the chances of survival may be measured in terms of the group's ability to maintain itself in a steady state.

It takes a ground crew as well as an air crew to keep an aircraft in flight; and it is similar with groups. There are processes that enable a group to accomplish its task, but these processes and the group as a whole must be kept in working order through a maintenance system.

THE MAINTENANCE SYSTEM OF A GROUP

Four classes of things are being maintained in the maintenance system of a group:

1. The boundary of the group
2. Its resources
3. The group, itself, as a system
4. External relations

Boundary Maintenance

Boundary maintenance involves three processes: (1) the delineation of the boundary to indicate what is *in* and what is *out*, (2) the regulation of inputs and outputs, and (3) the varying of the openness and closedness of the boundaries as required by changes in internal and external conditions.

Input regulation must be corrected for either input deficiency or input overload. In output regulation, the problem is what is exported, in what quantity, and at what rate.

Resource Maintenance

A group is an open, organismic system, dependent for its survival on a ready source of people, materials, and ideas; many methods can be used to insure that supply.

Systems Maintenance

The group must be able to maintain itself in a tolerably steady state. This attempt, with all that it entails, can be regarded as system maintenance. A group in a steady state is not a group at rest; it is in dynamic equilibrium. It is a system in action with each of its subsystems perpetually in motion. What appears as a steady state is actually the result of a dynamic interplay of processes.

For a group to maintain itself in a steady state, every change in one of the subsystems must be accompanied by appropriate adjustive change in many, if not all, others. If a particular set of circumstances facing the group requires a particular degree and type of control, then a particular structure of positions, roles, and relationships will be necessary to permit or provide the required form of communication and locomotion.

If a system is to achieve and maintain a steady state, then it must have certain automatic feedback processes in operation. Whenever a change occurs in a part of the system, a signal must be transmitted through a feedback mechanism to the other parts, indicating how they are to adjust in order to keep the system in balance.

Member Maintenance

Because "healthy" groups require good group members, actions taken to enhance the well-being of the members serve also to promote the effectiveness of the group.

Subsystem Maintenance

To insure system maintenance, attention must be given to maintaining the critical subsystems: value, motivational, positional, role, relationship, communication, control, locomotion, and the maintenance system, itself.

Feedback Maintenance

Because feedback is essential to keeping the group functioning as a dynamic entity, the feedback processes must be kept in functioning order. If the wrong kind of feedback mechanism is operating, or if it is unresponsive or overresponsive, the group will be in trouble.

Maintenance of External Relations

A group is an open system, always exchanging material and energy with its environment. Consequently, a group must maintain a set of systemic linkages or relationships with its environment and the several relevant systems in its environment.

SUMMARY

There are two kinds of processes at work in a group: those that promote the accomplishment of tasks and those that maintain the group as a system. Consequently, there are two kinds of leadership in a group: task leadership and maintenance leadership. The task and maintenance functions usually are performed by different persons rather than by the same person; it seems natural for a kind of task and maintenance specialization to develop.

SELECTED BIBLIOGRAPHY

Bales, R. F., "The equilibrium problem in small groups," in T. Parsons, R. F. Bales & E. A. Shels (Eds.), *Working Papers in the Theory of Action*, Glencoe, IL: Free Press, 1953, 111-161.

Bales, R. F. & P. R. Slater, "Role differentiation in small decision-making groups," in T.

Parsons & R. F. Bales (Eds.), *Family, Socialization and Interaction Process*, Glencoe, IL: Free Press, 1955, 259-306.

Benne, K. D. & P. Sheats, "Functional role of group members," *J. Soc. Issues*, 1948, *4*, 41-49. Also in this volume.

Coffey, H. S., "Socio and psyche group process: integrative concepts," *J. Soc. Issues*, 1952, *8*, 65-74.

Grunsky, O., "A case for the theory of familial role differentiation in small groups," *Social Forces*, 1957, *35*, 209-217.

Hearn, G., *Theory Building in Social Work*, Toronto: University of Toronto Press, 1958.

Heinicke, C. & R. F. Bales, "Developmental trends in the structure of small groups," *Sociometry*, 1953, *16*, 7-38.

Jennings, H. H., *Leadership and Isolation*, New York: Langmorrs, Green, 1950, Chapter 13.

Klein, J., *The Study of Groups*, London: Routledge and Kegan Paul, 1956.

Loomis, C. P., *Social Systems*, New York: Van Nostrand, 1960.

Miller, J. G., "Toward a general theory of the behavioral sciences," *Amer. Psychologist*, 1955, *10*, 516-517.

Parker, S., "Leadership patterns in a psychiatric ward," *Hum. Relat.*, 1958, *11*, 287-301.

Simon, H. A., D. W. Smithberg & V. A. Thompson, *Public Administration*, New York: Knopf, 1956.

Stock, D. & H. A. Thelen, *Emotional Dynamics and Group Culture*, New York: New York University Press, 1958.

Thibaut, J. W. & H. H. Kelley, *The Social Psychology of Groups*, New York: Wiley, 1959, Chapter 15.

Zelditch, M., "Role differentiation in the nuclear family: a comparative study," in T. Parsons & R. F. Bales (Eds.), *Family, Socialization and Interaction Process*, Glencoe, IL: Free Press, 1955, 307-351.